Judging the Boy Scouts of America

LANDMARK LAW CASES

AMERICAN SOCIETY

Peter Charles Hoffer
N. E. H. Hull
Series Editors

RECENT TITLES IN THE SERIES:

Prigg v. Pennsylvania, H. Robert Baker
The Detroit School Busing Case, Joyce A. Baugh
The Japanese American Cases, Roger Daniels
The Battle over School Prayer, Bruce J. Dierenfield
Fighting Foreclosure, John A. Fliter and Derek S. Hoff
Little Rock on Trial, Tony A. Freyer
One Man Out: Curt Flood versus Baseball, Robert M. Goldman
The Free Press Crisis of 1800, Peter Charles Hoffer
The Treason Trials of Aaron Burr, Peter Charles Hoffer
The Woman Who Dared to Vote: The Trial of Susan B. Anthony, N. E. H. Hull
Roe v. Wade: *The Abortion Rights Controversy in American History*, 2nd ed., revised and expanded, N. E. H. Hull and Peter Charles Hoffer
Plessy v. Ferguson: *Race and Inequality in Jim Crow America*, Williamjames Hull Hoffer
Gibbons v. Ogden: *John Marshall, Steamboats, and the Commerce Clause*, Herbert A. Johnson
The Tokyo Rose Case, Yasuhide Kawashima
Gitlow v. New York, Marc Lendler
Fugitive Slave on Trial: The Anthony Burns Case and Abolitionist Outrage, Earl M. Maltz
The Snail Darter Case, Kenneth M. Murchison
Capital Punishment on Trial, David M. Oshinsky
The Michigan Affirmative Action Cases, Barbara A. Perry
The Sodomy Cases, David A. J. Richards
The Supreme Court and Tribal Gaming, Ralph A. Rossum
Obscenity Rules: Roth v. United States *and the Long Struggle over Sexual Expression*, Whitney Strub
Mendez v. Westminster, Philippa Strum
The Sleepy Lagoon Murder Case: Race Discrimination and Mexican-American Rights, Mark A. Weitz
The Miracle *Case*, Laura Wittern-Keller and Raymond J. Haberski, Jr.
Bush v. Gore: *Exposing the Hidden Crisis in American Democracy*, abridged and updated, Charles L. Zelden

For a complete list of titles in the series go to www.kansaspress.ku.edu

RICHARD J. ELLIS

Judging the Boy Scouts of America

Gay Rights, Freedom of Association, and the *Dale* Case

UNIVERSITY PRESS OF KANSAS

Published by the University Press of Kansas (Lawrence, Kansas 66045), which was organized by the Kansas Board of Regents and is operated and funded by Emporia State University, Fort Hays State University, Kansas State University, Pittsburg State University, the University of Kansas, and Wichita State University

Library of Congress Cataloging-in-Publication Data
Ellis, Richard (Richard J.), author.
Judging the Boy Scouts of America : gay rights, freedom of association, and the Dale case / Richard J. Ellis.
pages cm. — (Landmark law cases & American society)
Includes bibliographical references.
ISBN 978-0-7006-1950-4 (hardback) — ISBN 978-0-7006-1951-1 (paper) —
ISBN 978-0-7006-1984-9 (ebook)
1. Boy Scouts of America—Trials, litigation, etc. 2. Dale, James, 1970– —Trials, litigation, etc. 3. Freedom of association—United States. 4. Homophobia—Law and legislation—United States. 5. Boy Scouts—Legal status, laws, etc.—United States. 6. Gays—Legal status, laws, etc.—United States. I. Title.
KF229.D35E43 2014
342.7308'5—dc23

British Library Cataloguing-in-Publication Data is available.

Printed in the United States of America

10 9 8 7 6 5 4 3 2 1

The paper used in this publication is recycled and contains 30 percent postconsumer waste. It is acid free and meets the minimum requirements of the American National Standard for Permanence of Paper for Printed Library Materials z39.48-1992.

CONTENTS

ACKNOWLEDGMENTS

I have written longer books, but never one that took so long to write. It is appropriate therefore that I begin by expressing appreciation for the extraordinary patience shown by Michael Briggs of the University Press of Kansas. When other editors would have hectored and badgered if not given up, Mike continued to offer support and sympathy. His faith helped lift my spirits even if did not always dispel my doubts.

Those doubts stemmed in part from a political scientist's frustration at not being able to get more direct access to the decision-making process of the institutions I had chosen to write about. It soon became apparent that my original hope that I could tell the story of the behind-the-scenes maneuvering within the Boy Scouts of America and the US Supreme Court was hopelessly naïve. Both these august institutions work hard to prevent people from peering behind the curtains concealing their deliberations. Supreme Court clerks must even take a vow of secrecy in exchange for the privilege of serving the justices. BSA executives clam up almost as tight. The justices want us to believe that they are simply following the dictates of the law and the Constitution, just as Scouting's leaders have wanted us to accept that they simply follow the dictates of the Scout Oath and Scout Law and act in the best interests of Scouting. Neither the Court nor the Scouts want the public to see their institutions as political. At least I'm not that naïve.

Since beginning this book in the summer of 2008, I often asked myself whether it would be better to leave the writing of this book for another time and author. One day, after all, researchers will have access to the papers of the justices on the Supreme Court at the time of the *Dale* decision—though we will have to wait until all of these justices are dead (the youngest of whom, Clarence Thomas, is only sixty-five as of this writing) before Chief Justice William Rehnquist's papers will be available to the public. And although Dale's case is fast slipping into history, the controversy over admitting gays in the Boy Scouts is still as contentious as ever. Perhaps in several decades, when the morality of gay and lesbian relationships no longer divides the nation as sharply and when the principals involved have exited the stage, the Boy Scouts will be prepared to open their archives to researchers. That seems too long to wait, however, to begin to tell such an important story.

Fortunately, I encountered many people willing to help me tell this story. I am especially grateful to David Peavy, who devoted untold hours to answering an endless stream of questions. David's encyclopedic knowledge of the Boy Scouts is unrivaled, as is his generosity in helping those who wish to understand the Scouts. I also benefited greatly from the wide array of resources that he makes available to the public on two websites: http://www.bsa-discrimina tion.org/ and http://paxtu.org/index.html. David also was kind enough to read the completed manuscript and he saved me from countless embarrassing errors, large and small.

I also owe a particular debt to Merril Hirsh, an attorney at Troutman Sanders who represented Michael Geller and Roland Pool, two gay men who challenged the Scouts' exclusionary policy two years after Dale did. I contacted Hirsh looking for a few depositions and ended up with a massive box full of relevant materials from that case that enriched the story in countless ways. Roland Pool was also eager to help and he, too, sent me an entire box of documents and filings from the case.

Also deserving of special thanks is Kenneth Ritchie of the New Jersey State Law Library. In the course of my research I benefited from many acts of generosity and kindness, but nobody came close to putting in more time on my behalf than Ken, who graciously scanned for me an immense trove of New Jersey court documents related to the *Dale* case. Willamette University's librarians Melissa Treichel and Rich Schmidt were also unfailingly helpful in locating needed documents. Several Willamette University undergraduate students also helped me tremendously in gathering information related to the *Dale* case. In particular, I would like to thank Catie Theisen, Katie Johannsen, and Will Nevius.

A few other individual also deserve thanks for helping me track down hard-to-find documents. Tim Curran not only answered my questions related to his pioneering case, he also dug up from his files several important documents, most notably a revealing five-page letter sent to him by BSA attorney Malcolm Wheeler in July 1981. Jon Davidson, legal director of Lambda Legal, also gathered up a number of documents that I asked about and, most important, sent me a several-hundred-page deposition by Edelman's Blake Lewis that I had been unable to find elsewhere. Thomas Moloney of Cleary Gottlieb also dug out several important briefs that I had been unable to locate.

The cooperation and assistance of many of the principals involved in the *Dale* litigation were also critically important in reconstructing events. Among those who gave generously of their time to talk with me and educate me were Evan Wolfson, James Dale, Ruth Harlow, David Buckel, Donna Costa, Mark Agrast, Jim Hough, and Deborah Poritz. I also learned from conversations with Richard Socarides, Robert Raben, Dan Marcus, and Kinga Borundy.

Notably lacking from this list of names, unfortunately, are the officials and lawyers representing the Boy Scouts of America. My requests to speak with BSA officials were almost always rebuffed or ignored. Local officials directed me to the national office, specifically the then BSA corporate counsel David Park. I did have a brief telephone conversation with Park in August 2008, but he insisted that I submit all questions in writing—and then never responded to the questions I did submit. Requests for interviews to various others, including Edelman's Blake Lewis and several BSA attorneys, specifically Sanford Brown and George Davidson, also went unanswered or were declined, though toward the end Davidson did respond helpfully via email to some specific factual questions. An Edelman representative was willing to tell me when the company began operations in Dallas, but once I asked about the public relations firm's connection with the Scouts their representative stopped communicating. I recognize that this book is poorer for my lack of access to those on the other side of this story. My only consolation is that the voluminous court records—not just in Dale's case but in several other similar cases—go a significant way toward compensating for that lack.

One part of the story that I opted not to tell here is the Clinton administration's aborted involvement in the writing of an amicus brief on the side of Dale. That the Clinton administration considered such a brief and that the question was contentious is clear from many interviews I conducted and email communications I received. However, the accounts were sufficiently contradictory, imprecise, or secondhand that I did not feel confident telling the story without more direct access to the Clinton administration's internal deliberations regarding the brief. I have submitted a Freedom of Information Act request related to these internal deliberations, but since the administration's aborted brief is at best a side story in my tale I decided against further delaying publication of the book for the sake of its inclusion.

There would have been no book at all without the financial support I received from several quarters. Completion of the book was made possible by a timely grant from Willamette University's Center for Religion, Law, and Democracy, directed by my colleagues Steve Green and David Gutterman. Early work on the project was supported by Willamette University's Atkinson grant program and by the National Endowment for the Humanities. My special thanks to Jay Mechling and Karen Orren for writing in support of my NEH application. Both Karen and Jay also kindly read the completed manuscript and offered encouraging words leavened, in Karen's case, with loving criticism and constructive suggestions. This isn't the book Karen would have written, but it's better for her having read it.

This book is also better for the close attention and critical reading given it by Chuck Myers, now director of the University Press of Kansas. One of the embarrassing measures of how long this book took me to finish is that by the time I got around to delivering the long-promised manuscript, UPK had reshuffled some of its internal responsibilities, with Chuck taking over from Mike Briggs the in-house handling of the Landmark Law Cases series. Any concerns I might have had about being handed off from one editor to another were quickly dispelled by Chuck's deft touch and sound judgment. *Judging the Boy Scouts* is the sixth book I have published with UPK, and I am so profoundly grateful to everyone at the press—most especially my friend and mentor Fred Woodward—for their incredible support over the past two decades. I have always found the entire UPK staff to be consummate professionals dedicated to their craft, and this time has been no different.

Finally, I need to acknowledge my debt to Nancy Rosenblum's wonderful book *Membership and Morals: The Personal Uses of Pluralism in America*. My interest in writing about Dale's case stems directly from teaching *Membership and Morals* in my course on Liberalism and Its Critics. Rosenblum's nuanced discussion of the freedom of association challenged students to think deeply about the dilemma at the heart of liberal democracies. On the one hand are the freedom from discrimination and the importance of equal treatment. Allowing powerful, socially favored groups to discriminate against marginalized minorities perpetuates prejudice and fosters hate, and thereby undermines liberal democratic life. On the other hand is the importance to a free society of private, voluntary groups. Empowering the state to dictate a group's membership poses a threat to liberal democracy that seems every bit as great as the threat of untrammeled discrimination and prejudice.

Dale's case is not discussed in *Membership and Morals*. At the time the book was published in 1998, Dale's case had not even reached the New Jersey Supreme Court, let alone the US Supreme Court. But in teaching the book between 1999 and 2005, I became drawn to Dale's case as a prism through which to think about Rosenblum's provocative analysis of the importance of associational life in a liberal society. For the final essay assignment, I asked students to imagine that the US Supreme Court's ruling in *Boy Scouts of America v. Dale* had been appealed to a "higher court," upon which sat nine of the political theorists they had read during the semester—along with Rosenblum, the others on this august court included Isaiah Berlin, Amy Gutmann, Friedrich Hayek, Mary Ann Glendon, Susan Okin, Michael Sandel, and Judith Shkar. I tasked students with determining the court's decision and writing the majority and dissenting opinions.

Although I no longer offered the class after 2005, the experience of teaching the Scouts' case stuck with me. It was impossible not to be moved by how profoundly the case engaged students' intellect and emotions and how it provoked classroom debate of the highest order. Those memorable classroom discussions—and equally memorable final papers—planted the seed that would eventually grow into this book. Without those discussions and without those wonderful students I would never have dreamed of suggesting to Fred Woodward, in the spring of 2008, that I write a book on Dale's case for UPK's Landmark Law Cases and American Society series. For better or for worse, that is how someone who had never been a Boy

Scout, never been to law school, and had little connection to the LGBT community decided to write a book on *Boy Scouts of America v. James Dale*. Whether that was a wise or foolhardy decision, I leave the reader to judge.

Judging the Boy Scouts of America

Freedom of Association and the Right to Exclude

Few things are more fundamental to liberal democracy than freedom of association. Without the freedom to associate, there would be no political parties, no labor unions, no churches, indeed no groups of any kind, except those sanctioned by the state. For most of us, free speech would mean little if we could not band together and pool our resources with others who share our views. In joining with others, we also build what social scientists call "social capital" by learning to trust, cooperate, and negotiate with others. But freedom of association is more than an instrumental value; choosing who we associate with is an essential part of what it means to be free. If you cannot choose your comrades and companions, then you can hardly be said to be free.

Yet there is a dark side to the freedom of association. For the freedom to associate, if it is to be meaningful, must include a right to exclude. What happens, then, when my freedom to associate comes at the expense of *your* freedom of association and your right to live free from discrimination? One response is to say, "tough, go find your own group." But even the most vigorous defenders of voluntary associations typically concede some limits on the freedom to associate, particularly when the exercise of that freedom involves serious injury to others. This concession is a version of John Stuart Mill's famous "harm principle," which states that "the only purpose for which power can be rightfully exercised over any member of a civilized community, against his will, is to prevent harm to others." However, if the harm principle is construed too expansively, there would be little left of the freedom of association. In the quest to eradicate discrimination we would have all but abolished the freedom of association. The question, then, as the political theorist Stuart White poses it, is, "When is the freedom to exclude essential to meaningful freedom of association and, therefore, something which a state may not legitimately restrict or prohibit: and when may, and should, a state legitimately curtail the freedom to exclude in the interests of securing other important values?"

Some cases are easy. Clearly we don't want the state picking our friends for us. It certainly might hurt your feelings and damage your self-esteem to be excluded from a circle of friends, but that's not a harm that the government should seek to remedy, no matter how arbitrary or hurtful the grounds for exclusion (though bullying or harassment might justify state action). Matters become more complex when we enter the realm of formal associations, groups like the American Legion, Red Cross, Elks, National Rifle Association, League of Women Voters, and Boy Scouts of America. Should groups such as these be allowed to exclude anybody for any reason? Or can we distinguish between acceptable and unacceptable reasons?

The British sociologist Paul Hirst thinks we should distinguish between exclusions based on beliefs, such as political ideology or religious affiliation, and exclusions based on inherent characteristics, such as race or sex. Under Hirst's "associative ethics," the former type of exclusion is fine since those wishing to join a group have only to change their beliefs. There is no problem, then, with Catholics excluding Protestants or Republicans shutting out Democrats. Excluding individuals based on sex or race, on the other hand, is unacceptable, Hirst tells us, because individuals do not choose their race or sex.

At first blush, this distinction may seem appealing, but it quickly runs into a host of difficulties. There is, to start with, the problem that one's race may be itself a choice—the United States census, after all, allows individuals to choose which racial group they identify with. And many Americans would regard their religion not as a choice but as a given part of their identity. The problem is compounded if we think about sexuality, where the question of whether sexual orientation is freely chosen is itself a point of contestation. Things get messier still if the exclusion is premised on sexual conduct: would Hirst's associative ethics prevent a group from barring lesbians and gays because we do not choose our sexual orientation but allow that same group to bar "practicing homosexuals" since sexual conduct is a choice? The difficulties run still deeper. Should the state bar a women-only health and fitness club from excluding men? And does it make sense to prevent civic groups from excluding Asians or African Americans on the basis of their skin color yet allow them to exclude Muslims or Sikhs based ostensibly on their religious beliefs? Is the latter exclusion less unjust than the former? And do we really want to compel an avowedly white supremacist group to admit nonwhites?

Instead of looking at whether an individual characteristic is innate or chosen, it perhaps makes more sense to weigh the harm done to those who are excluded against the harm done to those who are forced to include. The harm of compelled association appears particularly troubling when it undermines or contradicts the group's express purposes. Race may be innate and religious belief a choice, but the white supremacist group compelled to admit blacks suffers a harm that is every bit as great as the Catholic Church compelled to admit atheists. But by resting the right to exclude on the association's expressive message, we end up with a paradoxical result in which classic voluntary associations such as the Elks, Odd Fellows, Jaycees, and Boy Scouts of America may have less freedom of association than hate groups such as the Ku Klux Klan or the Aryan Nations. Even worse, it may encourage civic groups to adopt and espouse a discriminatory expressive message so as to justify their right to exclude.

Even if we allow that the harm of compelled association should be evaluated in terms of the damage done to a group's expressive message, that does not answer the question of who gets to decide the group's message. Is the association the sole judge of its expressive message, or can judges second-guess the association? It is disturbing to contemplate the state—acting through judges—telling an organization what its expressive purpose is; yet if judges reflexively defer to the organization, then almost any exclusionary practices will be sustained.

Things don't get any easier when we try to weigh the harms inflicted by exclusion from voluntary associations. What kinds of harm should we protect an individual against? Many would agree that exclusions that mark people as second-class citizens should be outlawed. But what exclusions are markers of second-class citizenship? One answer would be that exclusion denotes second-class citizenship when it involves denying equal access to public establishments. Although helpful, this answer doesn't relieve us of the need to make contentious judgments about what counts as a public establishment.

Laws banning discrimination in "places of public accommodations" date back to the post–Civil War era. These laws typically targeted racial discrimination in privately owned businesses that served the public, such as railroads, theaters, and inns. Today, almost everybody accepts that government can and should bar restaurants and hotels from refusing to serve people based on their race—though the US Supreme Court infamously concluded otherwise in 1883, when it invalidated the public accommodations provisions of the Civil Rights Act of 1875 on the grounds that the Civil War amendments (the Thirteenth, Fourteenth, and Fifteenth) were aimed only at discrimination by the federal government, not discrimination by private entities. Although there is broad agreement today that the Supreme Court got it wrong in 1883, courts and scholars disagree sharply about how broadly to construe public accommodation statutes. Is Little League a place of public accommodation? How about privately run day camps or swim clubs, or membership organizations such as the Jaycees or the Rotary Club? Even more difficult is reaching agreement on whether the Boy Scouts of America are a place of public accommodation. Some judges say "yes," others "no."

Even if we reach agreement that a group qualifies as a place of public accommodation under state (or federal) law—and the precise standards are different in different states—that should not necessarily absolve us from evaluating the extent of the harm caused by an exclusion, nor does it settle the level of harm that warrants state intervention. Even if we were to decide—as the New Jersey courts did in the early 1970s—that Little League is a place of public accommodation, it does not necessarily follow that excluding girls would mark them as second-class citizens (unless, of course, we make it true by definition). What makes an exclusion a mark of second-class citizenship may have less to do with whether a given entity is a place of public accommodation and more to do with the basis on which a group is being excluded. Exclusion on the basis of race may create second-class citizenship in a way that exclusion based on other immutable characteristics might not.

Perhaps, though, the standard of second-class citizenship sets the bar too high. Others have suggested that the proper standard is injury to a person's sense of self-worth and the perpetuation of harmful stereotypes. Exclusions may stigmatize even while not relegating a group to the rank of second-class citizens. Stuart White suggests that if this measure is not to become "overly subjective," then the reasonableness of such claims has "to be tied to the background pattern of status inequality in the community." The weaker the group, the stronger the claim against exclusion. However, as the political theorist Nancy Rosenblum notes, if white-only or male-only or straight-only organizations are singled out for compelled association, those groups will almost certainly see themselves as "victims of powerful, hostile social forces." Certainly the Boy Scouts of America see themselves this way. Can we say they are entirely wrong?

Faced with the difficulty of adjudicating between the competing values of freedom of association and freedom from discrimination, it is perhaps tempting to take refuge in absolutism. Some liberals say that my right to be free from discrimination should invariably trump your right to exclude, particularly if you are powerful and I am weak. The state should have "zero tolerance" for exclusion because even apparently minor exclusions stigmatize and subordinate vulnerable groups. In a democracy, righteous liberals contend, equality (or equal freedom) must win out. Some conservatives, on the other hand, warn of a very different slippery slope. Allow the state to decide which groups are powerful and which are weak, which need protection against discrimination and which do not, and you are on "the road to serfdom." Like the hypersensitive liberal, the libertarian conservative warns that there is no principled stopping point once one sets out to balance equality and liberty. In a free country, the libertarian insists, private associations must be free to exclude whomever they wish.

Against these absolutisms stands the political philosophy of Isaiah Berlin, who teaches that in a liberal democracy "we must engage in what are called trade-offs—rules, values, principles must yield to each other in varying degrees in specific situations." According to Berlin, "The concrete situation is almost everything. There is no escape: we must decide as we decide. . . . To force people into the neat uniforms demanded by dogmatically believed-in schemes is almost always the road to inhumanity."

Law, of course, is all about the concrete situation. In the *Boy Scouts of America v. James Dale*, the concrete situation pitted a gay assistant Scoutmaster against an iconic American institution. Judges had to decide how to balance the harm done to James Dale by his exclusion from the Boy Scouts against the harm done to the Scouts by having to admit somebody whose presence, the organization's leaders said, would be inconsistent with their core principles. In doing so, they had to decide whether to privilege the freedom of association or the freedom from discrimination.

For those who believe that judges are like umpires, the notion of judges weighing harms and balancing rival values is anathema. Balancing seems too subjective, not at all like calling balls and strikes or a runner out. Some will insist that Dale's case is an easy call if judges simply follow the law or do as the Constitution commands. In some cases, of course, the law or the Constitution will be sufficiently clear and precise so that virtually all jurists will reach the same conclusion. But Dale's case is not one of those unambiguous cases. To start with, no public accommodation statute mentions the Boy Scouts of America. And, of course, the Constitution nowhere mentions the freedom of association. Certainly there is no precise formula that can tell us the relative values a judge should attach to voluntary association and the freedom from discrimination.

Uncomfortable with the idea that they are ranking rival values, judges—like the litigants—often obscure the depth of the conflict by exaggerating the harms done to one side and minimizing the harms inflicted on the other side. But we do better in a difficult case like Dale's to acknowledge honestly and fully the trade-offs between competing values: what we gain and what we lose through the choices we make. Dale's case has an enduring fascination precisely because it requires us to weigh liberty against equality, to balance the freedom to live as we like against the right to be treated with equal dignity. In law, as in life, choosing between values is inescapable.

PART ONE

The Scouts Take Their Stand

CHAPTER I

The Model Boy Scout

The story ran on page 11 in the Health and Fitness section of the Sunday edition of the *Newark Star-Ledger*, nestled among reports of a New Jersey doctor's trip to a remote Guatemalan village to treat needy children, a state clinic that cared for multiple sclerosis patients, and the advisability of testing children for high cholesterol. Under an earnest, low-key headline, "Seminar Addresses Needs of Homosexual Teens," the story told of a one-day conference hosted by Rutgers University that addressed how New Jersey's social service system could better respond to the pressures and challenges facing gay and lesbian adolescents. Neither the *Star-Ledger*'s reporter nor its editor could have suspected that this run-of-the-mill story would spark a legal conflict that would be carried all the way to the US Supreme Court.

The bulk of the article related the words and thoughts of one of the seminar's main speakers, Mary Leddy, director of community and counseling services at the Planned Parenthood League of Middlesex County. Leddy spoke of the confusion and insecurity that inevitably accompanied teen sexuality. These feelings, she noted, were often intensified for homosexual teenagers, who sometimes felt cut off from their peers and believed that their sexual preferences were abnormal, hateful, or sick. Leddy recited a few harrowing statistics about gay teens: anywhere from one-fifth to one-third attempted suicide and at least one-half of homeless teenagers in cities were gay. By failing to foster an honest dialogue about sex, Leddy argued, schools and other institutions in society frequently drove teenagers, gay and straight, "underground" to find out about sex, with dangerous results, most notably the spread of Acquired Immune Deficiency Syndrome (AIDS) and other sexually transmitted diseases. Some of Leddy's comments may have offended a few readers—such as her characterization of "family life curriculums" as little more than "courses in plumbing"—but none of her remarks had anything to do with the controversy that unfolded after the article's publication.

Instead, the controversy centered around three sentences in the middle of the article that related the teenage experiences of James Dale, the nineteen-year-old co-president of the Rutgers University Lesbian/Gay Alliance. Together with his fellow co-president, Sharice Richardson, Dale had been invited to speak about the experience of being a gay teen. Dale told of the "double life" he had led in high school, pretending to be straight, suspecting he was gay. He recalled dating girls and laughing at homophobic jokes to disguise his homosexuality from his peers, and perhaps even from himself. Only during the past year, his second at Rutgers, had Dale finally found the acceptance and community of support to give him the courage to come out as a gay man. A picture of Dale conversing with Leddy and Richardson accompanied the story.

Although Dale had recently told his mother and father that he was gay, most people in the community of Port Monmouth, less than one hour's drive from the Rutgers campus, still did not know. Dale's father, a military man, was not immediately accepting, and his parents had certainly not broadcast the news to friends and neighbors. So when the *Star-Ledger*'s reporter, Kinga Borundy, approached Dale at the conference and asked if she could quote him, Dale was initially reluctant and asked that she please not identify him by name. Borundy pressed Dale. His comments, after all, had been made at a public event about teen homosexuality. Had Dale pushed back, emphasizing the harm and upset that might be caused by divulging his name, Borundy says that she "probably" would not have identified Dale by name or used his picture in the story. Dale, however, relented, without necessarily thinking through the repercussions of coming out in a newspaper with the largest circulation in New Jersey.

The morning the story appeared on July 8, 1990, James Kay began getting phone calls. Kay was the head of Monmouth Council of the Boy Scouts of America (BSA), one of fourteen councils in New Jersey and one of four hundred BSA councils nationwide. As the executive of Monmouth Council, Kay oversaw more than two hundred Scouting units—seventy-seven of which were Boy Scout troops—that included about eight thousand boys and nearly three thousand adults. To Kay, who had been in his post only two years, the *Star-Ledger* story would have meant little. Kay would not have recognized Dale by sight or name, and the *Star-Ledger* story made no mention of Dale's affiliation with the Scouts. But Dale was sufficiently well known to the old hands in the Monmouth Scouting community that the story would not go unnoticed. Volunteer Scout leaders who knew Dale contacted Kay to inform him of what they had read: there in black and white in the state's most read newspaper was the assistant Scoutmaster of Monmouth Council's Troop 73 admitting that he was gay. A number of *Star-Ledger* readers even cut out the article and mailed it to Kay.

A professional Scout since 1965, the forty-eight-year-old Kay had essentially spent his entire adult life working for the Scouts. Kay was well aware that the Boy Scouts' policy was not to admit those who openly professed their homosexuality, and that the Scouts were currently in litigation over precisely this issue. Knowing that he could not ignore the *Star-Ledger* story—especially now that other Scouts had brought it to his attention—Kay notified BSA headquarters in Irving, Texas. The national office instructed Kay on the action that needed to be taken and the letter to be used—the same form letter the Scouts used in every case of dismissal.

On July 19, Kay wrote to Dale to inform him that after "careful review" the Scouts had decided to terminate Dale's involvement with the Scouts. Membership in the Boy Scouts was "a privilege," explained Kay. And the Scouts reserved the right not to extend that privilege "whenever there is a concern that an individual may not meet the high standards of membership which the BSA seeks to provide for American youth." The letter also informed Dale that he could have the decision reviewed by a BSA regional review committee, and that if he wished to do so he had sixty days to write to the BSA regional director "explaining [his] version of the facts."

The letter stunned Dale. A few friends had congratulated him on the *Star-Ledger* story, but he had thought little more about it. Certainly he had never considered the possibility that his minor role in a back-page article could rupture his relationship with the Scouts, a relationship that had begun when he joined Cub Scout Pack 242 at the age of eight.

Dale was no casual Scout. He came from a family that was deeply invested in Scouting, and from the time he was eight until he turned eighteen Dale had immersed himself in the activities of Scouting. It was the Scouts who first provided this sometimes "insecure and fearful kid" with a sense of belonging and acceptance in a group. Dale recalls trying "soccer, band, karate—all the activities that little boys growing up in my middle-class New Jersey suburb were supposed to enjoy," but found that he "spent most of [his] time on the sidelines." Scouting, in contrast, gave him "positive reinforcement, a direction, shared goals." Dale remembers that his "fellow Cub Scouts didn't judge me because I couldn't hit a home run. We were taught to appreciate each other's strengths because each of us was a unique and necessary part of a larger whole."

Many adolescents leave the Scouts when they hit their teenage years. Not James Dale. If anything, his involvement in the Scouts only intensified. His teenage life revolved around the Boy Scouts. He earned thirty merit badges and became an Eagle Scout at seventeen. Dale was also elected to the Order of the Arrow (OA), the BSA's national honor society, which recognizes "Scouts and Scouters [a "Scouter" is a registered adult member of BSA] who best exemplify the Scout Oath and Law in their daily lives." So exemplary was Dale's conduct that he was awarded the Vigil Honor, a "high mark of distinction . . . reserved for those Arrowmen who, by reason of exceptional service, personal effort, and unselfish interest, have made distinguished contributions" to the Scouting community. A model Scout, Dale was asked to chair his local Vigil Honor selection committee and was regularly tapped by his elders to represent the Scouts at civic and fund-raising events. Upon turning eighteen, Dale was asked to continue his association with the Scouts as an assistant Scoutmaster. Although college-bound, Dale agreed to volunteer his time to aid an organization that he adored—and that he thought adored him.

Now that organization was rejecting him, and without providing any information about what he had done wrong or why he had been expelled. Dale could not quite believe it. He felt "very, very betrayed." Dale explained: "When they wrote me that expulsion letter saying basically they want nothing to do with me, I took all my Scouting stuff, my merit badges, my uniform, knapsack, every bit of paraphernalia and put it in a box, and put the box in the attic." On August 8 (Kay's letter from July 19 did not reach Dale until August 5), a devastated Dale wrote to Kay seeking an explanation. Kay's response, dated August 10, was immediate. "The grounds for this membership revocation," Kay explained, "are the standards for leadership established by the Boy Scouts of America, which specifically forbid membership to homosexuals."

The first letter had felt like a sucker punch; it had come without warning and without explanation and had left Dale feeling confused and betrayed. The organization that had given him "a sense of belonging" no longer wanted him. Now that he had his answer, though, Dale felt the blow even more keenly. Confusion gave way to outrage and anger at a policy he regarded as profoundly unjust. He could see no rational reason why being gay should make him unfit to be a Scout leader. The Scouts, he told people, had taught him "to stand up for what is right," and he was determined to fight back against what he deeply believed was an injustice and a perversion of the true teachings of the Boy Scouts.

Dale knew those teachings as well as anyone and nowhere did he find anything to suggest that being gay was inconsistent with being a Scout, nor was he aware of any written policy that forbade homosexuals from being Boy Scouts. Like every other Scout, Dale had been required to memorize the Scout Oath:

On my honor, I will do my best
To do my duty to God and my Country and to obey the
Scout Law;
To help other people at all times;
To keep myself physically strong, mentally awake, and
morally straight.

To ensure that every young Scout knew the meaning of their solemn promise, the Scouts instructed boys on the meaning of each part of the oath. In the tenth edition of the *Boy Scout Handbook*, published in 1990, youth were taught the meaning of the pledge to be "morally straight": "To be a person of strong character, guide your life with honesty, purity, and justice. Respect and defend the rights of all people. Your relationships with others should be honest and open. Be clean in your speech and actions, and faithful in your religious beliefs. The values you follow as a Scout will help you become virtuous and self-reliant." The ninth edition of the *Handbook*, in circulation between 1979 and 1990, included a two-page explication of the meaning of "morally straight" that ended with the solemn injunction: "Let your conscience be your guide. Know what is right. Do what is right." In none of the many editions of the *Handbook* dating back to 1911 did the explanation of "morally straight" make any mention of sexual orientation. Nor had anyone in the Scouts ever suggested to Dale that the words referred to sexual orientation. In openly acknowledging his homosexuality, Dale believed that he was following the Scouts' teachings to follow one's conscience and "not to lie about who we are."

In taking the Scout Oath, Dale pledged to obey the Scout Law, which the *Handbook* described as "the foundation on which the whole Scouting movement is built." The moral credo by which all Scouts are expected to live, the Scout Law consists of twelve commandments. Boy Scouts are famously required to be trustworthy, loyal, helpful, friendly, courteous, kind, obedient, cheerful, thrifty, brave, clean, and reverent. Again Dale found nothing in these words to suggest that a Scout must be heterosexual.

The 1990 edition of the *Handbook* explained that the Scout Law's injunction to be clean meant that a boy must avoid the "kind of dirt . . . that shows up in foul language and harmful thoughts." To be clean in "body and mind" meant avoiding the use of "swear words, profanity, and dirty stories" because they were "weapons that ridicule other people and hurt their feelings." For the same reason, the clean Scout must avoid "racial slurs and jokes making fun of ethnic groups or people with physical or mental limitations." Knowing that "there is no kindness or honor in such mean-spirited behavior," a Scout not only avoids this type of insulting behavior in "his own words and deeds" but also actively "defends those who are targets of insults." Nowhere did the *Handbook* suggest that a gay person lived an unclean life.

Nor did Dale find any hint of an antigay policy in the venerable Scout Motto (Be Prepared!) or Scout Slogan (Do a Good Turn Daily!), which were the other principal components of the Scouting code that every "true Scout" was required to understand and live by.

On Dale's reading, the Scouting code that he had been taught had nothing to say about homosexuality but a great deal to say about personal and collective responsibility and about standing up for oneself and helping others.

Although Dale believed that he had been wronged, it was less clear what he could do about it. The Scouts were a private organization. And in the summer of 1990, New Jersey—like almost every other state in the nation—had no law that forbade discrimination on the basis of sexual orientation, even by public entities. Moreover, the US Supreme Court had never held that sexual orientation was a suspect classification subject to heightened judicial scrutiny under the Equal Protection Clause of the Fourteenth Amendment. It was unclear that the Scouts had done anything illegal in terminating Dale's membership.

It also wasn't clear that it was worth the fight. This was the *Boy* Scouts, after all, and Dale was now a man. The Boy Scouts had been an integral part of his adolescent development, but the Scouts needed volunteers like Dale more than he needed them. Some friends urged him to forget the matter. If the Scouts wanted to deny themselves the services of a model Scout and citizen, then it was their loss. A lawsuit would also be expensive, and Dale was a full-time college student with few resources. His mother and father shared their son's sense of outrage, but they were of modest means too.

Challenging his expulsion would also mean broadcasting his homosexuality to the nation. As a youth, Dale remembered "hoping to God [he] wouldn't be gay," and it had taken all his courage to finally come out to his family and close friends. Was he ready for the whole world to know he was gay? This would be a daunting prospect for any young man. But imagine how much more difficult for someone whose conservative upbringing had included graduating from a military high school—the Marine Academy of Science and Technology (MAST) in Sandy Hook, New Jersey—at a time when the military did not permit gays to serve in the military. And like all his high school classmates, Dale had been required to be a member of Naval Junior Reserve Officer Training Corps. (Dale was no ordinary cadet; he was selected as one of a handful of "company commanders" at the school.)

Dale was also an unlikely candidate for gay "activist." As a teen he had largely been politically quiescent. He had not even been "a news junkie." For Dale, the phrase "gay activist" conjured up stereotypical images of AIDS protesters chanting slogans, waving signs, confronting police, marching on buildings. Dale had been trained—by family, schooling, and the Scouts—to think of himself as a leader and dutiful citizen, not as a defiant protester or angry activist.

Nonetheless, Dale decided that he needed to do something to protest a policy that he believed was profoundly unfair and incompatible with the true spirit of Scouting. After all, the first and most famous point of the Scout Law demanded that a Scout be "trustworthy." The Boy Scouts had long taught that this meant that "a Scout tells the truth" and that honesty is "a part of his code of conduct." Yet now the Scouts were terminating Dale for having told the truth about who he really was, for having followed the Scout Law as every Boy Scout pledged to do. Dale felt that the Scouts had not only wronged him but were doing an injustice to every gay Scout by requiring them to lie in order to remain a Boy Scout or a Scout leader.

Dale decided to seek legal counsel and was advised that before proceeding with legal action against the Scouts, he would need to exhaust the internal appeal procedures offered by the Boy Scouts. Kay's initial letter dated July 19 had included a copy of the procedures for requesting a review of the decision by the BSA's regional review committee. Those procedures included the opportunity for Dale to attend the review hearing. At the end of September, Dale wrote to the director of the northeast region—one of the BSA's four administrative regions—to request a review of the expulsion decision and to indicate that he wished to attend the review hearing, as was his right under the Scouts' procedures that he had been sent. Dale also requested that the regional director send him a copy of the BSA's "standards for leadership" that Kay had invoked in his letter from August 10.

A week later Dale received a brief letter from the assistant regional director Charles Ball that acknowledged receipt of Dale's request and notified him that a review committee had been appointed to review his file. No mention was made as to when or where the review hearing would be held. And no copy of the requested "standards for leadership" was forthcoming. Dale wrote again, reminding Ball that he wished to attend the hearing and therefore needed to know when and where the meeting would be held. Dale heard nothing from the Scouts for six weeks. Finally, at the end of November, Dale received a letter, again from Ball, informing him that the regional review committee had affirmed the decision to terminate Dale's registration with the Scouts.

Clearly the appeals process was getting Dale nowhere. Indeed the Scouts weren't even following their own procedures. The only way forward was legal action. Back in August, Dale had sought advice about legal representation from an acquaintance at the New Jersey Lesbian and Gay Coalition. Dale was given the names of two brilliant young lawyers in the gay and lesbian community: Ruth Harlow of the American Civil Liberties Union of New Jersey and Evan Wolfson of the New York City–based Lambda Legal Defense and Education Fund. Dale talked first with Harlow, whom he had met before. Harlow was sympathetic to Dale's plight, but she had only recently begun work at the ACLU and thought that Lambda Legal would be better suited to helping Dale. So Dale drove to New York City to meet with Wolfson in hopes of persuading Lambda Legal to take the case of a gay Boy Scout.

CHAPTER 2

In Dale's Defense

The Lambda Legal Defense and Education Fund opened its doors as a public interest law firm in 1973. The brainchild of a young New York lawyer, William J. Thom, Lambda Legal was established to provide free legal assistance for gay men and lesbians and to educate gays and lesbians about their legal rights. In requesting incorporation, Thom modeled his application word for word on the paperwork filed by the recently established Puerto Rican Legal Defense and Education Fund, only substituting lesbians and gay men for Puerto Ricans. Under New York law at the time, an entity practicing law could not be incorporated unless it was "organized for benevolent or charitable purposes, or for the purpose of assisting persons without means in the pursuit of any civil remedy." A New York court unanimously rejected Thom's application for incorporation because the organization's purposes were "neither benevolent nor charitable, . . . nor, in any event, is there a demonstrated need for this corporation." The court rejected the analogy with Puerto Ricans, arguing that while Puerto Ricans were poor and therefore could not afford a lawyer, gay and lesbians were not similarly disadvantaged in obtaining legal help. Only upon appeal to the state's highest court was the lower court's judgment reversed and Lambda allowed to start work.

In its early days Lambda operated on a shoestring budget, with Thom as "president and chief cook and bottle washer" and his partner as general counsel. Lambda was "pretty cautious" at first, Thom recalls, preferring to take cases in which there was "close to an optimum set of facts." Although Lambda lacked a publicity budget, its work steadily attracted attention within the gay and lesbian community. With the increased attention came more financial support, which in turn enabled Lambda to expand its legal staff.

By the time James Dale arrived in Evan Wolfson's office in August 1990, Lambda had been serving gay and lesbian clients for nearly twenty years. However, in 1990 it was still a relatively modest organization, with only four lawyers handling all the casework. Taking on the Boy Scouts would be a huge undertaking. Some within Lambda were skeptical that Dale's case was worth pursuing. They even wondered why a grown man would want to be a Boy Scout in the first place. There were scores of important discrimination cases that involved gays and lesbians losing their jobs. Was it really worth going to court so that Dale could be reinstated in a volunteer position? For an adult to be excluded from the Boy Scouts hardly seemed a big deal compared to the scourge of AIDS that was then ravaging the gay community.

Since the onset of the AIDS epidemic in the early 1980s, Lambda had devoted much of its limited legal and educational resources to combating discrimination against people with AIDS. In 1983, in one of the nation's first lawsuits dealing with bias against people with AIDS, Lambda joined with the New York attorney general to block tenants in a cooperative apartment house in Greenwich Village from evicting a doctor who treated HIV-positive patients. Lambda had also played a pivotal role in pressuring the manufacturers of the antiviral drug AZT (azidothymidine) to significantly lower its price. In 1989 Lambda achieved a landmark legal victory when it persuaded a federal judge in California that a rehabilitation clinic had violated federal antidiscrimination laws by discharging a man after he had tested positive for HIV. By the end of the 1980s, almost 40 percent of Lambda's legal docket was devoted to AIDS litigation. Some at Lambda doubted the wisdom of diverting the organization's precious resources away from the front lines of the war against AIDS discrimination in order to fight a skirmish that seemed at the periphery of the battle for gay rights.

There was also a worry that taking on the Boy Scouts could be bad for Lambda. The tragedy of AIDS had been a financial windfall for Lambda. Between 1985—the year that legendary movie star Rock Hudson revealed to the nation that he had contracted AIDS—and 1986, Lambda's revenue stream tripled, shooting up from $300,000 to $900,000; by way of contrast, at the opening of the decade Lambda had taken in only about $50,000 a year. Lambda's

AIDS-related litigation had enabled it, for the first time in its history, to attract grant money from mainstream foundations that had previously kept their distance from Lambda's gay rights agenda. In 1980, Lambda received only $6,000 in grants and the following year nothing at all. In contrast, by the end of the decade, in 1989, Lambda pulled in $275,000 in foundation grants. Might taking on a case like Dale's jeopardize the huge strides the organization had made?

Moreover, Lambda's philosophy was to select cases that they believed were winnable and that would therefore establish positive legal precedents. No one could dispute that Dale was a model Boy Scout. It would be difficult to find a better vehicle for combating stereotypes about gay men than James Dale. But taking on an iconic American institution like the Boy Scouts hardly seemed like a winning strategy. And losing could establish negative legal precedents that would set back the cause of gay rights.

The attorneys at Lambda were especially sensitive to the dangers of creating negative precedents because of the outcome in *Bowers v. Hardwick*, the controversial case from 1986 in which the Supreme Court upheld the constitutionality of a Georgia statute outlawing sodomy. Writing for a 5–4 majority, Justice Byron White sneeringly dismissed the contention that the constitutional right to privacy afforded to heterosexuals protected homosexual sex as well. To this sixty-nine-year-old former professional football player, the idea that there was "a fundamental right to engage in homosexual sodomy" was laughable; it was, he said, "at best, facetious." The Court's ruling not only set back the cause of those challenging sodomy statutes in the twenty-six states that still had them, but provided a disastrous precedent that guided lower courts in a host of cases involving discrimination against gays and lesbians. For instance, in *Padula v. Webster* (1987), the DC Court of Appeals invoked *Bowers* in explaining why the FBI could not be faulted for refusing to hire a lesbian. The court reasoned that "if the [Supreme] Court was unwilling to object to laws that criminalize the behavior that defines the class, it is hardly open to a lower court to conclude that state sponsored discrimination against the class is invidious. After all, there can hardly be more palpable discrimination against a class than making the conduct that defines the class criminal." Pressing ahead with the

Bowers case—a controversial decision within the gay rights community—ended up legitimating the very discrimination that Lambda was dedicated to combating.

Making Dale's case seem even more quixotic was the fact that the Supreme Court appeared to be moving in a more conservative direction. Although Lewis Powell, who had sided with the Court's majority in *Bowers*, had retired, Court watchers saw no reason to believe that his conservative Republican replacement, Anthony Kennedy, would be more sympathetic to gay rights. And Justice William Brennan, one of the four dissenters in *Bowers* and the most vocal supporter of gay rights on the Court, had stepped down in the summer of 1990 after suffering a stroke. When the Supreme Court had refused in 1985 to hear an appeal from a high school guidance counselor who had been fired because of her sexual orientation, it was Brennan (joined only by the reliably liberal Thurgood Marshall) who dissented, chiding his colleagues for ignoring that

> homosexuals constitute a significant and insular minority of this country's population. Because of the immediate and severe opprobrium often manifested against homosexuals once so identified publicly, members of this group are particularly powerless to pursue their rights openly in the political arena. Moreover, homosexuals have historically been the object of pernicious and sustained hostility, and it is fair to say that discrimination against homosexuals is "likely . . . to reflect deep-seated prejudice rather than . . . rationality."

Little was known about Brennan's reclusive replacement, David Souter, but what little was known prompted Lambda's legal director, Paula Ettelbrick, to testify against Souter's confirmation at the Senate Judiciary Committee hearings in September 1990. Ettelbrick based her opposition largely on the grounds that in 1987 Souter had joined an unsigned advisory opinion by the New Hampshire Supreme Court that declared that a statute prohibiting gays and lesbians from becoming adoptive and foster parents violated neither the federal Constitution nor the state constitution because the state's goal of providing "a healthy environment and role models" was "rationally related" to the ban. Among the reasons that the state could legitimately decide that gays and lesbians were not suitable role models was the concern that gay parents might negatively affect a child's "developing sexual identity." Lambda's anxiety about the direction of the Court was heightened by rumors of Marshall's failing health, which made it look increasingly likely that President George Herbert Walker Bush would get to name his replacement (as indeed happened the next year when Marshall resigned and Bush nominated Clarence Thomas). Given the makeup of the Court, it was difficult to see where five votes in favor of Dale would come from.

Wolfson was not naïve. He could count votes as well as the next lawyer. And he was only too well aware of the disastrous legal consequences of the *Bowers* litigation. Indeed it was Wolfson, working in a pro bono capacity, who had authored Lambda's amicus brief in *Bowers*. Wolfson knew that Dale's case was risky, but he believed it was a gamble worth taking. And winning wasn't everything. Creating positive legal precedents was important, of course. But just as important in Wolfson's eyes was using the law "to impact the public dialogue and conversation."

And on that score, *Bowers*'s legacy was not as negative as it first appeared. Wolfson saw the Court's decision in *Bowers*, along with AIDS, as one of "the two towering paradigm shifters of the '80s." In Wolfson's view, *Bowers* had a "galvanizing effect" on the gay rights movement because it "energized a grass-roots movement . . . and politicized people." Anger at White's derisive words helped to spark the 1987 March on Washington for Lesbian and Gay Rights, which attracted a half million marchers. Six hundred people were arrested on the steps of the Supreme Court building in what political scientist Ellen Ann Andersen described as the "largest single act of civil disobedience in the United States since the anti–Vietnam War demonstrations." One telling indication of the impact of *Bowers* on the public dialogue came in October 1990 when Powell confessed that he had "made a mistake" in siding with the *Bowers* majority.

Wolfson also knew that the legal setback in *Bowers* had boosted Lambda's fund-raising. Lambda had sent out solicitation letters immediately after the *Bowers* ruling, and for the next year the case was "the cornerstone" of the organization's fund-raising appeals. Individual contributions in 1986 exceeded a half million dollars, three times what it had been in the year before *Bowers*. Indeed, so deep-seated was the disappointment and anger at *Bowers* within the gay and lesbian community that the case would remain an important component of Lambda's fund-raising appeals until 2003, when, in *Lawrence v. Texas*, the Supreme Court finally overruled *Bowers*.

In helping to expand Lambda's budget, the "paradigm shifters" of *Bowers* and AIDS had created litigation opportunities that had been unthinkable in the organization's first decade. But with enhanced resources and broader litigation opportunities also came sharp and sometimes bitter disagreements among Lambda's staff in the late 1980s and early 1990s about the direction the organization should take and the causes it should champion.

Among the most divisive fights within Lambda during this period was whether the organization should get involved in the nascent movement for same-sex marriage. Many in the lesbian and gay community regarded marriage as an oppressive heterosexual institution that had no place in gay liberation. Among the leading proponents of this position was Lambda's legal director Paula Ettelbrick, who in 1989 authored a widely read essay titled "Since When Is Marriage a Path to Liberation?" Taking the other side in the debate in the pages of the gay and lesbian journal *Out/Look* was Lambda's executive director Tom Stoddard. Amid Lambda's public spat about same-sex marriage in 1989, Ettelbrick recruited the thirty-two-year-old Wolfson—who in 1983 as a third-year Harvard law student had written a thesis arguing that gays and lesbians should have the right to marry—to join Lambda.

Wolfson was smart, politically savvy, energetic, and intensely committed to advancing the cause of gay rights. Born in Brooklyn but raised in the suburbs of Pittsburgh, Wolfson was the eldest son of lifelong Democrats who hoped that one day their precocious offspring—how many thirteen-year-old boys invite the president of the United States to their bar mitzvah?—might just become the first Jewish-American president. As an undergraduate at Yale University, Wolfson was elected Speaker of the Yale Political Union, and his exemplary academic record got him admitted to Harvard Law School. First, however, he opted for a two-year stint with the Peace Corps in Togo, where he had his first gay relationship and a close-up look at a society in which the stigma against homosexuality stunted the lives of countless gay men. Upon graduating from Harvard Law School in 1983, Wolfson returned to his birthplace to take a job as an assistant district attorney, a position in which he quickly distinguished himself. While in the DA's office, Wolfson penned an amicus brief for a landmark US Supreme Court case that outlawed dismissing prospective jurors solely based on their race (*Baston v. Kentucky*) and authored another brief that helped to persuade the New York high court to eliminate the exemption that had permitted rape within a marriage (*People v. Liberta*). Wolfson's deepest passion, however, remained the cause of gay rights, and when the opportunity came to join Lambda—for whom he had already worked pro bono on several cases, including *Bowers*—he was quick to say yes.

Dale's case raised decidedly different legal questions from those raised by same-sex marriage, but it activated some of the same philosophical and personal fault lines within Lambda that had emerged in the fight over same-sex marriage. Ettelbrick believed that "justice for gay men and lesbians will be achieved only when we are accepted and supported in this society *despite* our differences from the dominant culture." Wolfson wanted Lambda to take Dale's case precisely because it would help heterosexual Americans see that there was nothing different about gay and lesbian Americans, apart from sexual orientation. In Wolfson's vision, justice for gays and lesbians depended on showing that they were as much a part of mainstream American culture as were heterosexuals—that, fundamentally, gay and lesbian Americans wanted the same things that all Americans wanted. Whereas Ettelbrick worried that Dale's case would skew the gay rights cause by highlighting a clean-cut, good-looking young man in a mainstream, conservative organization, Wolfson saw Dale's clean-cut conservative persona as a beautiful way to challenge societal stereotypes about gay men and help heterosexual Americans see themselves reflected in the image of homosexual Americans. Ultimately, Ettelbrick's challenge was overcome, and Wolfson—backed by Stoddard—was given the green light to pursue Dale's case.

Now Wolfson had to find a large law firm that would be willing to take the case on a pro bono basis. Despite its increase in funding and litigation capacity, Lambda did not have anything like the resources required to mount a successful legal case against an organization as well endowed as the Boy Scouts. Getting a law firm to help, however, proved to be exceptionally difficult. Some prominent firms turned down Wolfson immediately. One firm agreed to take the case and then abruptly dropped out, citing unspecified "conflict" within the firm. Others said they would have their lawyers do some research on the case, but after conducting the research they declined as well. Some of the firms may have been put off by the fact that this was "a gay case," but an even greater obstacle was the prospect of taking on an iconic American institution, one that many of the lawyers had belonged to as boys or were still involved with as adults.

There was still another problem, however. Like almost all states at the time, New Jersey did not have a law that prohibited discrimination based on sexual orientation. Passing nondiscrimination statutes had been a priority of gay and lesbian activists across the nation since the 1970s, and they had been reasonably successful at the local level. In 1972 the college towns of Ann Arbor and East Lansing, Michigan, became the first to pass local ordinances barring employment discrimination against gays and lesbians. And over the next decade and a half, major cities across the country, including San Francisco (1978), Los Angeles (1979), Philadelphia (1982), Boston (1984), New York City (1986), and Chicago (1988), barred discrimination against gays and lesbians in public and private employment as well as in public accommodations and housing. Progress had been much slower at the state level, however. In 1982 Wisconsin became the first state to pass a comprehensive law protecting gays and lesbians against discrimination in public and private employment, public accommodations, and housing. However, convincing other state legislatures to follow suit was difficult. Some governors, including in New York (1983), Ohio (1983), Washington (1985), Rhode Island (1985), Minnesota (1986), and Oregon (1987), had issued executive orders prohibiting discrimination against gays and lesbian public employees, but such unilateral executive action was necessarily limited in its scope.

Prior to 1990, New Jersey had not been in the vanguard of the movement to protect gays and lesbians from discrimination. An antidiscrimination statute had been introduced in the state legislature as early as 1984, but strong opposition from the New Jersey

Catholic Conference ensured that it never made it out of committee. Before 1990, not one New Jersey town had enacted an ordinance banning discrimination based on sexual orientation. But times were changing, in New Jersey as in the rest of the country. In 1990, New Jersey's largest city, Newark, as well as a couple of smaller localities, passed ordinances that outlawed discrimination against gay and lesbian city workers. More important for Dale's case was the momentum building within the state legislature for an antidiscrimination law. In the spring of 1991, the new Democratic governor Jim Florio signaled his willingness to support gay rights by issuing an executive order banning discrimination on the basis of sexual orientation in state employment. Buoyed by Florio's support, the New Jersey Lesbian and Gay Coalition spearheaded a lobbying campaign on behalf of a bill that would amend the New Jersey Law against Discrimination (NJLAD) to include sexual orientation. After eight years of failing to move the bill out of committee, the coalition finally succeeded in bringing the legislation to the floor of both houses for a vote. And on January 13, 1992, the final day of the legislature's lame-duck session, the legislation passed the Democratic-controlled general assembly and state senate by overwhelming margins (46–7 and 21–0, respectively). When Florio signed the bill the following week, New Jersey became only the fifth state in the nation—the others were Connecticut (1991), Hawaii (1991), Massachusetts (1989), and of course Wisconsin—to prohibit discrimination against lesbians and gay men in employment, public accommodations, housing, and credit.

With the new law in place, Dale's legal prospects suddenly looked brighter. Before the law's passage, Dale's case had understandably seemed a no-hoper to many of the law firms that Wolfson contacted. The new statute made Dale's case appear viable. Not coincidentally, Wolfson's frustrating eighteen-month, "scorched earth" search for a firm willing to take the case pro bono was about to come to an end.

Wolfson's breakthrough came via a young corporate lawyer he knew at the widely respected New York law firm Cleary Gottlieb Steen & Hamilton. Although the friend was not a litigator, he knew someone at the firm who was and who he thought might be interested in the case: Donna Costa. Costa was young—barely thirty—

but had recently been made a senior associate at Cleary. A corporate lawyer, she had "really strong feelings about gay rights" and jumped at the opportunity to represent Dale. But for Cleary to take the case, Costa's assent was not sufficient. First, she had to convince one of the partners at the firm to oversee the case. She approached Thomas J. Moloney, who agreed to sponsor the case. For Moloney, Dale's case was about "fairness." "If you can discriminate against gay Scouts," he explained, "then you can discriminate against black Scouts and Jewish Scouts." Moloney persuaded the partnership to back the case.

For the next eight years, Cleary would essentially foot the bill for a case that would end up requiring thousands of hours of pro bono work by the firm's attorneys, including many hundreds of hours taking depositions. According to Costa, almost everybody at the firm "wanted a piece of the case," and at least a dozen of the firm's talented lawyers worked on the case at one point or another over the next decade.

With Cleary now on board, Dale's legal team quickly readied their case. On July 29, 1992, almost two years to the day that Dale first learned that he had been booted from his beloved Boy Scouts, Dale's lawyers filed a complaint in New Jersey Superior Court alleging that the Boy Scouts had illegally discriminated against Dale. The complaint asked that Dale be reinstated as assistant Scoutmaster and that he be financially compensated "for the emotional pain and suffering he experienced and for the loss of his valuable privileges as a member of the Boy Scouts."

CHAPTER 3

The Three Gs

By the time Dale filed his suit in the summer of 1992, the Boy Scouts had grown accustomed to legal battles and political controversy. The previous summer the *New York Times* had featured the Scouts' legal troubles in a front-page article titled "Boy Scouts Try to Keep Identity as Outsiders Knock." The *Times* portrayed an organization whose leaders felt "besieged" by the demand for change; the story closed with a Scouting executive's lament that "society's views are changing and they are trying to get everyone loose in their moral standards." But the Scouts also had reason to be confident about their position. After having seen membership plummet in the 1970s, from 4.8 million in 1972 to 3.1 million in 1979, the Scouts' membership numbers climbed steadily in the 1980s, reaching 4.3 million in 1990—though much of this increase was because the BSA expanded Cub Scouts to include first (Tiger Cub Scouts) and second graders (Wolf Cub Scouts).

Scouting officials offered two somewhat conflicting explanations for their recent success. On the one hand, they credited programs that made the Boy Scouts more relevant to modern times. Under the leadership of Chief Scout Executive Ben Love (1985–1993), the Scouts initiated a campaign to combat the five "unacceptables": hunger, illicit drugs, child abuse, youth unemployment, and illiteracy. The Scouts also reached out aggressively to youth in inner cities and expanded coeducational "Career Awareness" Explorer posts, which enabled young people to meet professionals in fields such as law enforcement or medicine. The venerable *Boy Scout Handbook* added twenty-four pages on protecting children from sexual abuse and drugs. "We're not using the Norman Rockwell image anymore," Love boasted in a December 1990 interview with *Time* magazine.

Although determined to remain relevant to a changing society, Scouting officials also attributed their success during the 1980s to their steadfast adherence to Scouting traditions. Speaking to a *Los Angeles Times* reporter in September 1990, the director of the eleven-state Western region of the BSA explained the rebound in the Scouts' fortunes this way: "We were a victim of the '60s philosophy. . . . We like to think that people are coming back to values we never left." On this reading, the Scouts lost members in the 1970s because of a countercultural movement that made the Boy Scouts seem square. Now that society was returning to traditional mores the Scouts were flourishing once again. Only a month after Love had publicly distanced the Scouts from an idealized Norman Rockwell image, he defiantly told a reporter for *US News and World Report* that the Scouts would fight all the way to the Supreme Court to keep homosexuals and atheists out of the Boy Scouts. "A homosexual," Love explained, "is not the role model I want as the leader of my son's troop—and neither is an atheist." Becoming relevant and adapting to a changing society was one thing, but admitting homosexuals and atheists was quite another.

As Love's comment suggests, the Scouts' legal troubles were not limited to challenges from gays. Those who did not believe in God were challenging the Scouts' right to exclude individuals who did not affirm that they would "do [their] duty to God," as the Scout Oath required. Girls, too, were knocking on the Scouts' door, insisting that the Girl Scouts did not offer comparable opportunities to the Boy Scouts. Some in Scouting began to refer to this as "the three Gs" membership policy: no girls, godless, or gays.

Girls

When it came to gender, the Scouts by the early 1990s had begun to temper their defiance with pragmatic adaptation. Up until 1988 the Boy Scouts had resolutely refused to allow women to be Scoutmasters or assistant Scoutmasters. Fifty-six-year-old Catherine Pollard had thrown down the gauntlet to the Scouts after they twice denied her request, in 1974 and again in 1976, to become Scoutmaster of Troop 13 in Milford, Connecticut; she had been serving as leader of the troop in an informal capacity for several years because no men had been willing to assume the position. Calling the Boy Scouts' prohibition on women Scoutmasters "antiquated," Pollard took her complaint to the state's Commission on Human Rights and Opportunities. "What was good 30 years ago isn't today," she insisted. Chief Scout Executive J. L. Tarr (1979–1984) defended the Boy Scouts against the charge that they were old-fashioned or out-of-date: "If they mean by that that the Boy Scouts emphasizes patriotism, service to others, character and religious commitment in this selfish and Godless age, then I guess Boy Scouts would have to admit to the charge."

In 1984 the commission's hearing officer dealt the Boy Scouts an unexpected defeat. By refusing to allow Pollard to become the troop's Scoutmaster, the hearing officer ruled, the Boy Scouts had violated the state's public accommodations law, which prohibited discrimination on the basis of race, creed, color, national origin, ancestry, sex, marital status, or physical disability. The Scouts appealed and gained the sympathetic ear of Superior Court Judge Joseph J. Chernauskas, who rejected the notion that the Boy Scouts were a public accommodation and denied that the organization's ban on female Scoutmasters was discriminatory. "This is not," Chernauskas wrote, "an attempt by the National Boy Scouts Council to encourage the retention of 'traditional' sex roles, freezing biology into social destiny, but reflects only the initial and longstanding concept with respect to a male role model in certain Boy Scouts age groups." Pollard appealed to the state supreme court, where she lost again. According to the state's highest court, Connecticut's public accommodations law did not apply to Pollard because volunteering as a youth leader was a privilege rather than a protected right.

The Boy Scouts had prevailed, but at a substantial cost to their image. Battling against a widowed grandmother in her sixties was hardly calculated to burnish the Scouts' image. Moreover, the Scouts faced an acute shortage of male volunteer leaders. After the Scouts rejected Pollard, Troop 13 was forced to disband because it could not find a man willing to serve as a Scoutmaster. In addition, the principle for which the Scouts were fighting was muddied since the Scouts had long permitted women to serve as den leaders (formerly known as den mothers) for seven- to ten-year-old boys in

Cub Scout packs and as leaders of coed Explorer units that included boys between the ages of fifteen and twenty. Tarr's insistence that it was only in "the difficult developmental years" between ages ten and fourteen that boys required "a male role model and counselor" was not convincing, even to the BSA leadership.

Having won the legal right to exclude women, the national leadership of the Boy Scouts reconsidered the wisdom of a policy that had been in place for more than seven decades. In February 1988, a little over six months after its decisive victory in the Connecticut high court, the BSA voted unanimously to "remove gender restrictions on all Scouting leadership positions." Local troops from now on would be free to choose the best person regardless of their gender. "The time had come," the Scouts explained, "to recognize the valuable leadership women can provide." At the age of seventy, Pollard became the first official female Scoutmaster in the history of the BSA. By the end of 1991, the BSA had fourteen hundred female Scoutmasters—about 3 percent of the total number of Scoutmasters.

Although the Scouts decided to admit women as Scout leaders, they continued to cling to the exclusion of girls from the Cub Scouts and Boy Scouts. Back in 1971 the Scouts had made a partial concession to gender equality by permitting girls to register as Explorer Scouts, a program geared to fifteen to twenty year olds. The Scouts were adamant, however, that they would make no such concessions for the Cub Scout and Boy Scout programs, which were premised on the belief that "boys between the ages of 8 and 14 seek out and enjoy group activities with other boys." The Scouting program, the national office explained in a memo from June 1991, had been "carefully developed . . . to meet the emotional, psychological, physical, and other needs of boys between the ages of 8 and 14."

As far back as 1976 the BSA had been compelled to defend its all-boys policy before a state supreme court, after it had refused to allow an Oregon girl, Carla Schwenk, to become a member. Helping the Boy Scouts make their case to the Oregon high court were the Camp Fire Girls and the Girl Scouts, both of whom feared that opening the Boy Scouts to girls would increase competition for members as well as undercut their own ability to exclude members of the opposite sex. Although the court's chief justice agreed with Schwenk that Oregon's public accommodations statute should extend to a noncommercial entity like the Boy Scouts, the rest of the Oregon high court concluded that the Scouts could not be compelled to admit girls because the state's antidiscrimination law did not apply to the Scouts.

Neither Schwenk's case nor the other complaints filed on behalf of excluded girls in the 1970s and 1980s attracted much public attention. That changed, albeit briefly, in the summer of 1991 when Margo Mankes, an eight-year-old girl from Miami, Florida, challenged her exclusion from the Cub Scouts. Scouting ran in the Mankes family: both her brothers were Boy Scouts, her mother was an assistant Scoutmaster, and her father was the leader of Cub Scout Pack 350, the pack that Margo wanted to join. Her Scouting registration had been accepted in January 1991, but her money was returned and her membership revoked after the BSA national office figured out that Margo was a girl. Margo continued to participate in her pack's meetings and activities, but when she applied to attend a Cub Scout day camp that summer, she was turned down because she was not a member of the BSA. Margo's parents then took the BSA to court, asking a judge to compel the Scouts to admit Margo and let her attend the day camp. The Mankes family argued that the Girl Scouts did not offer the same range of opportunities and challenges as the Boy Scouts. As Margo explained to one reporter, the Brownies "did tie-dying and played on water slides," whereas "Cub Scouts have cookouts, canoe, play sports, learn about tools, [and] learn to make fires." Margo's attorney pressed the case that the separate organizations were not equal; the purpose of the Girl Scouts was "to make women better homemakers," whereas the Boy Scouts were "training boys to be successful" in life. Margo's legal challenge attracted the attention not only of the *Miami Herald* but of national outlets such as the *New York Times* and *Time* magazine.

Although the Mankes case stood out for the media attention it received, Margo did not fare any better in the courts than any of the other girls who had been excluded over the past two decades. First a federal judge and then a state judge refused to intervene on Margo's behalf, and the Dade County Human Rights Board also denied Margo's appeal. Following their decisive legal victories, the Scouts terminated the membership of Margo's parents on the grounds that they had knowingly violated BSA policies by permitting their daughter to participate in Pack 350. Although the Scouts had relented on the leadership issue, they drew the line at admitting girls. As Love told the *New York Times* in the summer of 1991: "If we [admit girls] it would not be the Boy Scouts of America anymore."

The Godless

That the Scouts had spent the past fifteen years fending off efforts to compel the organization to open its ranks to girls and women was hardly surprising. During this same period, organizations such as Little League, the Boys Club, and the Rotary Club had faced similar legal challenges, though unlike the Scouts they consistently lost in their bid to exclude females because courts deemed them public accommodations. In the spring of 1990, however, the Scouts came under assault on a new front when the family of seven-year-old Mark Welsh, from the affluent Chicago suburb of Burr Ridge, sued the Scouts for refusing to allow atheists and agnostics to join the Scouts.

In September 1989, Mark's first grade teacher had given each of the boys in the class a flyer that invited them to join the Tiger Cubs and "Have Lots of Fun!" Enthused by the prospect of "a lot of camping, swimming, [and] parties," Mark got his dad, Elliott, to take him to the meeting in a public school gymnasium where he could sign up to join the fun. The flyer promised that "any boy . . . can join," but Mark's father, Elliott, found that the membership application required one to affirm the Scout's Declaration of Religious Principle, which meant agreeing that "recognition of God as the ruling and leading power in the universe and the grateful acknowledgment of His favors and blessings are necessary to the best type of citizenship and are wholesome precepts in the education of the growing members." Because a boy could not join the Tiger Cubs without an adult joining as a Tiger Cub Partner, it was necessary for Elliott to attest to his belief in God. For Elliott, however, the religious affirmation was no small thing. In the 1960s he had been convicted of draft evasion and sentenced to three years in prison; the court ruled that atheists and agnostics could not be exempted from the draft as conscientious objectors because they did not have religious objections to war. His historic case (*Welsh v. United States*) reached all the way to the US Supreme Court, which in 1970 overturned his conviction and affirmed that a person did not have to believe in God to be a conscientious objector. Now, two decades later, the Scouts were asking him to retract his deeply held views so that his son could join the Scouts.

Elliott requested that he and his son be permitted to become members without accepting the religious declaration, but was told that nonreligious families could not participate in the Scouts. Elliott was stunned. As a youth he had been a Boy Scout, as had his father before him, and back then religious devotion had not seemed "a particularly big point" in Scouting. An indignant Elliott felt that "this was just a taste of what it must have been like to be Black in the South before segregation." He filed suit in federal court, alleging that the Scouts' policy against admitting the nonreligious violated the Civil Rights Act of 1964, which made it illegal for public accommodations to discriminate on the basis of race, color, religion, and sex.

The case began well for the Welsh family. Judge Ilana Rovner, a Republican and Reagan appointee, rebuffed the Scouts' motion to have the case dismissed. For Rovner the question of religious persecution was intensely personal. As a child, she had been among the last Jews to leave Latvia before the Nazis arrived; other family members were not so lucky and died in concentration camps. Her initial response breathed sympathy for the Welsh boy's plight and skepticism that admitting nonbelievers or the "religiously ambivalent" would require the Scouts to "alter any of its activities." After all, the Scouts' own literature affirmed that the organization was "absolutely nonsectarian in its attitude toward religious training," that "it was not the role of the Boy Scouts of America to give theological interpretations," and that religion was "the responsibility of the Scout's family and religious leaders." She was puzzled why an organization that seemed to tolerate nearly every conceivable religious belief needed to exclude atheists and agnostics. The Scouts' concept of God was "sufficiently vague," Rovner noted, that it was "difficult to understand how the Boy Scouts can actually use, in practice, belief in God as a criterion for membership." Rovner also seemed unimpressed with the Scouts' contention that as a private organization they had an unlimited freedom to associate with like-minded individuals. Would the court also have to defer, she asked, if the BSA declared itself a whites-only organization united by a belief that blacks are inferior to whites?

When the trial opened in June 1991, the Scouts' legal team was better prepared to persuade the skeptical judge. The Scouts called witnesses to testify that duty to God was—and always had been—one of the "basic tenets" of Scouting. The BSA also impressed upon the judge that well over half of the nation's Scouts were in troops sponsored by churches; in fact, six of the top eight sponsors were churches: Methodist, Mormon, Catholic, Lutheran, Presbyterian, and Baptist. Charles Rommel, leader of a Catholic-sponsored troop, informed the court that Scouts earned religious badges, participated in activities involving Bible readings, thanked "the Lord" before meals, and even attended Mass at Scouting camps. Although conceding that these religious activities were optional, Rommel stressed that including nonbelievers would inevitably make Scouting a "totally different program." The Scouts' star witness was a Southern Baptist minister, James E. Johnson, who laid claim to being Chicago's first black Eagle Scout and who had served in a high-ranking position in the Nixon administration. Professing to speak for thirty-seven Baptist denominations (he was the chairman of the Association of Baptists for Scouting), Johnson promised the court that all Baptist churches would cut their ties to the Scouts if atheists and agnostics were allowed to join. Johnson also ridiculed the idea that the Scouts' exclusion of religious nonbelievers was comparable to discrimination faced by African Americans because of the color of their skin. As the son of a sharecropper, Johnson had experienced "raw prejudice" firsthand, and he assured the judge that there was nothing prejudiced about the Boy Scouts' policy against admitting atheists and agnostics.

In March 1992, Rovner announced her decision: the Scouts were not a place of public accommodation or public entertainment and so were not bound by the Civil Rights Act of 1964 that banned discrimination on the basis of race, color, religion, or sex. As a private organization, the Scouts had the right to "select its membership according to its own criteria and conscience." To the surprise of both sides, Rovner fully vindicated the Scouts' position. Three months later, Rovner was selected by President George H. W. Bush to serve

Scouts = private

on the US Court of Appeals for the Seventh Circuit, becoming the first woman ever to hold the position. Had Rovner ruled against the Scouts, it seems unlikely that Bush, who at the time faced a strong primary challenge from the conservative culture warrior Pat Buchanan, would have nominated her for the post.

The Welshes appealed Rovner's ruling but lost again. The appellate court, in May 1993, affirmed that Rovner was right: the Scouts were not a public accommodation and therefore did not have to comply with the Civil Rights Act. Writing for a 2–1 majority (the sole Democrat on the three-judge panel dissented), Judge John Coffey, a Reagan appointee, wrote that for the state to regulate the Scouts' membership policies risked "undermining one of the seedbeds of virtue that cultivate the sorts of citizens our nation so desperately needs," particularly at a time when the country was afflicted by "single-parent families, gang activity, [and] the availability of drugs."

Usually it is the loser who appeals a verdict, but the Scouts were so confident of their position that they took the unusual step of asking the US Supreme Court to hear *Welsh v. Boy Scouts of America*. The Scouts wanted the Court to affirm the organization's First Amendment right "to form an association for the purpose of expressing, transmitting and reinforcing certain values and beliefs, including religious ones, and to limit membership to those who share those values and beliefs." By having the nation's highest court weigh in as soon as possible, the Scouts hoped to bring an end to the mounting number of legal challenges to the Scouts' exclusionary policies. In 1991, for instance, two atheist twins in Orange County, California, William and Michael Randall, had sued the Scouts after having been kicked out for refusing to say the word "God" while reciting the Cub Scout Oath. In May 1992, the trial judge found that the Boy Scouts counted as a "business establishment" under the terms of the state's civil rights act and ordered the twins be reinstated. The Scouts would eventually—six years later—prevail in that case, but appeals were time-consuming and costly. "There are limits," the Scouts' attorney George A. Davidson pleaded with the US Supreme Court, "on the financial and administrative capacity of any volunteer organization to litigate these cases in forum after forum." The Scouts were to be disappointed, however. At the end of 1993, the Court announced that it would not review the appellate court's judgment in *Welsh*. As Davidson feared, the court of appeals's ruling in *Welsh* had done little to halt the proliferation of litigation. As the Scouts' position on religion continued to harden, atheists and agnostics became increasingly willing and even eager to challenge their exclusion.

Interestingly, at precisely the moment that the Boy Scouts of America were insisting on the exclusion of nonbelievers, the Girl Scouts of America were moving emphatically in the other direction. In October 1993, while the Boy Scouts were asking the US Supreme Court to uphold their right to exclude the nonreligious, the Girl Scouts of America voted overwhelmingly (1,560 to 375) to allow members to substitute a word or phrase in place of "God" when reciting the oath. Instead of promising to "serve God," a girl could pledge, for instance, to serve her family or her conscience. The president of the Girl Scouts boasted that the vote demonstrated that the Girl Scouts were on the "cutting edge" of social change and that they were an "inclusive organization" that was proud of its diversity. The voices emanating from the Boy Scouts could not have been more different. Without the oath to God, declared Chief Scout Executive Ben Love, "Scouting is just not Scouting." The BSA's general counsel David Park underscored that the Scouts were "not going to cut our cloth to fit any particular fashion. We are what we are and have been since 1910."

Gays

In fighting to keep out the godless, the Boy Scouts had no difficulty producing documents, dating all the way back to the organization's founding in 1910, that proclaimed a belief in God to be central to what it meant to be a Scout. The Scout Oath, for instance, begins with a pledge "to do my duty to God." And the twelfth and final point of the Scout Law is that a Scout must be reverent, defined explicitly as "reverent toward God." However, the third G—gays—presented a greater challenge for the Scouts. For nowhere in the material that the Scouts circulated to its members was there a comparably explicit statement that Scouting was incompatible with homosexuality.

During the summer of 1990, just as James Dale was grappling with his expulsion from the Scouts, the Scouts were preparing to go to trial in Los Angeles County Superior Court in a case that was much like Dale's. Already a decade in the making, the case involved another Eagle Scout, Tim Curran. Like Dale, Curran had been featured in a newspaper article (in the *Oakland Tribune*) about gay youth; the story described Curran as a "gay youth activist" and included a photograph of Curran holding hands with his male date at his high school prom. And as with Dale, when the local Scout executive learned of the article—which nowhere mentioned Curran's connection with the Scouts—he informed Curran that he would no longer be welcome in the Scouts. "Homosexuality and Scouting," the executive told Curran, "are not compatible." With the aid of the ACLU, the nineteen-year-old Curran sued the Boy Scouts for discrimination under California's civil rights act.

By 1990, Curran's case had been a ten-year rollercoaster ride of setbacks, victories, and delays—a journey that would continue for another eight years before the California Supreme Court finally decided in favor of the Scouts. In 1981 a superior court judge had dismissed Curran's complaint, ruling that the Scouts were a private organization, not a business establishment, and so the state's civil rights law did not apply to the Scouts' membership policies. Two years later, a state appellate court reversed the lower court's judgment, holding that the state statute did apply to the Scouts and that the Scouts could not refuse membership to Curran without evidence that Curran's homosexuality would negatively affect the Scouts. Then the delays began. First the case was put on hold while the trial court awaited the US Supreme Court's ruling in a case involving whether the Rotary Club had the constitutional right to exclude women (the Supreme Court unanimously ruled in 1987 that the club did not have that right). The case was then delayed further because the initial trial judge retired and the next judge assigned the case was promoted to the appeals court.

Curran's trial finally got under way in September 1990. The first phase of the trial focused on the question of whether the Scouts qualified as a business establishment under California law. Curran's lawyers noted that the Boy Scouts were a "massive, national enterprise" that boasted two thousand retail shops and annual revenues of nearly $100 million. The Mount Diablo Council, to which Curran had belonged, had twenty-two full-time paid employees and an annual budget of more than $1.7 million. The Scouts' attorney George Davidson retorted: "A duck has feathers and lays eggs but it doesn't necessarily mean it's a chicken." The judge sided with Curran: given its size, nonselectivity, and visibility, the Scouts fell within the purview of the California statute barring discrimination based on sexual orientation in business establishments. The second phase, which got under way in December 1990, focused on whether applying the state's civil rights law to the Boy Scouts in this case would violate the Scouts' constitutional rights of expressive association. To prevail on this second question, the Scouts needed to show that opposition to homosexuality was a core part of the Scouts' expressive message.

The Scouts also felt they needed to show that in refusing to admit Curran they were following their well-established membership policy. To demonstrate this, the Scouts placed into the court record internal documents that had never before been made public. The earliest of these was a memorandum on "homosexual unit members" dated February 13, 1978. Addressed to Scout executives, and written by public relations director Russ Bufkins, the memo was a response to an incident in Mankato, Minnesota, in which two Scouts, aged seventeen and sixteen, had been kicked out of a Scouting group (the Blue Earth County Law Enforcement Police Explorer Post 243) because of their homosexuality. The boys had never divulged their homosexuality to the Scouts, but the mother of one of the boys had approached the post's advisor about getting counseling for them. The advisor, a police sergeant, expelled the two boys. When the boys challenged their expulsion before the Mankato Equal Opportunities Commission, the media contacted the Scouts' national office to inquire if the Scouts "supported the action of the Post Advisor." The memo from Bufkins informed Scout executives of the three points that the national office had communicated to the media: (1) the national office supported the decision to deny membership to those "who declared themselves to be homosexuals," (2) the Scouts were a private organization and membership was "a privilege, not a right," and (3) the Scouts reserved "the right to deny membership to individuals upon the basis of our own standards, consistent with the laws of the land." Scout executives were instructed to direct any "queries on individual cases" either to Bufkins or to David Park, the BSA's legal counsel.

The second, longer memorandum, dated March 17, 1978, came right from the top. Signed by the BSA's president Downing Jenks and Chief Scout Executive Harvey Price, it was addressed to the members of the BSA's regional executive committee. The memo began by noting that "homosexual activist groups across the country" had been trying to enact "non-discrimination ordinances and laws." This had led to "many" inquiries about "the chartering of units to openly homosexual organizations, membership of homosexuals, and the appointment of homosexual volunteer and professional leaders." Having been asked to "express [their] official position to the field," Jenks and Price distributed "a statement of our policies and procedures relating to homosexuality and Scouting." The policy statement took the form of five questions and answers; the procedures were encapsulated in an additional three questions and answers.

The first policy question was whether a person who "openly declares" himself homosexual can be a voluntary Scout leader, such as a Scoutmaster. The answer was "no" because the Scouts did not "believe that homosexuality and leadership in Scouting are appropriate." The second question was whether a person who "openly declares" himself homosexual can be a member of the Scouts. Again, the answer was "no." The explanation was that the Scouts did not "feel that membership of such individuals is in the best interests of Scouting." The third question was whether professed homosexuals can obtain a charter unit, and again the answer was "no." The reason: because the Scouts "reserve the right to grant or withhold charters as we see fit."

The fourth and fifth questions addressed Scout employees, whether "professional," such as a Scout executive, or "nonprofessional," such as secretaries or janitors. Here the answers were more guarded. On the question of whether an open homosexual could be employed by the Scouts, the answer was that the Scouts did not "knowingly employ homosexuals" and were "unaware of any present laws which would prohibit" them from refusing to hire homosexuals. The other question asked whether the Scouts should fire an existing employee if the person openly declared his homosexuality. Here again the answer was more circumspect: "Yes, in the absence of any law to the contrary." The answer reiterated that the Scouts knew of no law or ordinance that prohibited employment discrimination "on the basis of homosexuality." However, "in the event that such a law was applicable, it would be necessary for the Boy Scouts of America to obey it." Nonetheless, the Scouts' position was that "homosexuality and . . . employment in Scouting are not appropriate."

To further substantiate the existence of a written policy on homosexuality, the Scouts submitted into evidence a document from 1983 prepared by the Scouts' legal counsel, David Park. Penned around the time that Curran's case was being heard by the state appellate court, the memo asserted, "Avowed or known homosexuals are not permitted to register in the Boy Scouts of America. Membership in the organization is a privilege, not a right, and the Boy Scouts of America has determined that homosexuality and Scouting are not compatible. No units will be chartered to known homosexual groups or individuals." Apart from the language of "avowed or known homosexuals," the wording of this statement was derived entirely from the 1978 memos.

These documents, particularly the statement of policy from March 1978, verified that prior to 1980 the Scouts had a written policy that open homosexuals could not be Scout members or serve as volunteer leaders. In refusing to allow Curran to register with the Scouts in 1980, therefore, Scout officials had followed their written policies and procedures. However, the documents also revealed other facts that the Scouts were less eager to highlight because they undercut key aspects of their argument. First, there was no evidence that the Scouts had a written policy about homosexuality prior to 1978; presumably if there were such a policy the Scouts would have produced it in court since it would have bolstered their case. Moreover, neither memo from 1978 claims to reaffirm a long-standing policy. Second, the Scouts had made no effort to publicize the memorandum of March 1978; it was an official position that was revealed to Scouting professionals but not to members or volunteer leaders. Third, in the case of paid employees the Scouts were prepared in 1978 to concede that they would be required to abide by antidiscrimination statutes. Fourth, and most striking, the 1978 memos made no effort to link the exclusion of homosexuality to the "morally straight" clause of the Scout Oath or the "clean" in thought and deed provision of the Scout Law. Indeed the policy statement made no attempt to link the exclusion of homosexuals with any expressive purpose of the Scouts.

At the trial, Scout officials skirted around the problems raised by these documents. Instead, they testified that ever since the BSA's founding in 1910 it had been "clearly understood" by all "that homosexuality was an immoral behavior and had no place in Scouting for youth or leaders." The Scouts even produced a "handful" of scripted affidavits (the wording was drawn up by the Scouts' lawyers) signed by individuals who had been registered with the Scouts in 1916 to substantiate this claim. Being "morally straight," the BSA insisted, had always been understood as being heterosexual. Similarly, being "clean" in "thought" and "habits"—the Scout Law's eleventh commandment—had also been widely understood to rule out homosexuality. Scouting officials asserted that this view was communicated to Scout leaders and members whenever the issue of homosexuality arose. What had changed was not the Boy Scouts but society, specifically gay individuals' willingness to "come out" and to question the Scouts' traditional teachings.

It is true that when the Scouts found out about Curran's homosexuality, BSA officials did promptly and clearly communicate to Curran that homosexuality and Scouting were "incompatible." However, in July 1981, when Curran's lawyer first asked the Boy Scouts to point to the proscription against homosexuality in the organization's membership requirements, the BSA's lawyer, Malcolm Wheeler, floundered. In a five-page letter to Curran's attorney, Wheeler quoted from multiple sections of the Scouting *Handbook*, without producing anything that clearly referenced homosexuality. Wheeler included the entire Scout Oath and Scout Law, but never singled out the "morally straight" clause of the Scout Oath or the "clean" section of the Scout Law as a basis for the decision. Instead the Boy Scouts' lawyer highlighted sections in the *Handbook* that stressed the importance of obedience to the law and duty to God. Wheeler argued that being homosexual—or at least an "avowed homosexual"—was inconsistent with "the meaning ascribed by our society and by the Boy Scouts to terms such as 'duty to God and country.'" Homosexuals were ineligible for Scouting, the letter seemed to suggest, because homosexuals could not be "reverent to God" since homosexuality was against "His Plan."

In a particularly tortured closing argument, Wheeler maintained that when the Boy Scouts were incorporated by Congress in 1916, the statute required the Boy Scouts to use "the methods which were in common use by [the] Boy Scouts on June 15, 1916." Since "heterosexuality was a membership requirement on and before June 15, 1916, consistent with the statutes making homosexual conduct illegal in virtually every state," the Scouts were legally bound by federal law to exclude homosexuals. However, the letter produced no evidence that heterosexuality was a membership requirement in 1916. And the federal statute from 1916 made no mention of the Scouts' membership requirements. What the congressional charter actually said was that the Scouts were "to promote . . . the ability of boys to do things for themselves and others, to train them in Scoutcraft, and to teach them patriotism, courage, self-reliance, and kindred virtues, using the methods which were in common use by Boy Scouts on June 15, 1916."

Clearly, in 1981 the Scouts had not yet worked out a coherent rationale for why homosexuality was incompatible with Scouting. Certainly the Scouts had not yet decided that being "morally straight" and "clean" spoke to the issue of homosexuality. In their 1981 letter to Curran, the Scouts leaned most heavily on two arguments: (1) homosexuality was disobedient to God's will, and (2) homosexuality involved breaking the law. The problem with the first argument was that it made the Scouts sound like religious zealots. It was also in tension with a central plank of Scouting, namely, that Scouts should serve God "by worshipping him the way your parents and spiritual leaders taught you." That left the interpretation of whether homosexuality violates God's teachings in the hands of parents and ministers, not the Scouts. The second argument about sodomy laws was often used historically to justify discrimination against gays since it turned all "practicing homosexuals" into criminals. The problem with this argument in Curran's case, however, was that California had repealed its sodomy law for consenting adults in the 1970s, so Curran was no lawbreaker.

By the time of Curran's trial, the Scouts had jettisoned both the sodomy and "duty to God" arguments. However, the BSA underscored the religious basis of its exclusionary policy by summoning representatives from religious groups to testify that they would likely withdraw from Scouting if the court permitted homosexuals to join the Scouts. A priest from the National Catholic Committee on Scouting (the liaison responsible for communicating the official Catholic position to the BSA) told the court that if the Scouts were forced to admit gays it "would have such an effect that we would probably seriously consider breaking away." Such a change, he said, would be "anti-family, anti-everything." Jack H. Goaslind, a high-ranking official in the Mormon Church, was unequivocal. He promised that the Mormons "would withdraw from the Boy Scouts of America" rather than admit homosexuals into their ranks.

In the end, the judge was convinced. "Inclusion of a homosexual Scoutmaster who has publicly acknowledged his or her homosexuality," wrote Judge Sally Disco, "would either undermine the force of the Boy Scout view that homosexuality is immoral and inconsistent with the Scout oath and law, or would undermine the credibility of the Scoutmaster who attempts to communicate that view." In this case, the Scouts' First Amendment rights trumped the state law against discrimination.

Curran's legal team and the gay community expressed outrage at the judge's ruling. A spokeswoman for the ACLU called the ruling "crazy" because it essentially said that it was fine for the Scouts to discriminate "if part of their goal as an organization is to raise kids who shun homosexuality." That is, the more homophobic and hateful the Boy Scouts sounded, the stronger their right to discriminate became. The executive director of the Los Angeles Gay and Lesbian Community Services Center condemned the decision as "horrendous" because it perpetuated stereotypes that gay men could not be positive role models and sent "a horrifying message to kids that it's OK to hate gays and lesbians." The ruling triggered protests in San Francisco and a call for a boycott of United Way, a major Scouting benefactor.

The Scouts were not happy with the ruling either. Although gratified that the judge had upheld their right to exclude Curran, they were disturbed by Judge Disco's conclusion that the Scouts' "public orientation and prominence in the community" placed it within "the regulatory ambit" of the state's civil rights laws. The

Scouts worried that putting the burden on the Scouts to show that their exclusionary policies were linked to the organization's expressive purpose invited further legal challenges, not only in California but across the country. As a private organization, the Scouts believed that they should not have to justify their membership policies to the government. The Scouts were also displeased that by pitting their associational rights against "the state's interest in eradicating invidious discrimination," the ruling pushed the Scouts to be publicly explicit about something that many in the organization would have preferred remain implicit. As much as the Scouts insisted in court that opposition to homosexuality was at the core of their expressive identity, the organization's leaders were eager to avoid the adverse publicity that came with being portrayed as a discriminatory organization. Curran's legal challenge, however, seemed to leave the Scouts with little choice but to highlight an inextricable connection between Scouting and opposition to homosexuality.

CHAPTER 4

The Culture Wars

During the late 1970s and the 1980s, the Scouts' exclusion of gays, like its exclusion of atheists and girls, had attracted only sporadic press attention. That suited the BSA national office, which preferred not to draw attention to its discriminatory policies. Although Curran's case prompted scattered coverage in the California media in the early 1980s, interest quickly faded after the case became bogged down in procedural delays and legal maneuvering. Curran's trial in 1990 changed that. From that point forward, the Scouts found their exclusionary membership policies—especially their exclusion of gays—subject to intense media scrutiny.

Preparing for Curran's legal challenge made two things clear to Scouting's national leadership. First, the Scouts needed a formal policy statement on homosexuality so that the organization could prove in court that the exclusion of homosexuals was intrinsic to Scouting's mission. Second, and even more important, the Scouts needed a way of talking about their exclusionary policy in public that did not make the Scouts sound like bigots. For help with both of these tasks, the national office turned to the public relations professionals at Edelman Public Relations Worldwide, which in 1985 had opened a Dallas office, only a few miles from the Scouts' national headquarters in the Dallas suburb of Irving, Texas.

One of the largest and most well-known public relations firms in the world, Edelman had pioneered "litigation PR" in helping CBS fight the libel suit brought by General William Westmoreland after the network aired a documentary in 1982 asserting that Westmoreland had misled his superiors and the American people about enemy troop numbers in the Vietnam War. An Edelman vice president "sat with the press corps each day of the trial, provided documents to reporters, [and] congratulated writers who covered the trial in a way favorable to CBS." The company also showed off its crisis management bona fides in the late 1980s when it helped the H. J. Heinz Company rescue the reputation of its StarKist tuna brand, which had been battered by heavy criticism for using fishing nets that slaughtered dolphins. Edelman helped Heinz develop alternative fishing methods and then ensured that the American public knew that StarKist was—as their label said—"Dolphin Safe."

Impressed with Edelman's successes, the Scouts became Edelman clients in the summer of 1989. The Scouts had always been acutely aware of the importance of public and media relations in promoting positive messages about Scouting, but prior to 1989 the national office had relied on Scouting professionals to handle media relations. From 1967 to 1982, media communications had been the responsibility of the BSA's public relations director Russ Bufkins. During the mid- and late 1980s, media relations were managed by Raul Chavez, who had gradually worked his way up the Scouting hierarchy, starting from an entry-level position in which he was responsible for outreach to the Hispanic communities of East Dallas. Prior to working for the Scouts, Chavez had worked as an advertising executive, though his true passion was acting. He appeared in a number of Spanish-language films and commercials, including as the voice-over for Cap'n Crunch, and even played a brave Indian warrior who died in Tonto's arms at the end of an episode of the popular 1950s television series *The Lone Ranger*.

Chavez's limitations as a public relations man were exposed during an incident in 1985 involving a fifteen-year-old Scout, Paul Trout, who had been denied promotion to Life Scout when he told the board reviewing his application that he did not believe in a "Supreme Being." On the advice of the national office, Paul, a Unitarian, was then kicked out of the Scouts. Paul and his mother took their case to the national media, including a live appearance on the Phil Donahue Show. Chavez, who loved the lure of Hollywood, agreed to go on the show, together with Ed Dobson of the Moral Majority. By appearing alongside Dobson (whose introduction on the show was greeted with boos from the audience), Chavez seemed to align the Scouts with the religious intolerance of the Moral Majority. Moreover, Chavez struggled to explain how the BSA's insistence that all Scouts must affirm a belief in God as a "Supreme

Being" did not violate its claim to be a nonsectarian organization. Chavez's assertion that all religions shared a belief in God as a Supreme Being was sharply criticized for ignoring the world's many polytheistic religions, including Hinduism, Confucianism, and Buddhism. Stung by the adverse publicity, the Boy Scouts backed down. Trout was allowed back into the Scouts—he went on to become an Eagle Scout—and the "Supreme Being" language (which the Scouts had introduced in 1978) was dropped from the Scouting *Handbook*. The Scouting hierarchy understood that it could not afford a repeat of the Trout fiasco if it was to successfully defend its membership policies in the court of public opinion. Edelman's charge was to ensure that there were no more public relations debacles.

As the Curran trial wound to a close, Edelman executives, "with help from the Boy Scouts' office of External Communications," prepared a formal "position statement," "Homosexuality and the BSA," and presented it to the BSA executive board at its February meeting. Dated February 15, 1991, the statement read:

> For more than 90 years, the Boy Scouts of America has brought the moral values of the Scout Oath and the Scout Law to American boys, helping them to achieve the objectives of Scouting.
>
> The Boy Scouts of America also places strong emphasis on traditional family values as being necessary components of a strong, healthy society. The Scouting program is designed to be a shared family experience.
>
> We believe that Homosexual conduct is inconsistent with the requirements in the Scout Oath that a Scout be morally straight and in the Scout Law that a Scout be clean in word and deed, and that homosexuals do not provide a desirable role model for Scouts.
>
> Because of these beliefs, the Boy Scouts of America does not accept homosexuals as members or as leaders, whether in volunteer or in professional capacities.
>
> Our position on this issue is based solely upon our desire to provide the appropriate environment and role models which reflect Scouting's values and beliefs.

> As a private member organization, we believe our right to determine the qualifications of our members and leaders is protected by the Constitution of the United States.

Paragraphs 2 and 3 of the statement crystallized the arguments that the Scouts marshaled during Curran's trial. Inside the courtroom the Scouts leaned heavily on the arguments in paragraph 3: that the exclusion of gays was grounded in the "morally straight" provision of the Scout Law and the "clean in word and dead" portion of the Scout Law. Outside the courtroom the Scouts accented the argument of paragraph 2: that "traditional family values" were at the core of the Scouts' identity. As the BSA spokesman Lee Sneath told the *Los Angeles Times* in November 1990, the "bottom line" is that "we do not feel that homosexuality is consistent with traditional American family values that Scouting teaches."

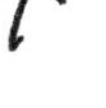

The new tactic of using "traditional family values" to explain the Scouts' policy reflected Edelman's influence. Prior to Curran's trial the Scouts had never defined their purpose in terms of traditional family values. Instead the Scouts strove to be as inclusive as possible in their public communications: their message was that the Scouts were open to all boys, not boys of a particular upbringing or family background. The original message, memorialized in a vintage Scouting patch, was "Scouting for All Boys." Or, as the Scouts' internal literature put it, the policy was to "band every boy, tag every boy, stick every boy," that is, make every boy a Boy Scout.

The embrace of traditional values was particularly discordant because during the late 1980s the Scouts had worked assiduously to shed the image of a traditional or old-fashioned organization in their effort to appeal to the broadest possible range of boys. In 1989, for instance, the Scouts had launched their "first paid national television campaign"—sponsored by American Airlines and the Phillips Petroleum Company and costing in excess of $1 million—the aim of which was explicitly "to dispel Scouting's old-fashioned image." The Scouts had typically relied on public service announcements to advertise, but these spots were usually broadcast at times when few people were watching. The new advertising campaign, in contrast, was broadcast during prime children's programming, and featured a "cool" young man "clad in a black leather jacket and tight Levis [and] talking the kind of hip language that young people understand. The announcer tells boys that in the Scouts they can 'chill out,' while the spot shows youngsters hiking along a frosty glacier. Then, he suggests that they 'get high' with the Scouts—as a scene of boys navigating a shaky bridge above a ravine flashes on the screen and the rock-and-roll background music swells." After Curran's trial, however, BSA officials altered their message to mesh with Edelman's new public relations campaign. Gone was the "be cool" and "get high" campaign. Now the Scouts became, in the words of a San Francisco Scouting official, quoted on July 1, 1991, "a private organization *aimed at traditional families*."

Scouting professionals received the new position statement and guidance for dealing with the media as part of a "comprehensive packet of information" sent out on June 24, 1991, by the BSA's new director of relationships and marketing, J. Carey Keane, a public relations professional who had until recently been RC Cola's marketing vice president. The day before, not coincidentally, the *New York Times* had published a front-page story on the Scouts that featured not only Curran's case but also the legal challenges of the eight-year-old girl Margo Mankes, who filed her sex discrimination suit on June 18, and the agnostic eight-year-old Mark Welsh, whose trial in federal court had begun the week before that. Included in the packet sent out by Keane was not only the position statement on homosexuality but also official position statements on "Duty to God" and "Girls in Scouting" and "suggestions for responding to local media inquiries on the issues of atheism, girls and homosexuality."

The enclosed "Suggestions"—drawn up by Edelman executives—began by noting that the Scouts were facing "high-profile" challenges on all three fronts: atheism, girls, and homosexuality. It acknowledged that legal challenges in these three areas shared "common elements." Each appealed to "emotions" and threatened the BSA's freedom of association, not to mention "the very values and ideals that have made the BSA successful in its mission." Moreover, all three had the "potential image of 'shaking the traditional organization.'" The document stressed that despite the parallels, it was vital that "each issue or specific challenge to an issue should be addressed individually" so as "to avoid an appearance that the fundamentals of the BSA are being challenged."

Scout executives were instructed on how to "be prepared" before participating in an interview with the local media. Helpful advice included clearing "your desk and your mind" prior to returning a reporter's call. In the interview itself, it was important to:

> Determine what key points you want to make in the interview and make them.
>
> Speak with conviction.
>
> Be concise. Rambling answers invite editing out of context.
>
> Be factual. If there's been a past problem in the council, provide the facts and then bridge to what's been done to resolve the situation and enhance Scouting.
>
> Don't speculate on "what if" type questions. That is asking you to deal with hypothetical issues, not the facts at hand.
>
> Bridge, or transition, the conversation to the positive work that the BSA and your council have done. Build on Scouting's excellent reputation for service to young people and the community at large.
>
> The same questions may be asked different ways to obtain different answers. Be consistent in your response, no matter how many times asked.
>
> Use only one spokesperson for the local council.

Council executives were also reminded that they were not to discuss any questions about the Scouts' national policy relating to the three Gs. All such inquiries were instead to be directed to Edelman. Council executives were also instructed not to comment on situations in other councils; those questions were to be directed either to Edelman or to the council in question. Executives who desired further guidance in talking with the media were told to contact one of three public relations professionals at Edelman: Blake Lewis, Greg Bustin, or Kaytie Daniell. To facilitate those communications, the Scouts even gave out the home phone numbers of all three Edelman employees. Underscoring Edelman's centrality in making and communicating the message, Keane's cover letter directed those who "need further information" on the policy to contact Blake Lewis.

Lewis became the principal spokesman for the Boy Scouts, though his relationship with Edelman was never mentioned in the press. Instead, he was always identified simply as a BSA "spokesman." In his many media appearances defending the Scouts' discriminatory practices, Lewis adhered closely to the language of traditional family values. In August 1991, for instance, Lewis explained to the *New York Times* that "Scouting represents tradition, or if you will, family structure and values." In another interview from later that same year, Lewis emphasized that the Scouts stood for "old-time family values." Time and time again, Lewis parried the charge of discrimination by highlighting that the Scouts' identity was "based on traditional family values."

Lewis readily acknowledged that Scouting's "traditional values" were "not . . . for every person in society to live by." Those who didn't share "the values of Scouting," he suggested in a November 1991 interview, could find "another organization better suited" to their own values and interests. The Scouts were not trying to impose their beliefs on others or tell others how to live. Instead, it was gay activists who were guilty of attempting to compel the Boy Scouts to abandon their deeply held and long-established values. "This issue," he explained, was "being raised by special interest groups trying to force their cause" on the Boy Scouts. In Lewis's narrative, the Scouts were the aggrieved party and homosexual activists were the ones intolerant of difference.

Edelman helped the Scouts hone their message, but the controversy and media attention surrounding the exclusion of gays continued to escalate, especially in the Bay Area. School boards in San Jose and San Francisco reacted to the *Curran* ruling by banning Scouting activities on school premises for the 1991–1992 school year. During the fall of 1991 a group calling itself the Forgotten Scouts formed with the goal of drawing national attention to the injustice of the Scouts' discrimination against gays. (James Dale would work as a volunteer for the group in the summer of 1992.) In December 1991, William Boyce Mueller, grandson of William D. Boyce, founder of the Boy Scouts of America, put added pressure on the Scouts by revealing that he was gay. "My grandfather," Mueller announced, "would not have tolerated discrimination. He founded the Boy Scouts for all boys, not just for some." That same month, a San Jose troop defied the Scouts' national office by passing a resolution that rejected the BSA's interpretation of the "morally straight" clause.

The Scouts' problems were compounded by groups such as the Forgotten Scouts and Queer Nation, which began to seek out gay men from across the nation willing to challenge the Scouts' policy in public and in court. In February 1992, for instance, Queer Nation arranged for seven gay men, including two Eagle Scouts, to descend on the Scouts' headquarters of the National Capital Area Council in Bethesda, Maryland, and try to submit applications to become local leaders. Their aim was not to become Scout leaders but to publicize the Scouts' policy and land the Scouts in court. The protest was successful on both counts. A *Washington Post* reporter and photographer were on hand to record the face-off between the applicants and the council's Scout executive, who explained that the Scouts did not feel that gay men were "acceptable role models for young boys as they develop into manhood."

Among those who read the *Post* story was Michael Geller, who—unlike the seven Queer Nation protesters—was registered as an adult leader of a Scout troop. The next day, Geller fired off a letter of protest to the DC Scout executive Ron Carroll (and copied it to several reporters), announcing himself as a gay man and proud Eagle Scout and accusing Carroll and the Scouts of teaching discrimination and fomenting prejudice and hate. The same day that Carroll received the letter, Geller's membership in the Scouts was revoked and his name placed in the Ineligible Volunteer Files, with the comment "an admitted gay leader." Six months later, Geller (together with Roland Pool, another Eagle Scout whose involvement was triggered by the *Post* coverage of the Queer Nation protest) sued the Scouts for violating the DC ordinance against discrimination on the basis of sexual orientation. The Pool and Geller case would absorb the Scouts' time and resources for the next decade.

Meanwhile, in Chicago, the Forgotten Scouts recruited Keith Richardson, a gay Eagle Scout, to file a complaint against the Boy Scouts. Richardson had worked for the Scouts in the early 1980s and now, at the behest of the Forgotten Scouts, he called up the Chicago Area Council to ask if the Scouts would hire him again knowing that he was gay. After receiving the expected answer—"no way"—Richardson sued the Scouts, seeking $1 million in damages.

Richardson's case, too, would wind its way through the legal system for the next decade.

Of even more immediate concern to the Scouts was a growing movement among gay rights groups to pressure organizations and businesses to stop funding the Scouts. Of particular importance was the United Way, which provided about 20 percent of the Scouting budget. In the fall of 1991 the Bay Area United Way convened a task force to study the question of whether to withdraw its financial support of the Scouts. In February 1992 the task force had readied a preliminary draft of its report, which called on the Scouts either to repeal its ban on homosexuals or to provide a local option for Bay Area troops that wanted to have gay leaders or members. If the Scouts did not make one of these two changes, then the task force recommended that the Bay Area United Way should withdraw the $1.2 million it donated each year to six Bay Area Scouting councils.

The BSA national office was in no mood to enter into a dialogue with Bay Area United Way about changing its policy. When it received the draft report, the BSA launched a preemptive strike by holding a press conference in San Francisco, at which it released the draft report and issued a stinging press release condemning the task force's "ultimatum" as "totally unacceptable." For over eight decades, the news release explained, the BSA had "represented a constancy of purpose—a rock-solid foundation of traditional family values that can serve as a beacon for America's youth." The task force, the Scouts insisted, was trying to "force Scouting to walk away from more than eight decades of good work and solid values upon which the BSA has been built." The Scouts refused to let that happen. They would not be bullied or blackmailed. "Our values and principles are not up for negotiation," the press statement declared. Chief Scout Executive Ben Love echoed the same point, telling the *New York Times*, "Our values aren't for sale."

The Scouts' response to the United Way report was shaped by Edelman's executives, who, on February 15, three days before the press conference, had drawn up a "Q&A for United Way of the Bay Area Task Force Issue." The Q&A emphasized that the Task Force had been formed with the aim of compelling the Scouts to conform to the Bay Area United Way's "'politically correct' values and standards." It described the task force report as "unacceptable" because it was an "ultimatum" that would require the Scouts "to sell out [their] long-held values based on traditional American families." The Scouts would "not negotiate [their] values," nor would they "desert the boys, youth and families that have come to depend on the Boy Scouts as their rock-solid foothold of values in an otherwise turbulent and confusing world." To the question of whether the Scouts' position was discriminatory, Edelman's answer was "no it isn't. We have no quarrel with gays and lesbians. They are free to pursue their lifestyle. The freedoms of America guarantee that right." But as a private organization the Scouts had the same right to support, as it always had, "traditional family values." Those same words appeared almost verbatim in a press release dated February 18, though as with most of the press releases, the words were attributed to Buford Hill, the BSA's western regional director.

In March 1992, Edelman produced an "Issues and Crisis Communications Guide" that was distributed to all local Scouting executives. The guide, which included a video, featured "general training" on dealing with the media and a mock interview and critique, as well as several "modules" on specific controversies facing the Scouts. One module focused on "Duty to God," another addressed "Girls," and a third covered "Homosexuality." The module on homosexuality began by noting that as a result of the *Curran* case "gay rights organizations have attacked Scouting to further their own agenda." Despite this challenge, the module stressed, "Scouting isn't changing. Scouting won't change." The local council's spokesperson was commanded to "convey this stance to the public through contacts with the media." The module also distilled the BSA's position on homosexuality to its essence: "THE BOY SCOUTS OF AMERICA HAVE EMPHASIZED TRADITIONAL FAMILY VALUES SINCE THE INCEPTION OF THE MOVEMENT. WE BELIEVE HOMOSEXUALS DO NOT PROVIDE A ROLE MODEL FOR SCOUTS THAT IS CONSISTENT WITH THESE TRADITIONAL VALUES. ACCORDINGLY, THE BSA DOES NOT ACCEPT HOMOSEXUALS AS MEMBERS OR LEADERS." Scout executives were instructed to remember that these three sentences were the "key points" they should reiterate in every interview. The position statement and the closing "issue review" put the accent where Edelman wanted it: on traditional family values, rather than on the Scout Law's commandment to be clean in word and deed or even the "morally straight" clause of the Scout Oath, although the latter was preserved in a question-and-answer segment of the module as a secondary reason for why Scouting was incompatible with homosexuality.

In the coming months, Scout executives across the country adhered closely to this communications guide in responding to the media. Take, for instance, the controversy that erupted in March 1992 in California's San Luis Obispo County when a Cub Scout leader barred the parent of one of the Scouts from bringing his gay partner to Cub Scout events. When the local Scout executive was contacted by the media, he explained that having the pair at pack meetings was "disruptive" and then proceeded to recite verbatim the BSA's position statement: "The Boy Scouts of America have emphasized traditional family values since the inception of the movement. We believe homosexuals do not provide a role model for Scouts that is consistent with these traditional values. Accordingly, the BSA does not accept homosexuals as members or leaders."

The Scouts' staunch defense of their exclusion of gays prompted the Bay Area United Way to announce in April that it would no longer fund the Scouts. That was a decision that the Scouts expected. More surprising was the success gay rights organizations had in persuading businesses to cut off funding for the Scouts. In May 1992, Levi Strauss & Co. announced that it would no longer support the Boy Scouts, and shortly thereafter several big banks, including Bank of America and Wells Fargo Bank, pledged to follow suit.

Still the Scouts remained defiant. Local Scout executives responded to the Bay Area United Way's decision with "a very aggressive fund-raising effort" that borrowed on the rhetoric fashioned by Edelman. The San Mateo Scout executive, for instance, sent a fund-raising appeal to all registered voters in the county that vowed to "refuse to bow down to United Way directions" that violated the Scouts' "basic principles." The Seattle Scout executive Dean Lollar echoed the same defiance in reacting to news that Seafirst Bank—a subsidiary of BankAmerica Corp.—would no longer support the Scouts. "We're not going to give in and change our standards and turn our backs on mainstream America," Lollar pledged. Scout leaders continued to express confidence that, as Edelman's Q&A put it, "the vast majority of American families fully support our values and will continue to be an overwhelming source of our funding for the BSA."

In the debate over funding, the Scouts framed the issue as one that pitted the lifestyle and preferences of a homosexual minority against what Edelman described as the traditional "standards that the vast majority of Americans want for their children and for society." Following Edelman's guidance, Scouting spokespersons increasingly emphasized that the BSA's position reflected not only the Scouts' own long-held values but the values and expectations of the mainstream American families that the Boy Scouts were committed to serving. The problem with admitting gays into the Scouts was not simply that the BSA leadership considered them inappropriate role models. Instead, as Lollar expressed it to a *Seattle Times* reporter, gays and lesbians were "not the proper role models that *our membership expects.*"

Whatever the views of "mainstream" Americans, conservative Christian organizations and Republican politicians were quick to rally to the Scouts' defense. After Levi Strauss's announcement, the Mississippi-based American Family Association—a conservative Christian group that proudly describes itself as having been on "the frontlines of the American culture war" since its founding in 1977—called for a boycott of Levi Strauss products. Christian radio stations across the country called on listeners to "start wearing Lees and Wranglers" and close their bank accounts with Wells Fargo and Bank of America. House Republicans took up the call for a boycott of those corporations that were, in the words of one Republican legislator, "mugging the Boy Scouts of America, trying to force them to lower their moral standards." Representative Tom DeLay (R-TX) encouraged the people of his state to "take off those Levi's and burn them in the streets" in protest of the company's "attack" on the Scouts. In July 1992, 130 House Republicans even backed an amendment introduced by Louisiana Republican Clyde Holloway that would have penalized any corporation that withheld funds from the Scouts. Allowing gay men to be Scoutmasters, Holloway warned, was akin to "the fox guarding the hen house."

By the summer of 1992 the Boy Scouts' exclusion of homosexuals had became so contentious that the Republican Party inscribed its support of the Scouts in its party platform. The 1992 platform declared:

> We . . . stand united with those private organizations, such as the Boy Scouts of America, who are defending decency in fulfillment of their own moral responsibilities. We reject the irresponsible position of those corporations that have cut off contributions to such organizations because of their courageous stand for family values. Moreover, we oppose efforts by the Democratic Party to include sexual preference as a protected minority receiving preferential status under civil rights statutes at the federal, State, and local level.

The platform also opposed "any legislation or law which legally recognizes same-sex marriages and allows such couples to adopt children or provide foster care." Never before had a platform of either political party declared its opposition to gay rights.

The 1992 platform was also the first in the Republican Party's history that invoked "family values" as shorthand for opposition to gays and lesbians. To be sure, the phrase "family values" had appeared sporadically before in Republican platforms, beginning with the platform in 1980. But in each case the term had been used in the narrow context of expressing opposition to activist judges, pornography, and abortion. In the language of the 1980 platform (and each subsequent Republican platform), the party declared its support for "the appointment of judges who respect traditional family values and the sanctity of innocent human life." In the 1992 platform, in contrast, "traditional family values" became a party mantra, and the tone was now shrill and urgent: "Now more than ever," the document declared, "the traditional family is under assault." Convention delegates heard the same message from Pat Buchanan, whose prime time address at the 1992 Republican National Convention announced that the country was in the midst of "a cultural war" that was "as critical to the kind of nation we will one day be as was the Cold War itself." For Buchanan and the cultural conservatives who supported him, gay rights were the front lines in the war over traditional family values. (Buchanan had infamously hurled himself into the controversy over gays in the Boy Scouts as far back as December 1983, when he invited Tim Curran, then twenty-three, on to his CNN debate program *Crossfire*, only to hound his young guest about NAMBLA, the North American Man/Boy Love Association, a group that advocated pederasty.)

Buchanan's clarion call for a culture war resonated with the Scouts' own public messaging in the summer of 1992. Indeed at the very moment that Republicans were gathering in the Houston Astrodome for their convention, volume 80, issue 4, of the Boy Scouts' venerable *Scouting* magazine was being delivered to the mailbox of every Scouter (that is, all registered adult BSA members, including volunteer leaders) in the United States. In it, the BSA for the first time disseminated and defended its exclusionary policy to all adult members of the Scouting family. The one-page unsigned manifesto, titled "Maintaining BSA Standards," crystallized the message that Edelman had honed over the past year.

The manifesto began by explaining that the BSA had "recently . . . been attacked by special interest groups" that were "intent on destroying the BSA this nation has come to expect and count on." Since its founding in 1910, the Scouts had "taken a strong stand for the teaching of traditional American values." Intent on using the BSA to gain a "platform for their own sociopolitical agenda," atheist and homosexual activists were seeking to force the Scouts to abandon "our long-held standards." But the Scouts would not be cowed: "Our values are not for sale." The Scout Oath and Law, which had "served as guideposts for more than 88 million young people," were "not up for negotiation." The Scouts "did not start this confrontation," nor would they shrink from "defending [their] commitment to upholding family values." Although careful not to "recommend, endorse, or condone" the boycotts of companies like Levi Strauss and Wells Fargo, the manifesto noted that such reactions "demonstrate the pent-up frustration felt by so many mainstream Americans for the deep erosion of our country's moral fiber." Pat Buchanan could not have said it better.

In short, by the time James Dale first filed his complaint in New Jersey Superior Court in the summer of 1992, the Scouts had become deeply mired in the culture wars. The Boy Scouts' language of traditional family values was indistinguishable from the language adopted by conservative Republican culture warriors like Buchanan. No less than Buchanan, the Boy Scouts believed that they were fighting on the side of righteousness. Retreat was not an option. Compromise would be cowardice. The Boy Scouts had taken their stand.

PART TWO

In the New Jersey Courts

CHAPTER 5

Dale's Case Begins

Dale's lawsuit was a media magnet. Immediately after filing his complaint in superior court on July 29, 1992, his story and picture were prominently featured in the *New York Times*. Titled "From Eagle Scout to Persona Non Grata," the article sympathetically related the tale of Dale's ouster. Readers learned of Dale's conservative upbringing, his exemplary Scouting accomplishments and record of public service, and his anguish at being thrown out of the organization he loved. Over half of the eight-hundred-word story was in Dale's own words, all of them earnest and compelling. The only quotation from the Scouts came in a terse comment from Monmouth Council executive James Kay, who declared, "The issue is purely and simply one that says we have a right to set standards for membership." The story pitted Scouting's "poster boy" versus the "people at the top" of the BSA who were "preaching hate."

From the Scouts' perspective, however, there was nothing special about Dale's case at this point. In the summer of 1992, Dale's complaint only opened one more front in a widening war of legal disputes. During 1992 the Scouts fielded lawsuits from aggrieved gay men across the country. In California, for instance, the Scouts were sued by Chuck Merino, a police officer and widely admired Scouting volunteer whom the Scouts expelled in August 1992 after finding out that he had revealed his sexual orientation at a community meeting on hate crimes. In the nation's capital, Roland Pool and Michael Geller filed complaints with the DC Department of Human Rights, and in Illinois Keith Richardson did the same with the Chicago Commission on Human Relations. Curran's suit was still by far the most high-profile challenge to the Scouts' exclusion of gays, and the Scouts were now in the midst of appealing Judge Sally Disco's 1991 ruling that the Scouts qualified as a business establishment under California law. The Scouts were also appealing the more recent setback they had been handed in another California case involving the atheist twins William and Michael Randall. In that case, decided in May 1992, the trial judge had not only found that the Scouts were a business establishment but ruled that the Scouts could not discriminate on the basis of religion and must therefore reinstate the twins. In the summer of 1992, then, James Dale was just one more headache for the beleaguered Scouts.

Dale filed his complaint in Monmouth County Superior Court's Law Division, which handles civil cases in which one party (the plaintiff) seeks damages (that is, money) from another party (the defendant) alleged to have harmed the plaintiff's body, property, reputation, or rights. Typical civil cases handled by the Law Division include auto accidents, medical malpractice, breach of contract, and workplace discrimination. In New Jersey a small number of civil cases are handled by a separate division called the Chancery Division. The Chancery Division treats those "General Equity" cases in which plaintiffs do not seek monetary damages from a defendant but rather seek an immediate court order to enforce a legal right. Typical cases handled by the Chancery Division involve businesses and property owners seeking a court order to end a labor strike, foreclose on a property, or enforce an easement. There are no juries in the Chancery Division and as a general rule these cases are settled much more quickly than cases heard in the Law Division.

Dale's lawyers filed their case in the Law Division because they were asking the court to award Dale "compensatory and punitive damages for the emotional pain and suffering he experienced and for the loss of his valuable privileges as a member of the Boy Scouts." But Dale's legal team also was asking the court to order the Scouts to reinstate Dale as assistant Scoutmaster. The latter request meant it was ambiguous whether the case should be assigned to the Law or Chancery Division. If the principal relief being sought was financial damages, then the Law Division was the proper place for Dale's case. But if the principal relief sought was a court order for reinstatement, then the Chancery Division was arguably a more appropriate venue.

The Scouts had hired Sanford Brown—an attorney from the Monmouth County law firm Cerrato, Dawes, Collins, Saker &

Brown—to help with the initial legal filings and proceedings. Brown was eager to take the case; he had been involved with Scouting all his life and would subsequently become president (a volunteer position) of BSA's Monmouth Council. Far more valuable to the Scouts was Brown's knowledge of the judges of Monmouth County Superior Court. Immediately after graduating from law school in 1978, Brown had clerked for Monmouth County Superior Court Judge Patrick McGann. Now the presiding judge in the Chancery Division, McGann handled all General Equity cases in the Chancery Division. Knowing that McGann would be sympathetic toward the Scouts' position, Brown pressed to change the venue to the Chancery Division. On November 6, 1992, Brown's motion to transfer the case to the Chancery Division was granted.

At the time the case was transferred to the Chancery Division, Judge McGann was sixty-four years old and had been a superior court judge for a quarter century. McGann was not only an experienced jurist but—as Brown well knew—a devout and conservative Catholic. McGann was a trustee and communicant of the Roman Catholic Church of the Precious Blood in Monmouth Beach and had been a member and president of their Holy Name Society, which is committed to "teaching, spreading and defending the Faith of Christ." Later in his life, McGann became president of the Monmouth County chapter of Serra International, a Catholic organization formed in the 1930s to "foster and affirm vocations to the priesthood and vowed religious life."

After Dale's legal team found out that McGann had been assigned the case, they did some digging into his record and discovered that they had drawn an outspoken judge who would almost certainly be hostile toward their case. Their research was quickly borne out by the legal proceedings. Donna Costa found McGann's courtroom demeanor to be at once bullying and condescending. Evan Wolfson vividly recalled McGann "glaring" at him and the "sneering smile" that thinly disguised his "unmitigated hostility." Initially, McGann even refused to allow the Lambda attorney to be part of the proceedings. Like each of the other attorneys in the case who were not licensed in the state of New Jersey, Wolfson had to present McGann with a motion (called *pro hac vice*) seeking permission to appear as an attorney in the case. The Boy Scouts' attorneys

George Davidson and Carla Kerr were admitted within two weeks of submitting their *pro hac vice* motion, and the following week Thomas J. Moloney and Donna Costa were admitted. Yet McGann rejected Wolfson's motion. Not until September 1993—nine months after the other attorneys had been admitted—did McGann grant Wolfson permission to appear before the court.

On the day that Wolfson was finally admitted, Dale's legal team submitted their brief in support of their motion for summary judgment, that is, for a judgment in their favor without holding a trial. Summary judgment, the brief explained, was "a prompt and inexpensive method of disposing of a case" when there was "no genuine issue of material fact requiring disposition at trial." Since there was no dispute about what had happened—the Scouts had terminated Dale after finding out he was gay—Dale's lawyers believed that a trial would invite unnecessary delay. In support of their motion, Dale's legal team submitted around one thousand pages of exhibits, including reams of Boy Scout publications as well as scores of affidavits and certifications by current and former Scouts.

Not surprisingly, Dale's legal team highlighted their client's sterling career as a Scout. But they also drew attention to Dale's broader involvement with the community, most notably his participation in a Lutheran Church youth group as well as a stint teaching Sunday school. They also played up his impressive achievements as a student. In high school, they informed the judge, Dale was ranked among the top five students academically. In addition, Dale had just graduated from Rutgers University, where he served on the student council and was among eighteen seniors (out of a graduating class of two thousand) inducted into the Cap and Skull Society in recognition of their outstanding leadership and academic achievements. Dale, they reminded McGann, was indeed a model Boy Scout.

Dale's attorneys cast the case as a "civil right action" brought to remedy an act of "illegal discrimination." Dale had been expelled from the Scouts "not because of anything he did, but solely because of what he is—a gay man." Such acts of "ignorance and bigotry" had been explicitly outlawed by New Jersey's 1992 statute that barred discrimination on the basis of sexual orientation in places of public accommodation and in employment. Moreover, this statute "codified" an already "well-established" state public policy against discrimination on the basis of sexual orientation, a policy reflected in numerous administrative rules, executive orders, and judicial decisions.

Dale's case, then, rested on three separate claims, or what lawyers call "causes of action." The first cause of action was that the Scouts' expulsion of Dale violated his "common law right not to be expelled from an association on grounds contrary to New Jersey public policy." The second and third causes of action were based on Dale's statutory rights under the NJLAD. One of these was that Dale was an employee of the Scouts and was therefore covered by the 1992 law's ban on discrimination in employment. The other was that the Scouts were a public accommodation and therefore were prevented by the 1992 law from excluding members based on sexual orientation.

Dale's lawyers sensed that the strongest of these three claims was the public accommodation argument, and spent far more space substantiating this cause of action than the other two (the employment argument received four pages, whereas more than thirty pages were devoted to elaborating the public accommodation argument). According to Dale's attorneys, there was no doubt that the Scouts qualified as a public accommodation as that term had been interpreted by New Jersey courts. They identified four questions that New Jersey's courts typically asked in determining whether an organization qualified as a public accommodation:

(1) Does the organization have a large and unselective membership?
(2) Does it advertise and engage in public solicitation to recruit new members?
(3) Is the organization educational and recreational in nature?
(4) Does it have a close and beneficial relationship with government entities or other organizations that independently qualify as places of public accommodation?

An affirmative response to any of these questions, the brief stated, meant that an organization was to be regarded as a public accommodation under the state's antidiscrimination statute. Dale's lawyers maintained that the Scouts met each of these criteria and so clearly qualified as a public accommodation under New Jersey law.

Dale's lawyers underscored the huge size of the BSA—four million youth and one million adults nationwide. They drew attention to the *Boy Scout Handbook*'s boast that Scouting was "the largest youth movement the free world has ever seen." By the Scouts' own accounting, nearly ninety million Americans had joined the Scouts since the organization's founding in 1910. Like Curran's lawyers, Dale's legal team noted that the Scouts advertised themselves as being open to all age-eligible boys. And they also drew attention to BSA recruitment drives and advertising campaigns that targeted boys "from all walks of life." In addition, Dale's lawyers had no difficulty showing that the Boy Scouts' own literature made abundantly clear that education and recreation were central objectives of the Scouting program.

The brief stressed the "close and beneficial relationship" between the Scouts and government entities, such as the military, police departments, and public schools. It pointed out that the BSA had been chartered by Congress in 1916, and that the charter required the BSA "to report annually to Congress regarding the organization's finances and corporate activities." Congress also authorized federal agencies to provide to the BSA "services and expendable medical supplies, as may be necessary or useful." Under this statute, federal departments, especially the Defense Department, regularly supplied the Scouts with "cots, blankets, commissary equipment, flags, and refrigerators for use at National or World Boy Scout Jamborees."

The brief highlighted the "particularly close" ties between the BSA and the military, noting that the army, navy, air force, and national coast guard each had an official whose responsibility it was to facilitate assistance to the Scouts, including transportation. Since 1981 the quadrennial national Scout jamboree had been held at Fort A. P. Hill, a seventy-six-thousand-acre army military training center in Virginia. Local councils were also frequently allowed to use local military facilities. The Monmouth Council, for instance, used Fort Monmouth on a regular basis. Dale's father, an employee in the Communications and Electronics Command at Fort Monmouth, certified that Scouting was "a part of my life at work." Not only was there a building at the fort "devoted to Scouting," but he witnessed Scouts and Scouters "around the military post on a regular basis" and was "often asked to help arrange transportation for Scouts." Military entities not only provided food, supplies, transportation, and meeting places for the Scouts, but also in many cases chartered local Boy Scout troops. In New Jersey, Dale's lawyers pointed out, "army bases and other military installations chartered more than two dozen Boy Scout troops in 1992."

Scouting's special relationship with government could also be seen in the fact that every president since William Howard Taft had served as the honorary president of the Scouts. The Scouts' first annual meeting in February 1911 was actually held at the White House, at Taft's invitation. In their literature, the Scouts celebrate this special relationship: "One of the causes contributing to the success of the Boy Scouts of America has been the thoughtful, wholehearted way in which each President of the United States since [the organization's founding in] 1910 has taken an active part in the work of the movement." What private organization could make the same claim?

The close relationship with government from which the Scouts benefited extended to the state and local level. In New Jersey, for instance, the legislature authorized the state Board of Fish and Game to "stock with fish any body of water" that the Boy Scouts owned or used. Tellingly, the statute extended this privilege to "other similar *public* organizations." The brief also pointed to the many local government entities that chartered Scouting units, including over fifty-five thousand fire departments and forty-two thousand police departments (usually as part of the Explorer Scouts program). Dale's attorneys counted more than two hundred Scouting units in New Jersey that were sponsored either by law enforcement, fire departments, or city governments, and more than thirty in Monmouth Council.

In addition, there was a "close and special" relationship between the Scouts and the public schools. The Boy Scouts' new "Learning for Life" program took place in classrooms during the school day and involved nearly seven hundred thousand students. But even apart from the school-based Learning for Life program, the BSA remained extraordinarily dependent on schools for recruitment, meeting spaces, and sponsors. Many children first learn about Scouting at school from announcements by teachers and administrators. Local councils commonly host "School Night for Scouting" on school grounds to distribute literature and explain Scouting to potential new recruits. In New Jersey, as in the nation as a whole, roughly one in five chartering organizations were public schools or parent-teacher associations (PTAs). In New Jersey there were about five hundred public schools and PTAs that chartered Scout troops, and in Monmouth Council there were at least fifty.

Dale's lawyers thought that this aspect of their argument was a legal slam dunk. The evidence of a long-standing and special relationship between the BSA and government entities seemed so indisputable that Dale's legal team asserted that there could be "no genuine issue of material fact in dispute regarding Scouting's close and beneficial relationship with government entities." Dale's lawyers believed that the key legal question to be decided was not whether the Scouts should be regarded as a public accommodation, but rather whether the Scouts' First Amendment rights trumped the law in this case.

To overcome the First Amendment objection, Dale's team knew that it was crucial to show that opposition to homosexuality was not part of the Scouts' core expressive message. In their brief, Dale's lawyers emphasized the same point that Curran's legal team had made forcefully: nowhere in the extensive literature—the BSA's membership applications, handbooks, recruiting materials, and training materials—distributed to Scouts, their parents, and troop leaders was there a statement of the BSA's "Anti-Gay Policy." The brief underscored Dale's assertion—backed by an affidavit from Dale's father—that prior to being kicked out of the Scouts in the summer of 1990 Dale had been unaware of any such policy.

To bolster their case, Dale's legal team did something that Curran's had failed to do. They submitted nearly 150 certifications from current and former Boy Scouts who attested that they had been unaware of the Scouts' antigay policy, at least until they read or heard of litigation challenging the policy. Each certification affirmed that "nothing that I learned while involved in the Scouting program suggested to me that homosexuals would not be eligible for membership in Boy Scouts of America." Dale's lawyers insisted that these certifications "easily distinguished" Dale's case from Curran's because they demonstrated what Curran had not, namely, that opposition to homosexuality was not one of "the views that brought . . . together" members of the Scouting program.

The certifications were drawn from a wide array of ages, backgrounds, and regions. There was an elderly man from Philadelphia who had been an Eagle Scout in the 1920s in Santa Monica, California. There was a software engineer with a doctoral degree from Stanford, married with four children, who had begun life in the 1950s as a Scout in the Tall Corn Area Council of Iowa and was now assistant Scoutmaster in the Stanford area. There was the Florida man who in 1981 had served as the National Explorer President, "the highest elected youth position in Scouting," before becoming an assistant Scoutmaster of a troop chartered by the Trinity United Methodist Church in Palm Beach Gardens, Florida. There was even a certification from the daughter of William D. Boyce, founder of the BSA.

Dale's legal team also bolstered their argument by submitting excerpts from a deposition given by James Kay in January 1993. In that deposition Kay admitted that he was unaware of any Boy Scout documents provided to Scouting youth, their parents, adult members, or chartering organizations that made explicit reference to the BSA's policy concerning homosexuals. Kay also admitted that he had never spoken to any member of the over two hundred Scouting units in Monmouth Council about whether the term "morally straight" referred to homosexuality. When asked about his own understanding of morally straight, Kay offered that "according to the Boy Scouts of America, it would be a life of—a character, a strong character exemplified by the virtues of justice [and] of cleanliness." Asked by Donna Costa how a homosexual failed to satisfy that standard, Kay faltered, prompting the Boy Scouts' lawyer George Davidson to intervene. The question, Davidson protested, was "tautological." How, he fired back, "can anybody answer that question?" "A moral view," he insisted, "is a moral view."

Dale's brief closed with a reading of three recent US Supreme Court cases that considered whether state antidiscrimination laws violated a membership organization's right of expressive association. In each of these cases (*Roberts v. United States Jaycees* [1984], *Board of*

Directors of Rotary International v. Rotary Club of Duarte [1987], and *New York State Club Association v. City of New York* [1988]), Dale's lawyers pointed out, the Court had "unequivocally rejected the claim that the Constitution licenses entities to engage in discrimination prohibited by state or local laws."

The *Roberts* case involved a challenge to the United States Jaycees' exclusion of women. Founded in 1920, the organization was known as the Junior Chamber of Commerce until changing its name to the Jaycees in the 1960s. (In 1990 the national organization voted to allow each state organization to choose whether to call itself the Jaycees or the Junior Chamber.) Membership in the Jaycees was limited to men between the ages of eighteen and thirty-five; women and older men were allowed to be "associate" members, but they could not vote, hold office, or participate in leadership training. When the Minneapolis and St. Paul chapters of the Jaycees started to admit women as full members in the 1970s, the national organization moved to revoke their charters. The two chapters then took the national organization to court, arguing that excluding women from becoming full members violated Minnesota's antidiscrimination law.

A federal court of appeals upheld the national organization's constitutional right to revoke the charter of the local chapters, but a unanimous Supreme Court overturned the lower court's judgment. Writing for the Court, Justice William Brennan acknowledged that government regulations that force a group to accept unwanted members "may impair the ability of the original members to express only those views that brought them together," but stressed that the "right to associate for expressive purposes is not . . . absolute." So long as the government was not aiming to suppress speech, then infringing on the right of associational freedom could be justified by regulations that served "compelling state interests" and that could not be achieved through other less restrictive means. Eradicating discrimination against women, Brennan concluded, was just such a compelling state interest.

Three years later, the Court again faced the question of the exclusion of women from a civic organization, in this case Rotary International, which was dedicated to promoting the idea of service among businessmen. ("He profits most who serves best" and "Service above self" were the long-standing Rotarian mottos.) Much as with the Jaycees, the case stemmed from a local Rotary club admitting women as members in violation of the organization's national policy and then filing suit in state court. And as in the Jaycees' case, the Supreme Court unanimously held that the state's antidiscrimination law—in this case California's—did not violate the First Amendment in requiring Rotary to admit women. Although granting that the organization engaged in "commendable service activities" that were protected by the First Amendment, the Court found that admitting women would not "affect in any significant way the existing members' ability to carry out those activities." And whatever "slight infringement" there might be was "justified by the State's compelling interests in eliminating discrimination against women and in assuring them equal access to public accommodations."

The third Supreme Court case introduced by Dale's lawyers involved a facial challenge by the New York Club Association to a new city ordinance that expanded the scope of the city's existing antidiscrimination law so that it would apply to a wider range of associations. Following its reasoning in *Roberts* and *Rotary*, the Court upheld the New York City ordinance on the grounds that it did not, on its face, require any group "to abandon or alter" First Amendment–protected activities. The new law did not affect "'in any significant way' the ability of individuals to form associations." Nor did the law infringe on an association's right to exclude "individuals who do not share the views that the club's members wish to promote." Instead, the law "merely prevents an association from using race, sex, and the other specified characteristics as shorthand measures in place of what the city considers to be more legitimate criteria for determining membership." The Court allowed that in a particular case a group might be able to show that it could not "advocate its desired viewpoints nearly as effectively if it cannot confine its membership to those who share the same sex, for example, or the same religion." However, the Court believed that "the large clubs covered by the Law" (the law only applied to groups with at least four hundred members) were unlikely to be that sort of club.

In short, Dale's lawyers contended, the Supreme Court over the past decade had consistently—and without a dissenting vote—rejected efforts to shield discrimination behind a right of expressive association. Under the standards established by the Court, Dale's team concluded, the Scouts' "Anti-Gay Policy [was] clearly not protected by the First Amendment." Indeed the policy could hardly be considered "an expressive goal of Scouting" when it was "not widely known by the members of Scouting." And certainly it did not express (in the language of the *Roberts* ruling) the "views that brought [the Scouts] together." Moreover, the antigay policy was "not essential to the [organization's] purposes," which were "teaching young people outdoor and camping skills, developing their leadership abilities and sense of community responsibility, and providing them with the tools to make moral choices over the course of their lives." Being compelled by the state of New Jersey to jettison its antigay policy would not, in sum, affect Scouting activities in any "significant way." Consequently, the Scouts' First Amendment rights of association must give way to New Jersey's "compelling interest in eradicating discrimination on the basis of sexual orientation."

CHAPTER 6

The Scouts' Response

Two months after Dale's attorneys submitted their complaint, the Boy Scouts' attorneys submitted their answer, together with fifteen hundred pages of supporting certifications and documents. The Scouts' brief opened by affirming that the organization "represents traditional moral values and teaches to youth members traditional moral values, including the value of living a 'morally straight' life." The Scouts' position was that an avowed homosexual—a person "who represents and advocates the morality of homosexual conduct"—could not live a "morally straight" life and therefore did not belong in the Scouts, especially not in a leadership capacity. The only questions for the court to decide were "whether New Jersey law authorizes, and, if so, whether the Constitution permits the state to decide a conflict of moral values in the context of a private, volunteer charitable association trying to teach moral values to youth." Like Dale, the Scouts saw no reason to go to trial and asked the judge for summary judgment.

The Scouts knew that the success of their constitutional argument rested on distinguishing *Dale* from *Roberts v. United States Jaycees*, the 1984 case in which the US Supreme Court required the Jaycees to admit women as full members. In 1984 the Scouts had been one of three groups to file an amicus brief in support of the Jaycees' right to exclude women. In that brief, on which George Davidson had worked, the Scouts made an expansive argument for an almost unlimited freedom of association, which they argued was "not a mere appendage to the rights enumerated in the First Amendment," but was instead "a separate human right inherent in the Constitution's plan for limited governmental powers." The "right to join together in voluntary societies," the Scouts explained, "lay at the heart of the American experiment" and was "fundamental to our Nation's concept of liberty." In support of this proposition, the Scouts enlisted the authority of Alexis de Tocqueville, who wrote:

> The most natural privilege of man, next to the right of acting for himself, is that of combining his exertions with those of his fellow creatures and of acting in common with them. The right of association therefore appears to be as almost inalienable in its nature as the right of personal liberty. No legislator can attack it without impairing the foundations of society.

At stake in *Roberts*, the Scouts claimed, was nothing less than the choice between "our free society" and the oppression and conformity of "totalitarian regimes."

The Scouts' decision to submit a brief on behalf of the Jaycees had been provoked by two recent setbacks the Scouts had suffered, first in October 1983 in California in the case of Tim Curran and then in January 1984 in Connecticut in the case of Catherine Pollard. In both cases, judges had ruled that public accommodation statutes applied to the Scouts. In their *Roberts* brief, the Scouts implored the Supreme Court to reject a "stunted" and "crimped" view of associational freedom by upholding the Jaycees' constitutional right to exclude whomever they wanted to exclude. The Jaycees were not a commercial business, the Scouts pointed out, but instead were "an association of like-minded people devoted to advancement of particular beliefs and purposes." In a free society the state had no business telling groups of like-minded people who they could associate with, no matter how "alluring" the goal of combating "discrimination" (the Scouts put the term in quotation marks). The Scouts closed their brief with the ominous warning of Sir Thomas More: "What would you do? Cut a great road through the law to get after the Devil? . . . And when the last law was down, and the Devil turned round on you—where would you hide, . . . the laws all being flat?"

But now that the Supreme Court had cut that great road through the law and ordered the Jaycees (and the Rotarians in 1986) to admit women, the Scouts were compelled to take a different tack. Rather than make common cause with the Jaycees, they now emphasized the ways in which their case was unlike that of the Jaycees. They stressed that the Court had allowed the state to require the Jaycees to admit women because there was "'no basis in the record' for concluding that women have different ideologies from men and therefore no evidence that the Jaycees' expression would be affected" by admitting women. In contrast, in Dale's case there was "overwhelming evidence" that admitting "an avowed homosexual" would substantially interfere with the Scouts' expressive message. "Unlike the women in *Roberts* who had been excluded from the Jaycees," the Scouts argued, Dale harbored "'ideologies or philosophies different from' those of the Boy Scouts." In fact Dale's "very purpose" in bringing his suit was to subvert "Scouting's view of what the Scout Oath and Law require." And it was an undisputed fact in the case that the Scouts' "central purpose" was "to instill the values of the Scout Oath and the Scout Law in young people."

Dale interfered with the Scouts' ability to transmit their expressive message because of what he both advocated and represented. By his own admission, Dale had become "a gay activist" in his second year in college (1989–1990) and was "very active in gay politics" on campus, including serving as the co-president of the Rutgers University Lesbian and Gay Alliance. Whereas Dale had portrayed his legal challenge as stemming from having learned the nonpolitical values of honesty and courage that the Scouts had taught him, the Scouts' lawyers depicted a young man who was suing the Scouts because of a pro–gay rights philosophy that he had picked up in college. Dale had even gone on national television (on the Joan Rivers Show in July 1993) to publicize his criticism of the Scouts' exclusion of homosexuals. At stake in this case, then, was the advocacy of rival ideas or moral philosophies, and the *Roberts* Court had stated unambiguously that even a compelling state interest such as eradicating discrimination could only prevail over a First Amendment claim if it was "unrelated to the suppression of ideas."

The Scouts maintained that even if Dale had not been a self-described "gay activist" who openly advocated the morality of homosexuality, they still had a constitutional right under *Roberts* to expel Dale because of what he represented. Compelling the Scouts to accept a known homosexual as a Boy Scout leader would interfere with the Scouts' ability to "convey a message of traditional sexual morality to youth members through its leaders." Leaders, after all, were role models who taught lessons through their actions as well as through their words. The Scouts referred the Court to the 1972 edition of the *Scoutmaster's Handbook*, which preached:

> What you are speaks louder than what you say. . . . In his quest for manhood, every boy needs contact with men he can copy. Living, breathing men provide models of what manhood is like. Boys copy whatever models are available to them. . . . You are providing a good example of what a man should be like. *What you do and what you are may be worth a thousand lectures and sermons.*

Once Dale's homosexuality became known to others, it unavoidably became a form of advocacy "worth a thousand lectures and sermons."

To bolster this proposition, the Scouts introduced a certification from Ricky Slavings, an assistant Scoutmaster and recently tenured associate professor of sociology at Radford University. A little-known scholar who specialized in "small group dynamics" (his 1988 dissertation at the University of Missouri, Columbia, was on "Campus Housing, Identity Formation, and Student Retention"), Slavings had testified on behalf of the Scouts on at least three previous occasions, at the trials of Tim Curran, Mark Welsh, and the Randall twins. Slavings reported that he had observed over sixty Boy Scouts troops "as part of a professional study of the socialization process and methods of value transmission in Scouting"—a study, it turns out, that was never published or disseminated. In the Welsh and Randall trials, Slavings offered his professional opinion that allowing atheists into the Scouts would likely cause irreligious attitudes to "spread to other members of the group," which would "destroy group unity" as well as impair Scouting's ability to instill religious values in the other boys. Dale's case raised even greater concerns about the transmission of values because Dale, like Curran, would be a Scout leader and therefore a role model to whom young boys would look. Slavings explained that "a leader could not serve as an effective role model for a Scouting value which the leader did not live by; such a leader would instead serve as a role model for the values the role model actually practiced." According to Slavings, the "presence of a homosexual Scout leader would provide a role model to youth members for the view that homosexuality is moral."

The certification by Slavings left ambiguous whether the danger was that allowing known homosexuals to serve as Scoutmasters would lead to greater toleration of homosexuality in others (a change in values) or whether it would also lead to more homosexuality (a change in sexual orientation and behavior). In invoking language from the 1972 edition of the *Boy Scout Handbook*—"Boys copy whatever models are available to them"—the Scouts seemed to imply that they worried boys would be more likely to become homosexuals if they knew that their Scout leader was a homosexual. Dale's team summoned their own expert—Dr. Bryan Welch, a nationally prominent psychologist and senior policy advisor to the American Psychological Association—to push back on this second claim. Welch rejected the assumption that sexual orientation was a value or norm that could be transmitted from adult to child. In a supplemental certification, Slavings responded that Welch failed to take account "of the influence an avowed homosexual role model may have on a male youth's behavior." Among young people, Slavings maintained, "experimentation with homosexual identity or homosexual behavior is not uncommon, and may be influenced by a homosexual role model even if orientation is not affected." Admitting known homosexuals like Dale as leaders, in other words, might not turn more Scouts into homosexuals but it could make them more likely to engage in homosexual conduct.

The aim of the Scouts' brief was not only to distinguish *Dale* from *Roberts*, but also to show that Dale's case was "indistinguishable from the *Curran* case," which had been decided in the Boy Scouts' favor. In *Curran*, the trial judge found that the record showed that the BSA had "taken a consistent position that homosexuality is immoral and incompatible with the Boy Scout Oath and Law." After a lengthy trial, with scores of witnesses, Judge Sally Disco had found that "nothing in the evidence indicates that the BSA belief that homosexuality is immoral was adopted simply as a pretext or a post hoc justification for the exclusion of homosexuals from participation in the organization." And "unlike the evidence contained in the *Roberts* and *Rotary* records," Judge Disco concluded, "the evidence introduced in [*Curran*] establishe[d] the required nexus between the basis for the exclusion and the belief system which defines the organization." The Scouts' brief maintained that there was no reason for Judge McGann to reach a different conclusion since the BSA continued to adhere to the same position that homosexual conduct was "inconsistent with the promise to be morally straight and inconsistent with the requirement that a Scout be clean in body and mind."

In support of their reading of "morally straight" and "clean," the Scouts offered certifications from several individuals, including the Scoutmaster of a New Jersey Boy Scout troop, BSA's director of council services P. Karl Rowley, and a Catholic priest who served as chair of the membership committee of the National Catholic Committee on Scouting. Rowley affirmed that the belief that homosexual conduct was "not 'morally straight' under the Scout Oath or 'clean' under the Scout Law [had] been the position of the Scouting movement since Boy Scouts of America was incorporated in 1910." In addition, the Scouts' brief referenced certifications by the two adult volunteer leaders—Dale's Scoutmaster Earl Wightman and Paul Terzulli, chair of the troop committee—who had approved Dale's application to be assistant Scoutmaster of Troop 73. Both attested that they "understood homosexual conduct to be incompatible with Scouting principles" and that they would not have approved Dale's application had they known he was "an avowed homosexual." However, neither Wightman nor Terzulli mentioned their understanding of the meaning of "morally straight" or "clean."

In offering these certifications, the Scouts followed a script they had used successfully during Curran's trial. However, there was one obvious difference between the *Curran* and *Dale* records: namely, the roughly 150 certifications from former and current Scouts who swore that they had been unaware that the BSA had a policy against admitting homosexuals. The Scouts' brief thus took direct aim at these "100-odd" certifications in a bid to show that they had no real bearing on the case.

To begin with, the certifications were not, as the Dale team characterized them, "a broad cross-section of current and former Scouts from across the country." Instead, the Scouts countered, they were "solicited from Forgotten Scouts and other homosexual activists who are seeking to change Scouting's policy." Forgotten Scouts, the brief explained, was "a group of homosexual former Scouts committed to changing Boy Scouts' membership policies." The brief noted that Dale had also solicited certifications from those who had written to him in response to articles in the media, including gay magazines such as *OUT!* and *Gay Chicago*. By the Scouts' count, at least twelve of the certifications came from those who had "been written up in major newspapers as activists for homosexual rights and as members of homosexual advocacy groups." Another two dozen "identified themselves in correspondence [with Dale] as homosexuals or as Forgotten Scouts." In short, these certifications were not to be taken seriously because they came "entirely [from] those with an axe to grind."

But even if the certifications had included genuine "representatives of Scouting," the Scouts said that the statements would still not be relevant because they "miss the point." According to the Scouts, these "form" certifications—written by Lambda lawyers—"essentially [made] only two claims: (1) that while they were in Scouts they were unaware of a policy of excluding homosexuals, and (2) that they never knew it to be one of the central purposes of the Boy Scouts of America to exclude homosexuals." The latter point was irrelevant, the Scouts argued, because the BSA had "never contended that one of its *central* purposes was to exclude homosexuals." Instead, its central purpose was "to reinforce the values of the Oath and Law, including the values of morally straight and clean." The Scouts excluded "known or avowed homosexuals . . . because their admission would interfere with the central purpose of teaching boys to be morally straight and clean." None of the certifications suggested that the person "was unaware of the central importance of the values in the Oath and Law, including morally straight and clean."

The Scouts also brushed away the significance of the fact that these individuals claimed to have been unaware of the policy while they were in the Scouts. After all, there "would not be many occasions to discuss with youth a membership issue that arises predominantly with adult applicants or members, and with them only infrequently." It was also "not surprising that an adult trying to recall his early teens might not recall anything specific with respect to Scouting statements on homosexuality." This wasn't merely a dig at failing memories. Rather the Scouts' more important point was that the Scout Oath and Scout Law expressed "a positive code for living" rather than "listing 'don'ts' to avoid." And so it was natural that these former Scouts didn't recall conversations about the evils of homosexuality because "in seeking to reinforce the positive moral values of the Oath and Law, an absence of reference to homosexual conduct [was] precisely the environment Boy Scouts [sought] to preserve." In other words, the fact that ex-Scouts did not remember any discussion of homosexuality bolstered the Scouts' contention that they strove to inculcate traditional views of sexuality "based on marriage and family."

Another reason that the *Boy Scout Handbook*'s explication of morally straight did not explicitly mention homosexual conduct was that "in the moral and social climate that prevailed for most of Scouting's history, no one could reasonably have entertained any doubt that homosexual conduct was not 'morally straight.'" After all, during most of this period "homosexual conduct was regarded with such opprobrium that it was literally not spoken of." One could hardly expect the *Handbook* to mention a behavior that everyone knew was not only immoral but unspeakable. (This left unexplained, however, why even the latest [1990] edition of the *Handbook* did not mention homosexuality in its discussion of "morally straight," and why the previous [1979] edition's exegesis of morally straight warned against the dangers of sexual promiscuity leading to venereal disease.)

The opprobrium that attached to homosexual conduct explained, too, why for most of its history the Scouts did not have a written policy against such conduct. Prior to the emergence of a "homosexual rights movement" in the 1970s and 1980s, Rowley told the court, there had been "no occasion to prepare position statements with regard to homosexual conduct." Such position statements were unnecessary because "it was rare for anyone to declare himself to be a homosexual and inconceivable that an avowed homosexual would reasonably suppose that he would be eligible to serve as a Scout leader." Rowley conceded that the first position statement from 1978 was "never distributed" but this was "because there were no questions being raised as to whether avowed homosexuals could become Scout leaders." Only after Curran's suit did the Scouts feel it necessary to issue formal position statements, which they did in

1991, 1992, and then again in January 1993. Rowley entered into the record each of these three position statements.

Interestingly, Davidson chose not to reference any of these position statements in the brief. Despite the considerable energy the Scouts had invested in formulating the 1991, 1992, and 1993 position statements, the Scouts' attorneys evidently adjudged these statements to be not essential to the core constitutional case. From Davidson's perspective, the Scouts' constitutional case rested not on whether there was a written policy. Instead, the legal argument rested on demonstrating that the Scouts' central mission was to inculcate in young people the values of the Scout Oath and Law, and that the Scouts understood homosexual conduct to be inconsistent with the pledge to be morally straight and clean in body and mind. Forcing the Scouts to accept known or avowed homosexuals would thus trample on their First Amendment rights by preventing the Scouts from communicating their expressive message regarding the traditional family, marriage, and sexual morality. That the law could not do.

It was therefore unnecessary, the Scouts argued, for the court to consider whether the Scouts were a public accommodation under the NJLAD since even if they were judged to be a public accommodation the law still could not constitutionally be applied to the Scouts. Nonetheless, the brief proceeded to demonstrate why the Scouts were not in fact a place of public accommodation under the NJLAD. The Scouts dismissed the four-pronged "test" concocted by Dale's attorneys as having "no basis in law." The four strands of this phony test were derived not from cases dealing with a "bona fide membership organization" like the Scouts but rather from cases "involving businesses found to resemble the accommodations specifically listed in the LAD," such as taverns, hotels, stores, swimming pools, public libraries, and movie theaters. Indeed a Boy Scout troop was not even a place at all; instead, it was "a small group of boys and their leaders."

Moreover, that the Scouts were popular with boys did not make them public, any more than success in recruiting members meant that its membership criteria were unselective. The Scouts maintained that the requirement that all Scouts must promise to live by the Scout Oath was "in itself a sufficiently selective criteria to find that a Boy Scout troop is not a place of public accommodation." And adult members like Dale were subject to even more rigorous screening, including evaluation by the troop committee based on ten criteria, such as high moral standards, commitment to the ideals of Scouting, ability to relate to boys, organizational ability, energy level, and attention to detail.

The Scouts also objected that Dale's brief had "greatly overstate[d] the degree of government support to Scouting." The Scouts pointed out that thirty-five of the seventy-seven troops in Monmouth Council—including all three troops of which Dale had been a member—were church-sponsored. And nationally, nearly two in three Boy Scout troops were "sponsored by churches, synagogues, and church-related groups." Moreover, the fact that an organization received government aid did not make it a place of public accommodation. The brief pointed out that "ministers of religion, for example, receive free transportation from common carriers under federal law and transportation at special or reduced rates from railroads under New Jersey law." Indeed, as the Scouts might have added but didn't, every state plus the District of Columbia subsidizes churches by exempting them from property taxes but that did not make churches a place of public accommodation subject to antidiscrimination statutes.

The Scouts maintained, too, that they were exempt from the NJLAD because the law specifically exempted any "educational facility operated or maintained by a bona fide religious institution." The Boy Scouts, their brief argued, were "educational in nature," sought to "promote religious life," and taught boys "the importance of doing their duty to God and of behaving in accordance with a moral system based on religious principles." That religiously based moral system included condemnation of homosexuality.

Dale's Reply Memorandum

Dale's attorneys had the opportunity to respond to the Scouts' brief in their Reply Memorandum of Law. Mostly the reply restated and refined the arguments made in the original brief. But Dale's lawyers were anxious to respond to the Scouts' attempt to discredit the many certifications that had been submitted in support of Dale's motion. So Dale's attorneys contacted each of the individuals who had originally submitted certifications and solicited supplemental certifications that spoke more directly to the Scouts' claim about the widely understood meanings of "morally straight" and "clean." This time, each certified that "no one involved in Scouting ever told me—and no Scouting literature with which I am familiar ever suggested to me—that homosexuality is inconsistent with [the values of the Scout Oath and the Scout Law], or that a homosexual cannot be morally straight and clean." Moreover, each person swore that

> nothing I learned while involved in the Scouting program taught me that sexual orientation was relevant in any way to eligibility for membership in Boy Scouts of America, or to any aspect of the Scouting program. I never learned that it was a purpose of the Scouting program to exclude homosexuals. I never learned that admitting homosexuals would interfere with the fulfillment of Scouting's central purpose of teaching boys to uphold the values in the Scout Oath and the Scout Law, including being morally straight and clean.

Dale's team also submitted more detailed affidavits from five current Scouting leaders who attested to much the same thing.

Dale's team was also eager to replace the Scouts' portrait of these individuals as a motley crew of unreliable, homosexual ex-Scouts with "an axe to grind." To give the court a better idea of many of these individuals' deep involvement with Scouting, Dale's attorneys entered into the record a matrix that listed the "Scouting credentials" of the 153 current and former Scouts who had submitted statements on behalf of Dale's motion. The document showed that eighty-eight of the statements came from Eagle Scouts and forty-eight from members of the Order of the Arrow. These were not, then, casual Scouts but instead individuals who had been immersed in Scouting and who generally had, like Dale, "positive views of their Scouting experience." Nor were these all people who had, as the Scouts suggested, only been involved in Scouting in their distant "teen years." About a third of the statements came from individuals who had held adult leadership roles in Scouting.

Dale's lawyers also used the reply to introduce affidavits from religious leaders attesting that many religions and clergy did not teach that homosexuality was immoral or unclean. In support of this proposition, Dale's team offered affidavits from, among others, two Lutheran pastors, a rabbi, a Methodist bishop, an Episcopal bishop, and a Catholic bishop and priest. They also submitted statements culled from publications of the Unitarians, United Church of Christ, and Quakers. Drawing upon these affidavits, the reply brief noted that in the spring of 1992 the executive board of the Central Conference of American Rabbis had "called upon the BSA 'to open its membership and leadership to all men and boys without regard to sexual orientation,'" and that in the spring of 1993 the Council of the Episcopal Diocese of Newark had passed a similar resolution requesting that the BSA "admit to full membership otherwise qualified homosexual persons." Dale's team argued that these affidavits and statements showed that an understanding of homosexuality as unclean or not morally straight could not be, as the Scouts implied, "implicit in Scouting's '[Declaration of] Religious Principle' or in the requirement that Scouts strive to do their 'duty to God.'"

The most poignant of these affidavits came from the Reverend William A. Hanson, Dale's pastor at the King of Kings Lutheran Church in Middletown, New Jersey. Hanson had been pastor at King of Kings for nearly three decades and for some of that time the church had chartered a Scout troop, to which Dale belonged until the troop folded. Hanson told the court that during the time when the church sponsored a troop he had been unaware that the Scouts excluded homosexuals, and that had he known he "would have discouraged the leaders of the church from affiliating themselves or our church with Scouting." He took strong exception to the idea that sexual orientation had anything to do with being morally straight. "There was a time in history," he noted, "when left-handed people were thought to be of the Devil. Today we know that they can be as morally straight as anyone else, and that left-handedness has nothing to do with morality." Hanson found it equally absurd to suggest that "clean" in body and mind had any connection to sexual orientation. He assured the court that he had "never suggested to [his] congregation that homosexuals are not clean, either in a literal sense, or in the context of cleanliness of spirit." And finally he dissented from the notion that sexual orientation could be "relevant to whether an adult is a good role model." Hanson attested that Dale's impeccable character and integrity made him "an ideal role model." Indeed Hanson declared that he would have no hesitation in entrusting Dale, whom he had known since he was five years old, "with the care and responsibility of the children in my congregation," or even his own grandchildren. It was, he concluded, "sad and ironic that—at a time when it is increasingly difficult in our society to find young adults willing to devote their time and energy to serving their communities and helping others—a young man who would be welcome as a leader in his church [was] not similarly welcome in the Scouting organization."

The other Lutheran pastor solicited by Dale's attorneys, the Reverend George Wayne Freyberger, echoed Hanson's views of the teachings of the Evangelical Lutheran Church, by far the largest Lutheran denomination in the United States. Freyberger assured the court that members of the Evangelical Lutheran Church were "not taught by their religion to equate homosexuals with 'immorality' or 'uncleanliness.'" Freyberger's own view was that "the morality of sexual behavior is appropriately judged by considering whether a person engages in such behavior as an expression of a committed love or in a destructive or exploitative fashion." Freyberger also alerted the court to a recently circulated (October 1993) draft statement by the church's Task Force on Human Sexuality that declared that "sexual orientation should not become the basis for judging a person's overall character." In addition, Freyberger drew attention to the Lutheran Church's strong backing for the 1991 bill that amended the NJLAD to include a ban on discrimination on the basis of sexual orientation. As a good Lutheran, then, Dale had no reason to think, nor did his religious leaders instruct him, that being a homosexual was incompatible with taking the Scout Oath or Scout Law or signing the Declaration of Religious Principle.

The Scouts' Reply Memorandum

By this stage, the Scouts had said pretty much all they wanted to say. Whereas Dale's lawyers' reply memorandum was eighty-six pages, twenty pages longer than their original brief, the Scouts' reply memorandum was a mere twelve pages, a fifth the length of their original brief. The Scouts saw little need to counter the 153 certifications with scores of certifications of their own. At best, the Dale team's certifications only showed that "a handful out of about 1.2 million current volunteers disagree with Scouting policy." That was hardly surprising. However, the religious leaders' affidavits touched a nerve, provoking the Scouts into rounding up their own band of religious authorities. The Scouts presented certifications from seven clergymen from seven faiths: Catholic, Lutheran, Methodist, Presbyterian, Southern Baptist, Jewish, and Mormon.

Some of these clergymen the Scouts had tapped before, most notably the Mormon elder Jack Goaslind, who had testified in both the Curran and the Welsh trials in 1991. Goaslind was not just any Mormon; he was the general president of the Mormon Church's Young Men organization, responsible "for giving direction to all of the young men in the Church ages 12 to 18" and for coordinating the Scouting program for all Mormon-chartered troops. That meant that Goaslind was responsible for nearly 400,000 boys and 150,000 adults in 26,000 Scouting units across the United States. He was also on the BSA's National Executive Board (and in 1995 would receive Scouting's highest honor, the Silver Buffalo Award, for "distinguished service to youth"). When Goaslind spoke, the Boy Scouts listened.

In his affidavit, Goaslind did not repeat the threat he had made at the Curran trial: namely, that if a court forced the Scouts to admit homosexuals, all Mormon youth would leave the Scouts. But he did emphasize that the Mormon Church's "strong relationship" with Scouting was grounded in the congruence between the values the two organizations sought to transmit to young boys. Both the BSA and the Latter Day Saints (LDS) Church shared the conviction that homosexual conduct was immoral. Like Scouting, Mormonism taught "that a person must refrain from homosexual or lesbian relations to be morally clean." Indeed homosexual conduct was so abhorrent to the Mormon Church that it was "a ground for excommunication." The Mormon position on homosexual conduct, Goaslind explained, was "drawn from Scriptures," which condemn behavior "that is contrary to God's plan for family living."

The other clergy offered the same assurances that their churches' teachings on homosexuality were in close accord with the Scouts' policy. The Scouts' chosen Southern Baptist minister—an Eagle Scout and pastor from a tiny Texas town about an hour's drive south of the Boy Scouts' headquarters—affirmed that the Southern Baptists (sponsors of nearly five thousand Scouting units) believed that "homosexual conduct is immoral and unclean." As evidence he pointed to a resolution adopted at the Southern Baptist Convention in 1993 affirming "the biblical truth that homosexuality is sin." He also noted that the Southern Baptists did "not allow individuals who practice a homosexual lifestyle to be ordained members of the Church."

The Scouts presented these affidavits to show that their "moral position with respect to homosexual conduct [was] in accord with the moral positions of the religions to which a majority of Americans belong." As for the clergy summoned by Dale's team, either they were from denominations who "depart from the majority view" on homosexual conduct or they were "dissidents" who were "far out of the mainstream." As examples of the latter, Davidson pointed to the Methodist bishop Melvin Wheatley, who had "ordained a homosexual clergyman contrary to the tenets of his church, and been the subject of an ecclesiastical investigation," and the Catholic priest Paul Surlis, who had been an "advocate for the ordination of women and married men." Their heterodoxy was mild though compared to that of the Episcopal bishop John Shelby Spong, whose writings included the blasphemous claims (in Davidson's words) "that St. Paul was a homosexual, . . . that Mary's virginity is a 'myth,' . . . that Jesus Christ was conceived as a result of a rape, and . . . that Jesus Christ was married to Mary Magdalene."

To counter Dale's reform rabbi, the Scouts solicited a conservative rabbi who was also the vice-chair of the Jewish Committee on Scouting and had served as the Jewish chaplain at the most recent Scout jamboree. "Jewish morality," the rabbi explained, "is based on a strong sense of family tradition and values," which was why Orthodox Judaism "condemns homosexual conduct." According to Rabbi Arthur Vernon, "the Torah, the primary source of Jewish law, unambiguously describes homosexual conduct as an 'abomination.'" The rabbi added that both the "Scouting and Jewish tradition strive to instill traditional, heterosexual family values in youth," which is why he believed a homosexual could not serve as "a role model for emerging adolescents who are developing values and making lifestyle decisions." Homosexual Scout leaders would breed homosexual youth. Alone among the Scouts' witnesses, the rabbi closed with a warning that if he "lost the right to exclude known or avowed homosexuals from leadership positions in Jewish Scouting units," he would "withdraw [his] support of Scouting."

The Scouts parried the certifications of Dale's Lutheran ministers with a minister (Jerald Joersz) from the Lutheran Church–Missouri Synod (LCMS), the country's second largest—and much more conservative—Lutheran denomination. Joersz cautioned that the Task Force on Human Sexuality's draft statement from October 1993 that Freyberger invoked was not adopted as policy by the Evangelical Lutheran Church and had in fact drawn intense opposition from church leaders and members. Moreover, the LCMS president had denounced the draft in a press release in which he reiterated the Synod's long-standing view that "the Holy Scriptures teach . . . that homosexual behavior is intrinsically sinful." Joersz enlisted the authority of a report on human sexuality that *was* adopted: a 1981 report by the LCMS Commission on Theology and Church Relations. In that report, the church affirmed that, whatever its causes, homosexuality was "profoundly 'unnatural,'" and that even if there was a genetic element it could not be used "by homosexuals as an excuse to justify homosexual behavior." The homosexual, according to the report, must be "accountable to God for homosexual thoughts, words, and deeds." The report did not take a position on whether the sin of homosexuality meant that homosexual behavior should be made illegal, but it did state (and Joersz underlined this part for emphasis) that "even if one felt that such relationships were not a fit subject for legislation, . . . the law would still have a legitimate interest in protecting children from homosexual influence in the years when their sexual identity is formed." The Boy Scouts' policy was not only in keeping with the Scriptures but prudent.

The Methodist minister solicited by the Scouts (John Giffin) challenged Bishop Wheatley's reading of the church's *Book of Discipline*, which sets out Methodist doctrine and law. Whereas Wheatley quoted the book's affirmation that "homosexual persons no less than heterosexual persons are individuals of sacred worth," the Scouts' Methodist minister—who had served as the Methodist chaplain at the 1993 Scout Jamboree—quoted the book's admonition that "the practice of homosexuality is incompatible with Christian teaching." And whereas Wheatley highlighted the book's insistence that "all persons, regardless of . . . sexual orientation, are entitled to have their human and civil rights ensured," Giffin noted that the book stated that "self-avowed practicing homosexuals are not to be accepted as candidates, ordained as ministers, or appointed to serve in the United Methodist Church." Remarkably, a legal and constitutional dispute had descended into a debate over religious doctrine.

CHAPTER 7

Judging an "Active Sodomist"

Despite Judge Patrick McGann's reputation for efficiency and impatience with delay, it took him a very long time to issue his opinion. Not until three years after the trial had been transferred to the Chancery Division and twenty-one months after the two sides presented their final arguments did McGann finally deliver his decision. Filed on November 3, 1995, the opinion was seventy-one pages, far longer than is typical for a Chancery case. The length of the opinion, and the time it took to write it, reflected McGann's sense that this was an uncommonly important case. The judge was so fascinated by the case that he even asked his law clerk, a woman of Indian descent, to research Hindu attitudes toward homosexuality to help him with the opinion.

McGann began by laying out the undisputed facts of the case. His first sentence recorded that Dale had been born James R. Dick (Dale changed his name after his eighteenth birthday). McGann then reviewed Dale's "most commendable" record as a Scout and recounted the events that led the BSA to terminate Dale's registration. The judge acknowledged that "no serious hearing was ever accorded Dale on the merits of whether an actively homosexual assistant Scoutmaster could be or should be compatible with the goals of Scouting." McGann passed over the question of whether the Scouts had violated their own procedures by refusing Dale the opportunity to attend the regional review hearing. To McGann, such "procedural niceties" did not matter because it was "clear that all of the hearings which might have been accorded would not have changed the result" since Dale did not deny that he was a homosexual and the Scouts' position was that no "avowed homosexual" could remain in the Scouts.

McGann's initial framing of the question was revealing. David Park's letter of December 21, 1990, to Dale's counsel had explained that the BSA's policy was not to admit "avowed homosexuals." On McGann's reading, Park's "use of the modifier 'avowed' was intended to describe the BSA's understanding that Dale was a sexually active homosexual." In addition, according to McGann, "the context of the correspondence" made it "apparent that . . . it was so understood by Dale and his counsel when they read the letter." In fact, though, there is no reason to think that Park used "avowed" in anything other than its ordinary meaning: to "acknowledge openly, boldly, and unashamedly." The Scouts' position was that Dale was ineligible because he had announced himself to be a homosexual. Whether he was sexually active was not important to the Scouts' policy or to their legal position. So why was it important to McGann? The answer to that question would become clear when the judge reached his "Legal Analysis" in the second half of the opinion. First, however, McGann set about explicating "The Nature of Scouting in the United States."

He began with a brief history of Scouting, starting with its founding in England in 1907 by the army officer Robert S. Baden-Powell. McGann—who himself had been an army officer during the Korean War and served in the navy during World War II—noted that because Baden-Powell had been a military leader, Scouting possessed "many military attributes," including the wearing of uniforms "with insignias and badges," a "chain of command," and organizational units called "Posts, Troops and Patrols."

He recounted that the Boy Scouts of America had been incorporated as a not-for-profit corporation in 1910, and then granted a new corporate charter by Congress in 1916. The charter established that the governing body of the Scouts would be an executive board comprised of US citizens. The number of board members, their terms of office, and the mode of selection were left to the BSA to determine through its bylaws.

McGann then laid out the BSA's formal organizational structure:

- An executive board that meets at least three times a year (more if there are special meetings) and made up of no more than sixty-four members, each of whom is elected annually by the voting members of the national council.

- A national council that meets once a year (typically in May) and numbers well over a thousand people, principally representatives from the local Scouting councils; each local council is allotted two voting members, plus one for every five thousand registered youth members.
- An executive committee of the board that meets at the call of the BSA national president (about once a month), consists of around sixteen members, and acts as the BSA's governing body between executive board meetings.

Each voting member of the national council, executive board, and executive committee is a volunteer with the lone exception of the Chief Scout Executive, who is responsible for the day-to-day governance of the national office and is chosen by the executive board and serves at its pleasure. McGann underscored the centrality of volunteers in BSA governance. "Except for necessary professional and administrative personnel," he observed, "Boy Scouting from top to bottom is conducted by adult volunteers." In Monmouth Council, for instance, there were nearly three thousand adult volunteer leaders and only four professional Scouters (a Scout executive and three district executives), although this number, which McGann derived from Monmouth Council Executive James Kay's deposition, didn't count the council's two rangers, six full-time and part-time salaried support personnel (such as the administrative assistant, registrar, and shop manager), and the seasonal employees needed to staff the summer camp program.

McGann also detailed the BSA's decentralized administrative structure, beginning with its division into four regions (central, southern, western, and northeast), each governed by a regional committee. Each region is then subdivided into areas (today, for instance, the southern region is divided into nine areas, the western region into six) governed by an area committee. Each area in turn is made up of an array of local councils (like the Monmouth Council), each of which must be chartered annually by the BSA executive board. The BSA executive board, on the recommendation of the local council, issues charters to the organizations (for example, a civic group or church) wishing to sponsor a Scouting unit, such as a Boy Scout troop or Cub Scout pack.

After delineating at length the BSA's organizational structure, McGann took up the factual issue about which the two sides disagreed most sharply: did Scouting have a policy against admitting homosexuality that was or should have been known by Scouts such as James Dale? The judge zeroed in on two documents. The first was the section on "Sexual Responsibility" in the 1990 *Boy Scout Handbook*. McGann quoted it in its entirety, declaring that "in itself it is a declaration of policy by BSA":

> As you grow into manhood, your friendships will change. People around you are also changing. Girls you know are becoming young women. They are growing both physically and emotionally. Your relationships with them will become closer and more meaningful to you and to them.
>
> You are maturing sexually, too. As a young man, you are capable of becoming a father. That is a profound responsibility with powerful consequences in your life and the lives of others. It is a responsibility that requires your very best judgment.
>
> Sex is not the most important or most grown-up part of a relationship. Having sex is never a test of maturity. True manliness comes from accepting responsibility for your actions toward others and yourself in the following ways.
>
> *Your responsibility to women.* Whenever you like someone, you want the best for that person. A healthy relationship is supportive and equal. You owe it to the women in your life to keep their best interests in mind. You can have a terrific time together enjoying your life and growing emotionally. However, the difficulties created by pregnancy can be enormous. Don't burden yourself and someone you care for with a child neither of you is ready to bear.
>
> *Your responsibility to children.* When you are fully grown and have become secure in yourself and in your relationship with another person, the two of you may decide to marry and have a child. That is a wonderful choice full of challenges and

rewards. By waiting until you are thoroughly prepared to be parents, you can give your own child a close, loving family in which to grow.

Your responsibility to your beliefs. For the followers of most religions, sex should take place only between married couples. To do otherwise may cause feelings of guilt and loss. Abstinence until marriage is a very wise course of action.

Your responsibility to yourself. An understanding of wholesome sexual behavior can bring you lifelong happiness. Irresponsibility or ignorance, however, can cause a lifetime of regret. AIDS and venereal diseases spread by sexual contact may undermine your health and that of others. Having a baby before you are ready may drastically limit your future chances for education, occupations, and travel.

You owe it to yourself to enter adulthood without burdens. You owe it to yourself to enrich your life by learning what is right. Your religious leaders can give you moral guidance. Your parents or guardian or a sex education teacher should give you the facts about sex that you must know.

Learn by asking, remember? If you have questions about growing up, about relationships, sex, or making good decisions, ask. Talk with your parents, religious leaders, teachers, or Scoutmaster. They have experienced much of life, and they are interested in what is best for you. Let them know your concerns.

If this constituted a declaration of the Scouts' policy not to admit homosexuals, it was a remarkably veiled way of announcing it. Nowhere does the statement mention homosexuality, let alone condemn it. True, the statement presupposes heterosexual relationships, but it takes a leap of imagination to get from anodyne advice about sexual responsibility—specifically the undesirable consequences of young boys getting young girls pregnant—to a policy barring homosexuals from being Scouts, let alone Scout leaders.

McGann's second key piece of evidence was the section in the 1972 edition of the *Scoutmaster's Handbook* that dealt with "Sex Curiosity." This section was designed to help Scoutmasters respond to questions that boys might ask about "sexual matters." The section offered three rules for dealing with such questions:

> Rule number 1: You do not undertake to instruct Scouts, in any formalized manner, in the subject of sex and family life. The reasons are that it is not construed to be Scouting's proper area, and that you are probably not well qualified to do this.
>
> Rule number 2: If Scouts come to you to ask questions or to seek advice, you would give it within your competence. A boy who appears to be asking about sexual intercourse, however, may really only be worried about his pimples, so it is well to find out just what information is needed.
>
> Rule number 3: You should refer boys with sexual problems to persons better qualified than you [are] to handle them. If the boy has a spiritual leader or a doctor who can deal with them, he should go there. If such persons are not available, you may just have to do the best you can. But don't try to play a highly professional role. And at the other extreme, avoid passing the buck.

From McGann's perspective, the passage that mattered most lay in the section's final paragraph that advised Scoutmasters on how to deal with "incidents of sexual experimentation." Such incidents "could run from the innocent to the scandalous" and "call for a private and thorough investigation, and frank discussion with those involved." McGann then underlined the last sentences for emphasis: "*It is important to distinguish between youthful acts of innocence, and the practices of a confirmed homosexual who may be using his Scouting association to make contacts. A boy of 15 cannot be assumed to be acting out of innocence, and should be separated from the Troop for the protection of younger boys.*" For McGann, those last two sentences were the smoking gun. They proved that the Scouts disapproved of homosexuality and had done so for a long time. "Thus," McGann concluded, "when Dale states that he did not know that BSA had a policy against commissioning a sexually active homosexual assistant Scoutmaster he is not worthy of belief."

The judge's attack on Dale's truthfulness is remarkable at several levels. First, this is the *only* mention of homosexuality in all of the Scouts' literature prior to the time that Dale was expelled. Second, the reference to homosexuality and "youthful acts of innocence" in the 1972 edition of the *Scoutmaster's Handbook* was subsequently *dropped* in the 1990 edition (it was also not in any of the five editions published prior to 1972). The discussion of sex curiosity in the 1990 edition urged Scoutmasters to "accept all youth as they are." "Your acceptance," explained the *Handbook*, "will reassure them that they are 'normal.'" Third, the passage emphasized by McGann warns against sexual predators using the Scouts to abuse minors; it does not affirm a policy that homosexuals cannot be Scoutmasters. And the BSA no longer maintained that sexual abuse of boys was a problem that was limited to or even more common with homosexual than heterosexual males. Indeed the BSA explicitly disavowed that position. Fourth, the statement speaks of the need to separate a boy from his troop, but it does not call for revoking his membership in Scouting. And the eighth edition, published in 1980, did not even go that far. Instead of calling for the boy to be separated from his troop, it only instructed the Scoutmaster to "assist [the boy] in securing professional help." In addition, McGann omitted altogether the final sentences that followed the ones he underlined. The closing sentences in the section on "Sex Curiosity" from 1972 read: "It is of greatest importance that such occasions be kept quiet. Avoid accusations and any loose talk. Avoid making a small and innocent act into a mammoth offense. Discuss these problems with the Scout's parents, religious leader, and troop committee." In short, there was no reason for Dale to have interpreted the 1972 statement on sex curiosity among Scouting youth as a statement of a policy "against commissioning a sexually active homosexual assistant Scoutmaster."

Even more telling is McGann's neglect of the explicit teaching about the relativism of morality in the 1972 edition of the *Scoutmaster's Handbook*. "What you consider moral or immoral," the *Handbook* instructed, "depends on your upbringing and background." Moral questions, Scoutmasters were taught, "often fail to come out nice and neat." For instance, "a young man who marches in a picket line is immoral to some. If you don't march, you are immoral to others." Scoutmasters were not to prescribe a particular position on moral questions. Instead, they were to evaluate *how* a boy approached a moral question. A Boy Scout demonstrated "moral fitness" by showing

- Courage about what he believes. Being called "chicken" doesn't divert him from doing what he believes is right—or not doing what he believes is wrong.
- Respect for other people's viewpoints when they differ from his.
- Compassion for others' feelings and needs.
- Acting as if the rights of others matter to him.
- Accepting others as equal in worth and dignity.

Judged by these criteria, Dale had arguably demonstrated remarkable "moral fitness." Certainly it was difficult to see how the *Scoutmaster's Handbook* could be read as a clear statement of a longstanding antigay position.

Indeed many Scouting professionals—including those who supported the policy—were not prepared to go this far. When asked in a deposition about how a prospective Scout would learn of the Scouts' policy against admitting homosexuals, James Kay responded: "If he became in violation. . . . If he were an avowed homosexual he would be informed of this policy." And the northeast regional director, Charles Ball, admitted in his deposition that the policy "never was in print or in writing, but we just knew." Not even the Scout officials who terminated Dale, then, accepted McGann's contention that the Scouting handbooks provided a clear statement of the Scouts' antigay policy.

Even if the Scouting literature did not provide a clear statement of an antigay policy, should Dale nonetheless have known that the Scouts would terminate his registration once they found out he was gay? After all, the *Curran* case was a decade old by the time Dale gave his interview to the *Newark Star-Ledger* reporter. And even some of the former Scouts from whom Dale's legal team had solicited certifications attested that they first heard of the Scouts' claim to have a policy excluding homosexuals in the early 1980s when they read about the *Curran* case. Was McGann right that on this question at least Dale was "not worthy of belief"? The answer is almost certainly not.

Nothing in the record suggested that Dale was not telling the truth. Dale was ten years old when Curran launched his legal challenge to the Scouts' policy. And although Curran's case attracted a flurry of media attention in the early 1980s, largely in California newspapers and the gay media, there is scant reason to think that the young Dale, who by his own admission was not a teenage "news junkie," would have been aware of these stories about a case on the other side of the country. The few Scouts who swore that they became aware of the policy in the early or mid-1980s were substantially older than Dale—by at least a decade—and usually hailed from California. Moreover, after the state appellate court found in favor of Curran in October 1983, Curran's case dropped out of the public spotlight until the start of his trial almost seven years later, in September 1990. In other words, Curran's trial—and the widespread publicity in the national media—did not begin until two months *after* Dale's name and picture appeared in the *Newark Star-Ledger*. It is not difficult to believe, then, that Dale was unaware of Curran's case and the Scouts' policy prior to Kay's letter of August 10, 1990, informing him that the Scouts "forbid membership to homosexuals." Making Dale's claim still more credible are the many affidavits and certifications submitted by former Scouts who attested that they only became aware of the Scouts' antigay policy in the aftermath of Curran's trial, testimony that is consistent with the fact, as we saw in chapter 4, that prior to the Curran trial the BSA did not publicize its policy.

Judge McGann's animus toward Dale came into even sharper relief in the second half of his opinion, titled "Legal Analysis." McGann opened the analysis with a sweeping affirmation that "it is abundantly clear from the proofs presented by BSA that from its inception Scouting has excluded from membership and adult leadership any person who openly declares himself a homosexual and that such policy has continued unchanged, to the present." McGann did not identify the "proofs" to which he was referring. In truth, the Scouts had presented no documentary evidence that this had been the policy since the organization's founding. The absence of such evidence is telling since the Scouts have long kept Ineligible Volunteer Files (aka the "red flag" or "perversion" files) for adult volunteers whose registration has been terminated because they are deemed unfit for a leadership position. For Dale and others terminated between 1980 and the early 1990s, the Scouts recorded notations such as "an admitted gay leader" on their Ineligible Volunteer record sheet kept as part of a permanent file in the national office. To demonstrate that excluding "avowed homosexuals" was a longstanding policy, the Scouts would have needed only to produce redacted files showing that since its inception the Scouts had placed individuals in the Ineligible Volunteer Files on the grounds that they were known to be gay. The Scouts produced no such examples.

Why was McGann so sure that opposition to homosexuality had always been the Scouts' policy? The answer in one word: sodomy. Although the Scouts' brief did not explicitly mention sodomy, McGann made it the starting point of his legal analysis. He explained that homosexuality meant not just "sexual desire for others of one's own sex" but, according to the dictionary he consulted, "sexual activity with another of the same sex." Therefore homosexuality, in this second meaning, "becomes sodomy—i.e., 'anal copulation of one male with one another.'" McGann thought it relevant to point out that "buggery" was a "vulgar equivalent of sodomy."

McGann then offered a short history of the origins of the word "sodomy." The term, he explained, was "derived from the name of the biblical city, Sodom, which, with the nearby city of Gomorrah, was destroyed by fire and brimstone rained down by the Lord because of the sexual depravity (active homosexuality) of their male inhabitants." McGann helpfully affixed a citation to Genesis 18:16–19:28 of the King James Bible. He noted, too, that "in the Judeo-Christian tradition the act of sodomy has always been considered a gravely serious moral wrong." This was also true, he added, of the Muslim and Hindu religions.

Moving seamlessly from religion to law, McGann pointed out that "the criminal laws of Western civilization," including those of the United States, had long "imposed penal sanctions in addition to moral culpability" upon those who committed sodomy. In the half century after the founding of the Boy Scouts, McGann observed, sodomy was "a serious criminal offense" in every state as well as the

District of Columbia. Although many states had subsequently repealed their statutes criminalizing consensual sodomy—including New Jersey in 1979—McGann observed that as of 1986 (the year that the US Supreme Court, in *Bowers v. Hardwick*, upheld Georgia's sodomy statute on the grounds that the Constitution did not confer "a fundamental right to engage in homosexual sodomy") roughly half the states still criminalized sodomy.

In light of this long-standing moral and legal disapproval of sodomy, McGann concluded that it was "*nonsense* . . . to suggest that BSA had no policy against active homosexuality":

> It was an organization which from its inception had a God-acknowledged moral foundation. It required its members, youth and adult, to take the Scout Oath that they would be "morally straight." It is *unthinkable* that in a society where there was universal governmental condemnation of the act of sodomy as a crime, that the BSA could or would tolerate active homosexuality if discovered in any of its members.

McGann acknowledged that in New Jersey the criminal law had changed in 1979. But just because New Jersey no longer regarded sodomy as a criminal act did not change the unwavering "moral stance" of the Boy Scouts. This held true not just for the Scouts but for society more broadly. "The criminal law has changed," McGann insisted, but "the moral law—as to the act of sodomy—has not." "All religions," McGann declared, continue to "deem the act of sodomy a serious moral wrong," just as all religions still deemed the acts of "adultery and fornication" to be "morally culpable." This religiously based "moral law" against the act of sodomy was as true "today in New Jersey" as it had been before the state decriminalized sodomy prior to 1979.

Reduced to its essentials, McGann's reasoning was simple: The Boy Scouts of America is a "moral organization." Sodomy is universally considered to be an immoral act. Therefore being "an active sodomist is simply incompatible with Scouting." To suggest otherwise was "nonsense," even "unthinkable."

McGann's syllogism allowed him to avoid the thorny question of whether "morally straight" had always meant what the Scouts now claimed it did, namely, that homosexuality was incompatible with Scouting. Specifically, it enabled McGann to sidestep the awkward fact that nowhere in the pages of the *Boy Scout Handbook* that were devoted to explicating the meaning of "morally straight" did the Scouts ever make any reference, veiled or otherwise, to homosexuality.

The syllogism was, in any event, flawed, a flaw suggested by McGann's analogy with adultery and fornication. If the acts of adultery and fornication are also considered "morally culpable," why did the Scouts not refuse membership to all those who had committed fornication—that is, sexual intercourse by unmarried individuals—and adultery? As McGann's supposedly "apt" analogy made clear, many acts widely deemed immoral were not grounds for expulsion from the Scouts.

A similar logical problem attached to sodomy itself. The legal and moral condemnation of sodomy that McGann invoked was not limited to homosexual sex. Sodomy statutes typically criminalized oral sex as well as anal sex, and often applied—at least in law—to homosexuals and heterosexuals. For instance, the Georgia sodomy statute that the Supreme Court upheld in 1986 specified that a person "commits the offense of sodomy when he or she performs or submits to any sexual act involving the sex organs of one person and the mouth or anus of another." Moreover, those same major religious traditions that condemned anal sex also condemned oral sex as perverse and immoral. Yet the Scouts did not have a policy forbidding membership to heterosexuals who engaged in oral sex (or anal sex, for that matter).

In any event, McGann's syllogism did not dispose of the central legal question, which was whether the NJLAD forbade the Scouts from discriminating against James Dale. McGann did not dispute that the Scouts "did discriminate (in the broad sense) against [Dale] because of his . . . sexual orientation." The question then was whether the law required the Scouts to change its policy and to reinstate Dale.

In responding to the legal question, McGann began by comparing Dale's actions with those of a criminal. "Clearly, if Dale had engaged in criminal activity such as using or dealing in controlled dangerous substances" or "if he were a rapist or murderer or pederast," he could not claim that the NJLAD protected him from being dismissed by the Scouts. McGann observed that the BSA in such cases would be duty bound—"to keep faith with the avowed purposes of Scouting and with the parents who entrust their boys between 8 and 18 to BSA"—to remove such persons from positions of leadership since those "who do those criminal and immoral acts cannot be held out as role models." Although "active homosexuality . . . is no longer a crime" in New Jersey, McGann reiterated that "BSA and the major religions of the civilized world all deem it immoral." McGann then closed with a baffling rhetorical question: "Should NJLAD be read to compel the BSA to accept that form of immorality [homosexual conduct] when it is perfectly clear that NJLAD could not protect from adverse treatment, one [that is, a murderer, rapist, pedophile, or drug dealer] whose immoral activity violates the criminal law as well?"

McGann asks us to accept that if the NJLAD did not protect the rights of rapists and murderers, then surely "common sense" suggested that it could not be read to protect the rights of homosexuals since both were acting in ways that others considered immoral. The problem, of course, is that the NJLAD says nothing about discriminating against rapists, murderers, and drug dealers. What it does state is that it is illegal in the state of New Jersey for public accommodations to discriminate against people on the basis of their sexual orientation, regardless of whether one views homosexuality as immoral.

One would expect, then, that the first order of business in a case of this sort would be to determine if the BSA was a place of public accommodation under the meaning of the NJLAD. In the *Curran* case in California, for instance, the first part of the trial was devoted to deciding whether the Scouts were "a business establishment" under state law; only after answering that question in the affirmative did the judge proceed to the second half of the trial. Obviously if the BSA was not a place of public accommodation under New Jersey law, then the NJLAD would not apply and Dale's case would collapse, unless one accepted the plaintiff's argument that Dale had a claim under "some prior common law policy." But McGann summarily waved away the common law argument, which meant that Dale had no case if McGann concluded that the Scouts were not a public accommodation covered by the NJLAD. Given McGann's analogy between homosexuals and murderers—not to mention his emphasis on the universal religious condemnation of sodomy and the centrality of an antigay message to Scouting—one might think that he was building a case for why the Scouts should prevail despite the NJLAD. But in fact McGann's conclusion, announced more than two-thirds the way through his opinion, was that the BSA was not a place of public accommodation after all and that therefore the NJLAD did not apply, leaving the reader to wonder why McGann felt it necessary to question Dale's truthfulness, declare sodomy abhorrent, and vindicate the Scouts' antigay policy.

McGann agreed with the Boy Scouts that they were not a place of public accommodation because they were neither "public" nor "a place," under the meaning of the law. The BSA, McGann wrote, "neither owns or controls a 'place' from which Dale has been excluded." The Scouts were not "a physical place to which one may point" but an organization united by "certain moral concepts and values." Moreover, the Scouts' activities and meeting places were not "open to the public." Dale's troop, for instance, met in a hall provided by the Methodist Church, but while that hall was a "place" it was not a public accommodation because it was "private property" used at the "invitation and sufferance" of the sponsoring church. But even when the meeting place was a public school, it was not a public place under the meaning of the law because only those who had taken the Scout Oath and pledged to live by the Scout Law were invited to participate.

McGann rejected Dale's argument that the Boy Scouts were similar to Little League, which had been determined to be a public accommodation by the New Jersey Court of Appeals in 1974. McGann personally believed that the appellate court had erred in finding Little League to be a public accommodation and in forcing Little League to admit girls, but his opinion stuck to enumerating the "many" differences between Scouting and Little League. Whereas Little League coaches largely taught baseball skills and good sportsmanship, McGann noted, "Scoutmasters are teachers and role models of 'what a man should be like' in all aspects of male adulthood." Moreover, whereas Little League was "open to all age-eligible persons who want to play baseball," Scouting was "limited to those who subscribe to the Scout Oath and Law." And whereas Little League "thrives on public (i.e., family members and friends) attendance," Scouting is "personal and social [and] there is no public attendance." In short, while Little League might qualify as a place of public accommodation under the NJLAD, Scouting did not.

McGann underscored that New Jersey's law explicitly provided that the NJLAD did not apply to "any institution, bona fide club, or place of accommodation, which is in its nature distinctly private." And for McGann, there was no doubt that the Scouts were "an institution which is distinctly private not public." As evidence McGann pointed to the Scouts' "membership requirements," "distinctive uniforms and insignia," "distinctive traditions and ceremonies," and "values and goals."

McGann also rejected Dale's secondary argument that New Jersey's law against employment discrimination applied to his situation. McGann agreed with the Scouts that Dale was a volunteer and therefore not an employee covered by the statute. Dale, McGann wrote, "did not work for BSA," nor did he receive any "remuneration or benefits" from the BSA or Monmouth Council. That left open the possibility that the Scouts might have been in violation of New Jersey employment law had they fired James Kay for being an "avowed homosexual," but that was not a question that McGann needed to address to decide Dale's case.

In sum, McGann concluded, nothing in New Jersey law prevented the Scouts from terminating Dale's registration. But McGann did not want his decision to depend solely upon a narrow reading of the NJLAD. Even if the Scouts were found to be a public accommodation, McGann maintained, the law would be unconstitutional as applied to the Scouts because it violated the organization's constitutional right to "expressive association."

McGann took his constitutional bearings from *Roberts v. United States Jaycees*, the 1984 case in which the US Supreme Court held that Minnesota's antidiscrimination law required the Jaycees to admit women as full members. However, McGann focused not on Justice Brennan's majority opinion but instead on Sandra Day O'Connor's concurrence, which emphasized that because the Jaycees were a "predominantly commercial association" it was "therefore subject to rationally related state regulation of its membership." In contrast,

O'Connor reasoned, an association whose activity was "predominantly expressive" would enjoy "First Amendment protection of both the content of its message and the choice of its members." McGann drew attention to O'Connor's observation that "a broad range of activities can be expressive." Protected expression might include not only "expressive words . . . that are strident, contentious, or divisive," but also "quiet persuasion, inculcation of traditional values, instruction of the young, and community service." Citing the Boy Scout and Girl Scout handbooks, O'Connor added that "even the training of outdoor surviving skills . . . might become expressive when the activity is intended to develop good morals, reverence, patriotism and a desire for self-improvement." Clearly, then, under O'Connor's standard, the Boy Scouts were an expressive association deserving of the most stringent First Amendment protections.

In McGann's view, opposition to homosexuality lay at the core of the Scouts' expressive message. "Since its inception," McGann concluded, "Scouting has sincerely and unswervingly held to the view that an 'avowed,' sexually-active homosexual is engaging in immoral behavior which violates the Scout Oath (in which the person promises to be 'morally straight') and the Scout Law (whereby the person promises to keep himself 'clean')." In McGann's judgment, "the consequences of restoring Dale to a position of adult leadership would be devastating to the essential nature of Scouting" because homosexual conduct "is absolutely antithetical to the purpose of Scouting." The government could not compel the Scouts to articulate a message—that homosexuality was ok—that contradicted one of the organization's deepest, most firmly held moral beliefs. The First Amendment protection should be at its zenith in such cases, and so the New Jersey law, no matter how construed, must give way to the Scouts' First Amendment freedom to express their moral condemnation of an "active sodomist" like James Dale.

It was no surprise that McGann relied on O'Connor's concurrence in *Roberts*. More unexpected was his heavy reliance on a case from 1952, *Leeds v. Harrison*, in which the New Jersey Supreme Court held that the Young Women's Christian Association (YWCA) was a "quasi-religious" organization." The Scouts had briefly invoked the case to support their argument that they qualified for a religious exemption from the NJLAD, but McGann had rejected that argument on the grounds that the Scouts were not the kind of "bona fide religious or sectarian organization" that the law intended to exempt. Yet now in the final pages of his opinion, he quoted at length from the *Leeds* case to drive home his broader point about the Scouts' First Amendment rights as an expressive association.

Under the YWCA's bylaws, the only members allowed to hold office and vote were those women who belonged to "Protestant evangelical churches," showed "personal loyalty to Jesus Christ as Savior and Lord," and "subscribed to and will support the purpose" of the organization, which was "to promote growth in Christian character and service through physical, social, mental, and spiritual training and to become a social force for the extension of the Kingdom of God." The plaintiffs in the case were twelve women who wished to be accepted as full voting members even though they did not belong to an evangelical Protestant church and did not "subscribe to any statement of faith or dogma." The court dismissed the women's complaint. Even though the YWCA was "not formed for public religious worship and exercised no ecclesiastical control over [its] members," in New Jersey such a society is "deemed impressed with 'a religious use' and therefore [is] quasi-religious in the view of the law." The court concluded that quasi-religious associations such as the YWCA had a "kinship and identity" with "religious societies in the strict sense." And therefore the "the right of membership" in the YWCA, like in a church, "is not a justiciable question."

McGann found this case telling because in his view the Scouts were, like the YWCA, a quasi-religious organization. Admittedly, the BSA was "a non-sectarian quasi-religious organization," but McGann emphasized that nonsectarian did not mean "irreligious or religiously indifferent." Every Boy Scout, he noted, had to pledge a belief in God in both the Scout Oath and the Scout Law, and Scoutmasters were required to subscribe to a "Declaration of Religious Principle," which affirmed that "no member can grow into the best kind of citizen without recognizing an obligation to God." According to McGann, the BSA "has religious beliefs which it upholds as intrinsic to its purpose." In fact, on McGann's reading, religion lay at the core of the "noble ideal" of Scouting, which was "molding . . . the character of growing boys" so that they "could move into an adult world armed with strong moral principals [*sic*] for their own good and for the good of those around them." That ideal (which, McGann noted parenthetically, "our society needs so desperately today") requires "a belief in God (the benevolent and loving Creator) and, through the Scout Oath, the Scout Law and the Scout *Handbook* an adherence to the Ten Commandments and the Golden Rule." As a quasi-religious organization with deeply held, religiously based moral objections to homosexuality, McGann concluded, it would be both unconscionable and unconstitutional to force the Boy Scouts of America to accept an "active sodomist" like James Dale as an adult leader or member.

CHAPTER 8

Eradicating the "Cancer of Discrimination"

James Dale's legal team had been prepared to lose. They had seen enough of Patrick McGann's courtroom demeanor to know that there was no possibility that he would side with them. Nonetheless, the language in McGann's opinion astonished Dale and his lawyers. Prepared for the worst, Evan Wolfson still found it "shocking to read such harsh anti-gay language coming from a judge." To Wolfson, the judge's attack on Dale as a lying "sodomite" was "vicious" and "gratuitous." But Dale's team grasped that the over-the-top, "almost cartoonish" quality of McGann's opinion had an upside. As Dale later observed, McGann seemed so "antiquated in his thinking" and "so homophobic" that the opinion helped to draw attention to the case and to build public sympathy for Dale.

An AP story that accented McGann's reliance on the biblical story of Sodom and Gomorrah was picked up by a number of newspapers across the country. The story made it into large city papers like the *Orlando Sentinel*, which had a circulation numbering in the hundreds of thousands, as well as small town papers like the *Titusville Herald*, which served a few thousand people in the northwest corner of Pennsylvania. The headline of *The Day*, a Connecticut paper, was typical: "Judge, Citing Bible, Upholds Boy Scouts' Ban on Gays." The press coverage brought Dale a host of supportive letters that helped to fortify his spirits against the hurt inflicted by McGann's opinion.

McGann's opinion also caught the attention of his fellow judges. Writing in his regular column in the *New Jersey Law Journal*, retired judge and former president of the New Jersey State Bar Association Martin Haines savaged McGann for his "rampant homophobia."

Homosexuality, Haines began, "is a word that strikes fear in the hearts of insecure men everywhere." That irrational fear, Haines charged, had prevented McGann from fairly and dispassionately applying the law. To reach the antigay result that he wanted, McGann had "skewed not only the facts, but the law." Haines lamented that McGann's was the sort of judicial opinion that was "bound to encourage proponents of judge-shopping."

The Scouts were delighted with the win even if they were not particularly happy with all of McGann's rhetoric. The Scouts would have preferred the judge avoid the word "sodomy"; in all their legal briefs and public statements the Scouts instead used the sanitized euphemism "homosexual conduct." Certainly they did not want the public conversation focused on biblical stories. Instead, they wanted their policy framed in the more politically palatable language of traditional morality and family values. But while McGann's opinion briefly upset the Scouts' carefully crafted public relations strategy, the flutter of adverse publicity was short-lived. McGann's ruling never became a major media event, and no national television network or magazine picked up the story.

McGann's ruling bolstered the Scouts' growing confidence in the strength of their legal arguments. Eighteen months before McGann's ruling, in the *Curran* case, the Scouts had prevailed in the California Court of Appeals, albeit in a sharply divided 2–1 decision. The court's majority determined that compelling the Scouts to admit openly gay leaders violated the organization's freedom of association under the First Amendment. "Unless Scouting can determine its own standards of morality," the court ruled, "it will be disabled as a teacher of moral views on any subject."

More recently, in the spring of 1995, the Scouts had also won in the Kansas Supreme Court in the case (*Seabourn v. Coronado Area Council, BSA*) of a Scout leader who had been kicked out after revealing his atheism. The Kansas high court ruled unanimously that the Scouts were not a public accommodation and so did not have to comply with the state's antidiscrimination laws. Unlike "business-like establishments" that had to abide by antidiscrimination laws, the court found that Scouting relationships were "continuous, close, personal and social, and take place, more or less, outside of public view."

Further buoying the Scouts' spirits was the June 1995 ruling by the US Supreme Court in *Hurley v. Irish-American Gay, Lesbian, and Bisexual Group of Boston*. The case presented the question of whether the South Boston Allied War Veterans Council could exclude the Irish-American Gay, Lesbian, and Bisexual Group of Boston (GLIB) from marching in the council's annual St. Patrick's Day parade. Two Massachusetts courts, including the state's high court, ordered the council to allow GLIB to march in the parade, reasoning that the parade was "not an exercise of [the council's] constitutionally protected right of expressive association" but was instead "an open recreational event . . . subject to the [state's] public accommodation law." The veterans appealed to the US Supreme Court, arguing that requiring them to include GLIB violated their freedom of speech.

After the Supreme Court agreed to hear the case, the Boy Scouts had filed an amicus brief on behalf of the South Boston Allied War Veterans Council. In urging the Court to reverse, the BSA amicus brief—written by George Davidson—emphasized that the veterans council "sincerely held or sincerely wished to hold" what the council itself characterized as "traditional religious and social values." As an expressive association, the group therefore had a constitutional right to exclude those messages or viewpoints, such as GLIB's, that it regarded as inconsistent with its values.

Writing for a unanimous Court, Justice David Souter agreed that the First Amendment protected the council's right to exclude GLIB from the parade. Souter reasoned that onlookers at a parade that featured members of GLIB marching beneath a banner proudly proclaiming their sexual identity would reasonably conclude that the parade's sponsors approved of the group's gay pride message. Thus by forcing the council to include GLIB in its parade, the government was essentially compelling the veterans to endorse a message of which they disapproved. This the government could not do because the First Amendment protected not only the right to speak but the right to choose "what not to say."

Admittedly, not all the legal battles were going the Scouts' way. In July 1994, Chuck Merino, the California police officer who lost his Scouting leadership position after the BSA discovered he was gay, prevailed in superior court. The trial judge ordered that the

Scouts reinstate Merino and pay $5,000 in damages. "Public acknowledgment of homosexuality," the judge opined, "does not translate into 'teaching' that homosexuality is proper or improper." Moreover, the Boy Scouts' assertion that a homosexual could not be an appropriate role model was "invidious discrimination . . . based on stereotyped notions." The Merino trial had been particularly embarrassing for the Scouts because one of their star witnesses—who inveighed against the immorality of homosexuality and the dangers of having "an openly gay individual teaching my children [and] exposing[ing] them to a lifestyle with which I disagree"—was identified at trial by two witnesses as a person who had engaged in sex with other men at gay bathhouses and adult video stores. Under the Scouts' policy, however, the homosexual conduct of their own witness—an Eagle Scout and member of the executive board of the local Scouting council—was not a problem because he was not an avowed or open homosexual but a closeted one. In his closing arguments, Merino's lawyer pointed to this as evidence of the "foolhardiness" of the Scouts' policy.

After McGann's ruling, Dale's legal team was down but far from ready to count themselves out. They believed that the unanimous *Hurley* decision involved a very different set of facts, and that the Boy Scouts were not the equivalent of a parade. They were convinced, too, that McGann's ruling said more about the judge's animus toward homosexuals than it did about the law. As Lambda's legal director Beatrice Dohrn told reporters, McGann was "so lost in his abhorrence of gay men that he fail[ed] completely to apply the law." Dale's lawyers remained confident that more impartial judges would agree with their contention that the Boy Scouts were a public accommodation under New Jersey law and were therefore required to comply with the NJLAD.

At the end of December 1995, a little more than a month after McGann's final order, Dale's team filed their notice of appeal. The nearly five thousand pages of affidavits and documents that had been submitted by the two sides were transmitted to the appellate court. And then once again it was time to wait. Two years would pass before the two sides would finally get their opportunity, on December 8, 1997, to argue their case in appellate court, before a three-judge panel.

Whereas McGann took two years to write his opinion, the New Jersey Court of Appeals needed less than three months. On March 2, 1998, Judge James Havey delivered the court's opinion. Havey agreed with the Scouts on one point. Dale's common law complaint should be dismissed as unnecessary since Dale already had a statutory basis for his legal action under the NJLAD. Apart from that, though, the news was almost all bad for the Scouts.

The court was unanimous that the Scouts qualified as a public accommodation under New Jersey law. Havey acknowledged that the question of whether the BSA qualified as a place of public accommodation had been the subject of "lively debate" in courts across the country. He took special note of a 1993 federal appellate court ruling (in *Welsh v. Boy Scouts of America*, discussed in chapter 3) that the BSA was not a place of public accommodation under the Civil Rights Act of 1964. However, Havey rejected the federal court's "narrow interpretation" of a place of public accommodation, pointing to a long string of New Jersey court rulings dating back to the late 1960s that held the NJLAD should be liberally construed to achieve its "overarching goal . . . of eradicating 'the cancer of discrimination' in New Jersey."

Havey's opinion was strongly influenced by the reasoning in *National Organization for Women v. Little League Baseball* (1974), in which the New Jersey Court of Appeals held that Little League was a public accommodation because "its invitation was 'open to children in the community at large, with no restriction (other than sex) whatever.'" To Havey it seemed clear that like Little League, the BSA "invites 'the public at large' to join its ranks, and is 'dependent upon the broad-based participation of members of the general public.'" As evidence, Havey pointed to a 1986 printing of a BSA publication titled *A Representative Membership*, originally published in 1975, which explained: "Our federal charter sets forth our obligation to serve boys. Neither the charter nor the bylaws of the Boy Scouts permits the exclusion of any boy. The National Council and Executive Board have always taken the position that Scouting should be made available for all boys who meet entrance age requirements." Drawing upon other documents submitted by Dale's legal team, Havey also noted the Scouts' extensive "advertising and public promotion to encourage new membership." To drive home his point, Havey quoted the BSA spokesman Lee Sneath, who in 1989 told the *New York Times* that he thought of Scouting "as a product and we've got to get the product into the hands of as many consumers as we can."

Havey rejected the Scouts' argument that their membership was selective because they only admitted those "willing and able to understand and live by the Scout Oath and the Scout Law." These membership criteria, Havey insisted, were "not significantly different" than the standards boys had to abide by to play Little League baseball, which included "requiring tryouts, demanding adherence to the rules of the game, and requiring physical attributes and skills to play it." In any event, the "undisputed invitation" that the Scouting literature extended to "all boys" made "the BSA's 'selectivity' criteria inconsequential." Havey also rejected the idea that in deciding whether the Scouts were a public accommodation the court should take into account the "more restricted and selective" criteria applied to adult leaders. By this logic, Havey noted, many if not all of the institutions that the New Jersey courts had previously determined were public accommodations, including private swim clubs and days camps, would no longer qualify because all organizations use more restrictive criteria in selecting leadership positions.

Havey also agreed with Dale's team that deciding whether the Scouts were a public accommodation required the court to examine more than membership selectivity. The court, Havey wrote, "cannot ignore the BSA's historic partnership with various public entities and public service organizations." The BSA's dense network of relationships with public schools, parent-teacher associations, firehouses, local civic associations, and the armed forces was mutually beneficial to the BSA and to the public and quasi-public organizations. In Havey's view, this "close relationship" between the BSA and these public and quasi-public entities "underscore[d] the BSA's fundamental public character."

Having established that the Scouts were a public accommodation, the question that confronted the court was whether the law unconstitutionally infringed on the Scouts' mission of instilling in boys the values of the Scout Oath and Scout Law. For guidance, Havey turned to the Supreme Court's "trilogy of cases" from the 1980s: *Roberts v. United States Jaycees* (1984), *Board of Directors of*

Rotary International v. Rotary Club of Duarte (1987), and *New York State Club Association v. City of New York* (1988). In these cases, Havey wrote, the Court had sensibly recognized the inherent "tension between the freedom to associate for the purpose of expressing fundamental views and the compelling state interest in eradicating discrimination." On Havey's reading of these cases, an organization that claimed a First Amendment protection had "a substantial burden of demonstrating a strong relationship between its expressive activities and its discriminatory practice." Otherwise it "invites scuttling of the state's anti-discrimination laws based on pretextual expressive claims."

Havey also found it necessary to confront the US Supreme Court's recent ruling in *Hurley*, a case that the Scouts highlighted in their brief. Havey emphasized that Souter's opinion in *Hurley* "focused on the Council's First Amendment freedom of speech, not its freedom of expressive association." To Havey, it was telling that the Court in *Hurley* "did not undertake a freedom of expressive association analysis under the *Roberts* trilogy of cases"; the reason they did not, Havey said, was that the Court recognized that "the parade itself constituted expression." In Havey's view, *Hurley* was different from *Dale* because "both the parade and GLIB's participation were pure forms of speech." In attempting to distinguish the two cases, Havey also pointed to a passage in Souter's opinion in which the justice accented that *Hurley*

> does not address any dispute about the participation of openly gay, lesbian, or bisexual individuals in various units admitted to the parade. The petitioners disclaim any intent to exclude homosexuals as such, and no individual member of GLIB claims to have been excluded from parading as a member of any group that the Council has approved to march. Instead, the disagreement goes to the admission of GLIB as its own parade unit carrying its own banner.

The *Dale* case, in contrast, involved the exclusion of a person merely because of his sexual orientation.

Havey found no evidence in the record that the Scouts' "expressive purpose" would be significantly compromised by admitting homosexuals. He started with "the undisputed fact" that the BSA's expressive purpose was "not to condemn homosexuality." Nor was there any disagreement that the Scouts did not exist "to provide a public forum for its members to expose the benefits of heterosexuality and the 'evils' of the homosexual lifestyle." Havey also found no evidence in the BSA's charter, bylaws, or literature that the Scouts' mission was, even in part, to advance "anti-gay views." Havey saw no reason to believe that enforcement of the NJLAD would significantly impede the BSA's ability "to instill in the Scouts those qualities of leadership, courage and integrity to which the BSA has traditionally adhered." Nor did the law "require the BSA to abandon or alter any of its laudable activities and programs." In short, the state's interest in eradicating discrimination on the basis of sexual orientation was compelling, and the application of the law had minimal or no effect on the BSA's ability to carry out its mission.

Havey also felt the need to address the relevance of the 1991 and 1993 position statements that the Scouts had submitted into the record. Havey noted that the "position statements" (the judge always put the term in quotation marks) were formulated by the Boy Scouts "at a time when their anti-gay policy was subject to judicial challenge" in the *Curran* case. It therefore seemed "not unrealistic to view these 'Position Statements' as a litigation stance taken by the BSA rather than an expression of a fundamental belief concerning its purposes." Havey added that the court certainly could "not accept the proposition that [a] 'Position Statement,' issued for the first time seventy-six years after Congress granted the BSA its Charter, represents a collective 'expression' of ideals and beliefs that brought the Boy Scouts together." Indeed, as far as the court could determine, the position statement "except during litigation, has not been presented to the public as representative of BSA's official position." Little wonder that Dale, as well as many "past and present boy Scouts and adult leaders, . . . had no knowledge that such a policy even existed." In contrast to McGann, who had charged Dale with lying when he claimed he did not know about Scouting's policy, Judge Havey implied that the Scouts were the ones who had acted dishonestly, by having concocted a "so-called 'position'" solely for the purpose of prevailing in court.

Having disposed of the legal questions, Havey dressed down Judge McGann for ignoring the law. He dismissed as "irrelevant" both McGann's description of Dale as "an active sodomist" and McGann's claim that the Scouts had reasonably determined that "an active sodomist [was] simply incompatible with Scouting." New Jersey law, Havey pointed out, said nothing about sodomy. The NJLAD outlawed discrimination on the basis of "affectional or sexual orientation." Moreover, the record clearly showed that the Scouts excluded Dale "because he was an avowed homosexual, not because he was an 'active sodomist.'" He also called out McGann for the effects of using homophobic language, which "raises, no doubt inadvertently, the sinister and unspoken fear that gay Scout leaders will somehow cause physical or emotional injury to Scouts, or will instill in them ideas about the homosexual lifestyle." Speaking more to the public than to the lawyers, the judge concluded,

> There is absolutely no evidence before us, empirical or otherwise, supporting a conclusion that a gay Scoutmaster, solely because he is a homosexual, does not possess the strength of character necessary to properly care for or to impart BSA humanitarian ideals to the young boys in his charge. Nothing before us even suggests that a male, simply because he is gay, will somehow undermine BSA's fundamental beliefs and teachings. Plaintiff's exemplary journey through the BSA ranks is testament enough that these stereotypical notions about homosexuals must be rejected.

The ruling brought a partial dissent from Judge David Landau. Landau doubted that in passing the NJLAD in 1945 the legislature intended a "private group" such as the Boy Scouts to be counted as a place of public accommodation. Lawmakers instead had in mind places such as hotels, restaurants, and theaters. However, the judge was persuaded by his colleagues that judicial interpretation had subsequently transformed the meaning of public accommodation to include organizations like the Scouts that "extend an open invitation to public membership." The Little League precedent was particularly telling for Landau since the legislature had made no effort in the subsequent two decades to correct the New Jersey courts' interpretation of Little League as a public accommodation.

However, Landau criticized his colleagues for failing to distinguish between membership and leadership. Landau agreed with the court that since the Scouts were a place of public accommodation they were forbidden by New Jersey law from revoking Dale's membership in the Scouts. But he disagreed that the New Jersey antidiscrimination law—or *Roberts*—required the Scouts to permit Dale to be a volunteer leader. By requiring the Boy Scouts to elevate "an avowed, practicing homosexual" like Dale to a leadership position, the state would force the Scouts to "endorse [Dale's] symbolic, if not openly articulated, message" that homosexuality was moral. This the state could not do because it violated the Scouts' "right of expressive association guaranteed by the First Amendment."

Judge Landau dismissed the court's argument that the Scouts did not in fact teach young Scouts that homosexuality was immoral. It was not for the court to decide what the Boy Scouts really professed. That was for the Scouts to tell the court. "Their consistent litigation stand in cases like this and the representation of their governing officials are enough for me." Nor did it matter that Scouting officials conceded that the BSA was "not organized for the primary purpose of advancing an anti-gay agenda." That was self-evident. But in Landau's view, whether the Scouts' stance on homosexuality was "fundamental to that organization's creation" was "entirely irrelevant." What mattered was only that opposition to homosexuality was *part* of what Scouting officials considered to be their expressive message.

Landau's split-the-difference approach would not have helped Dale, since Landau would have upheld the Scouts' right to strip Dale of his position as assistant Scoutmaster. To remain an adult "member" of Scouting who was ineligible to serve in a volunteer position would have been indistinguishable in practice from being an adult whose registration with the Scouts had been terminated. The only ones who would have been protected using Landau's approach were Scouts under the age of eighteen.

Landau never adequately explained, however, why requiring the Scouts to accept a volunteer leader infringes on their expressive message but requiring the Scouts to accept an all-gay troop or seventeen-year-old gay activists does not. In drawing a distinction between membership and leadership, Landau noted that in *Roberts* "only admission to membership was the issue." But this is misleading. The issue in *Roberts* was whether the Jaycees could limit women to associate membership; and as associate members women could not vote or hold local or national office. Both membership *and* leadership were thus at issue in *Roberts*. There is no reason to believe that the Supreme Court's position in *Roberts* would have been different if the Jaycees had allowed associate members to vote but excluded them from holding leadership positions.

Landau's dissent notwithstanding, the court's ruling was a tremendous triumph for Dale and Wolfson. It had been nearly eight years since Dale, now twenty-seven years old, had first received the letter from James Kay informing him that he must sever his decade-long connection with the Scouts. Now Dale experienced the thrill of vindication as the court affirmed what he had felt instinctively from the first: that he had been treated unfairly and discriminated against illegally. Reading the court's stern rebuke of McGann's "stereotypical notions about homosexuality" was particularly gratifying for Dale, who hailed the judges for "standing up against bigotry and discrimination."

For Wolfson, too, the ruling was sweet vindication. He remembered keenly the naysayers in the gay and lesbian community who had cautioned that the case was unwinnable or dismissed it as a sideshow in the real struggle for gay liberation. Now, for the first time since 1983, a court had ruled that the Scouts could not discriminate against gays. Wolfson had been proven right: the case was winnable and it certainly was important in confronting and exposing stereotypes about gay men.

The Monday the ruling was announced, National Public Radio (NPR) aired a story about the case on its weekday news program "All Things Considered." The segment included snippets from interviews with a nervous Dale, an ebullient Wolfson, and BSA spokesman (and Edelman vice president) Gregg Shields. Wolfson told NPR's Melissa Block that the court's opinion affirmed that "gay people can be just as morally straight as non-gay people," while Shields carefully repeated the talking points that Edelman had first honed during Curran's trial: "The Boy Scouts of America has long taught traditional family values that are held by the Scouting families. And a homosexual is not a role-model for those family values. So accordingly, we don't offer membership or leadership positions to avowed homosexuals."

Editorial pages across the country applauded the court's ruling. The *New York Daily News* hailed the court for going "beyond the dry legalese to deliver a written rap on the knuckles to the Boy Scouts." Sounding an optimistic note, the *Daily News* suggested that "slowly but surely, case by case, courts across the nation . . . are building a fortress of protection for gay rights," just as the courts had done in advancing civil rights for African Americans. Admittedly there was "still a long way to go," but the editors predicted that "increasingly [courts] will have to come to a common conclusion: Discrimination against homosexuals is indefensible."

The editorial page of the *New York Times* also championed Dale and his contributions to the cause of gay rights. Dale's case was so important, according to the *Times*, because it "remind[s] us what fights for civil rights in this country are usually about," namely, "the right to do the usual thing." Dale could have had "an easier run in life" if he had been willing to remain closeted, spending "his private time in the gay bars, churches, athletic clubs, and interests groups that formed a shelter for a whole population rejected from the usual places." But Dale "didn't want an exclusively homosexual life," a life of segregation and concealment. "He wanted an ordinary life," a life of assimilation and honesty. The "rub" was that Dale's desire to live an ordinary life was being thwarted by those who held outdated conceptions of homosexuals as "sinfully, criminally, mentally flawed." These misconceptions, the *Times* declared, "all grew from religious teaching," and it was thus no surprise that "it is in the most fundamentally religious and patriotic realms that American homosexuals have had to fight the hardest for acceptance." But the court's decision demonstrated that these "old definitions are fallen or falling back." The "fight," of course, was a "long way from over" and progress was slow, "sometimes inch by inch." But history, the *Times* suggested, was clearly on the side of Dale and gay civil rights.

Voices were also raised on the other side of the culture wars, especially in letters to the editor, but also in some visible op-ed columns, including one coauthored by Larry Arnn, founder and president of the conservative Claremont Institute (and soon to become the president of Hillsdale College). Arnn slammed the appellate court's decision as "a stunning blow to freedom of association," "a tragic blow to the family," and "a major victory for the homosexual agenda." For eighty years, he wrote, the Scouts had taught a "traditional sexual morality" that "sex finds its proper fulfillment in the relationship between a husband and wife," a position that was confirmed "by Biblical revelation, natural reason, and tradition." Arnn warned that if homosexuality was granted a "special status," as the New Jersey court was attempting to do, "every boy will be taught in school that it is a matter of personal choice whether he marries a man or a woman." It would also undermine "every family in the land" because the family depends on the "the triumph of love over lust" and "presupposes a morality grounded in nature, the natural distinction between men and women, and the natural union of a man and a woman in marriage."

Arnn strongly objected to the court's warning against the "sinister and unspoken fear that gay Scout leaders will somehow cause physical or emotional injury to Scouts." That fear, he allowed, was generally unspoken, but it was anything but sinister. Government statistics showed that in 1996 alone "60,000 offenders [were] convicted of child sexual abuse." It was therefore eminently sensible for the Scouts to "make scrupulous efforts to screen their Scout leaders." By preventing the Scouts from screening out known homosexuals, the court would "shatter the trust" that the Scouts had carefully built up with Scouting families, trust that was necessary for parents to send their boys to "participate in . . . retreats and camping trips" with adult leaders.

A few commentators expressed their unhappiness with both the court's ruling *and* the Scouts' policy. Nick Gillespie, an Eagle Scout and senior editor of the libertarian magazine *Reason*, said that he found the Scouts' discriminatory policy so disturbing that he would not want his son to join. The exclusion of gays (and atheists) seemed to Gillespie to be barely rational since sexual orientation or belief in a Supreme Being had "remarkably little to do with . . . [the Scouts' goals of] teaching teamwork, leadership, and service to the community." His own experience was that Scouting had "always been filled with gays and nonbelievers, dispositions that never much got in the way of building fires, tying knots, or doing a good turn daily." Yet it disturbed him even more that the policies of a voluntary organization were "being hashed out in the courts." He worried that compelling the Scouts to accept gays would set "a dangerous precedent." Would the National Association for the Advancement of Colored People (NAACP) be forced to accept a Klansman, or the B'nai B'rith an anti-Semite? It was, he said, better to allow the Scouts "to persist in their policy and be judged in the court of public opinion," a verdict that he predicted would likely be "quite harsh." But Gillespie's iconoclastic position was the exception to the rule. Most took sides in the culture wars by either condemning the ruling and defending the Scouts' policy, as Arnn did, or, like the editorial page of the *New York Times*, applauding the court and deploring the Scouts' bigotry.

The elation felt by Dale's supporters was short-lived. Three weeks after the New Jersey appellate court's decision, Dale's team received word of the long-awaited decision by the California Supreme Court in the *Curran* case as well as in a companion case involving the Randall twins, who had been kicked out because they did not believe in God. California's high court, comprised entirely of justices nominated by Republican governors, ruled unanimously that the Scouts were not covered by California's antidiscrimination law (the Unruh Act) and were therefore free to discriminate on the basis of both sexual orientation and religious belief. (Although the justices agreed that the Scouts were not a business establishment under the Unruh Act, the case spawned four separate concurring opinions that reflected the judges' inability to arrive at a shared understanding of how best to identify which organizations were subject to the Unruh Act.)

Because New Jersey's antidiscrimination statute and its case law were different from California's, Curran's case had no necessary effect on Dale's. But Dale felt the defeat keenly nonetheless, especially because Curran had become a mentor and friend to the younger Dale. Both men were deeply disappointed that the court had not only ruled in favor of the Scouts but had explicitly sidestepped discussing "the wisdom or morality" of the Scouts' actions and policies. For Curran, the California Supreme Court's narrow ruling spelled the end of an eighteen-year journey. Because the court had based its ruling on its interpretation of state law, there could be no appeal to the US Supreme Court. California's high court had made sure that it would be the final arbiter of whether the Scouts could exclude gays and atheists in California.

Although there was no appeal for Curran, there was never any doubt that the Scouts would appeal their loss in *Dale*. Even as partisans had lined up to applaud or deplore the appellate court ruling, the Scouts' legal team remained unfazed. George Davidson, who had defended the Scouts in every discrimination case over the past decade or more, publicly reminded everyone that this ruling was only "a step in the process. . . . Only the final word ends up making a lot of difference." Shortly thereafter, Davidson filed the requisite paperwork for an appeal. Next stop: the New Jersey Supreme Court.

CHAPTER 9

A Unanimous Court

The New Jersey Supreme Court is not your typical state supreme court. To begin with, the justices on New Jersey's high court never have to face the voters. In most states, citizens elect their judges or at least periodically vote on whether they should be retained. Some states, including California, even allow voters to gather signatures to recall judges who make unpopular decisions. Not in New Jersey.

New Jersey's 1947 constitution grants the governor the power to appoint justices with the advice and consent of the senate. After a seven-year probationary term, justices must be renominated by the governor and confirmed again by the senate. Once reconfirmed, a justice may serve until the constitutionally prescribed retirement age of seventy. Renomination and reconfirmation of judges in the twentieth century were rarely controversial. Every justice who sought to continue serving beyond the probationary period was renominated by the governor and reconfirmed by the senate—up until 2010, when Republican governor Chris Christie refused to renominate John E. Wallace Jr., an African American justice who had been appointed by Democratic governor Jim McGreevey. In 1999, however, at the time that Dale's case came before the New Jersey Supreme Court, Christie was still just a lobbyist, and the court still possessed a national reputation for impartiality.

Nonpartisanship or at least bipartisanship on the New Jersey high court was fostered by a tradition of partisan balance on the seven-person court. Although nowhere codified in statute or the constitution, the custom—adhered to by both Republican and Democratic governors—was that the court should consist of at least three justices from each party. Because tradition demanded a politically balanced court, governors routinely appointed justices affiliated with the opposing party. In 2006, for instance, Democratic governor Jon Corzine selected the Republican Helen Hoens to the court, and in 2004 Democratic governor Jim McGreevey appointed the Republican Roberto Rivera-Soto. Three of the six justices chosen by Republican governor Christine Todd Whitman during her two terms were Democrats. In contrast, the last time a Democratic president appointed a Republican to the US Supreme Court was in 1945 when Harry Truman, in a nod to bipartisanship, picked Harold Burton to replace a conservative, Justice Owen Roberts. The only Republican president in the last half century to nominate a Democratic justice to the US Supreme Court is Richard Nixon, who tapped the Virginian Lewis Powell in 1972.

New Jersey's distinctive tradition of judicial bipartisanship has been severely tested in recent years, most notably by Governor Christie's refusal to reappoint Wallace, followed by his vow in 2012 not to appoint any Democrats until he had transformed the ideological direction of a court that he deemed too liberal. Christie justified his stance on the grounds that one of the sitting justices (Jaynee Laveccia) who had been counted as a Republican ever since her appointment in 2000 was in fact a registered Independent and so should not count toward the quota of Republican justices, even though Laveccia had served in two Republican administrations, contributed money to Republican candidates, was picked by a Republican governor to replace a Republican justice at a time when there were only two other Republicans remaining on the bench, and occupied a seat on the court that had been occupied by a Republican continuously since 1948. The result was a bitter standoff with the Democratic-controlled senate, which took the unprecedented step of rejecting two Christie nominees (both Republicans) in quick succession, leaving the state's highest court with fewer than seven permanent members for over two years.

These high-stake partisan theatrics over judicial appointments, long familiar at the national level, played little part in late-twentieth-century New Jersey politics. Not that the state's high court was immune to political controversy. In fact, in the 1970s and 1980s the New Jersey Supreme Court issued a number of rulings that were sharply criticized by conservatives who complained of the court's judicial activism. In 1983, for instance, the New Jersey high court unanimously ruled that every municipality in a "growth area" had to ensure that a certain percentage of its housing was affordable to families of low and moderate incomes. The state's Republican governor Thomas Kean led the outcry against the "communistic" ruling, yet in 1986 Kean reappointed the opinion's author: the court's liberal chief justice Robert Wilentz, a former Democratic legislator who had been appointed to the court by Kean's Democratic predecessor Brendan Byrne. For Kean, the principle of judicial independence was too important to be sacrificed to partisanship or political ideology.

Wilentz's reappointment was undeniably contentious; he was reconfirmed in the Senate by a two-vote margin. However, the controversy stirred by Wilentz's reappointment was highly unusual. Far more typical was the unanimous vote in 1996 in favor of Wilentz's replacement, the Republican Deborah Poritz, who was confirmed as chief justice (by a Democratic-controlled senate) a mere seven days after being nominated by Republican governor Christine Todd Whitman. In fact, as figure 1 shows, all but one of the justices on the court at the time of the Scouts' case had been unanimously confirmed by the senate when first appointed; the one nonunanimous vote was 27–3. Of the five justices on the court who had faced a reconfirmation vote, four had been reconfirmed unanimously; the fifth was reconfirmed 31–5.

Several things stand out about the New Jersey high court circa 1999. First, the court was an extraordinarily experienced group as well as relatively old. Five of the seven justices had been on the court for at least fourteen years by the time the court heard oral arguments in the *Dale* case on January 5, 1999. A majority of the justices had served between seventeen and twenty-two years. All of the justices, even the two newest members, were in their sixties, born between 1930 and 1936. James H. Coleman Jr. had only been on the high court for a little over four years, but he was already sixty-five and had more than two decades of experience as a judge before becoming the court's first African American judge. The only justice younger than sixty-five at the time of the *Dale* case was the sixty-two-year-old Poritz. Although she had never been a judge before joining the high court, Poritz had been chief counsel to the governor, had more than a decade of experience in the state attorney general's office, and was New Jersey's attorney general at the time Governor Whitman nominated her to be chief justice.

Figure 1. Party Affiliation and Confirmation Votes for New Jersey Supreme Court Justices

Justice	Party Affiliation of Justice	Governor Nominated By	Senate Confirmation Vote	Governor Renominated By	Senate Reconfirmation Vote
Deborah Poritz	Republican	Whitman (R)	unanimous (June 24, 1996)	n/a	n/a
James Coleman	Democrat	Whitman (R)	unanimous (Oct. 20, 1994)	n/a	n/a
Gary Stein	Republican	Kean (R)	unanimous (Nov. 19, 1984)	Florio (D)	unanimous (Dec. 19, 1991)
Marie Garibaldi	Republican	Kean (R)	unanimous (Oct. 18, 1982)	Kean (R)	unanimous (June 19, 1989)
Daniel O'Hern	Democrat	Byrne (D)	27–3 (May 15, 1981)	Kean (R)	unanimous (June 27, 1988)
Stewart Pollock	Republican	Byrne (D)	unanimous (April 23, 1979)	Kean (R)	31–5 (June 23, 1986)
Alan Handler	Democrat	Byrne (D)	unanimous (March 21, 1977)	Kean (R)	unanimous (March 1, 1984)

The second notable aspect of the court was its bipartisan cast. Four of the justices were Republicans, three were Democrats. As figure 1 reveals, each Democratic justice had either been nominated (Coleman) or renominated (Daniel O'Hern and Alan Handler) by a Republican governor, and two of the four Republican justices were either nominated (Stewart Pollock) or renominated (Gary Stein) by a Democratic governor. Only the Republican Marie Garibaldi was nominated and renominated by a governor of the same party, and she had been (unanimously) confirmed on both occasions by a Democratic-controlled state senate.

Third, the court operated with a remarkable degree of civility and consensus. Decisions by a bare majority, so commonplace on the ideologically polarized US Supreme Court, were a rarity on the New Jersey court. The court frequently spoke with a single voice, especially on important questions. Most of the court's most controversial rulings dating back to the 1970s had been unanimous, including its affirmation in 1977 of the comatose Karen Quinlan's right to have life support withdrawn (*In re Quinlan*), its striking down in 1975 of zoning laws that prevented low-income people from living in a given municipality (*Southern Burlington County NAACP v. Township of Mount Laurel*), and its ruling in 1973 that financing public schools through local property taxes violated the state constitution because students in poorer school districts did not receive adequate funding relative to students from wealthier school districts (*Robinson v. Cahill*). Also unanimous was the pioneering 1992 ruling (authored by Handler) that broadened the definition of sexual assault so that the key legal question became not the use of physical force by the attacker (or resistance by the victim) but the presence or absence of consent (*State of New Jersey in the Interest of M.T.S.*). Because the court, notwithstanding its partisan diversity, so often spoke with a single voice, its pronouncements could not easily be dismissed as partisan or ideological.

Fourth, the court remained one of the most well regarded in the country, as it had been for the past half century. An article published in the *Santa Clara Law Review* in 2000 pronounced the New Jersey court the nation's most "important state supreme court," particularly in the area of individual rights. A decade earlier, the Harvard legal scholar Lawrence Tribe went even further, declaring the New

Jersey Supreme Court to be possibly "the best supreme court in the country—state or federal." In the early 1980s University of Michigan law professor Yale Kamisar, one of the nation's leading authorities on criminal law, hailed the New Jersey court as the "most innovative in the country." These expert judgments about the court's national reputation were borne out by a study published in 2007 in the *UC Davis Law Review* that examined the influence that state high courts exerted on courts in other states between 1940 and 2005. New Jersey ranked third in the number of decisions that had been followed at least three times by out-of-state courts; indeed New Jersey's high court influenced out-of-state courts at three times the rate of the average state supreme court. These findings closely paralleled results from another study of the reputation of state supreme courts published twenty-five years earlier.

Both sides in the *Dale* litigation were well aware of the New Jersey court's reputation as one of the most respected and influential state courts in the nation. Neither Evan Wolfson nor George Davidson viewed the case as a slam dunk for their side. The court's reputation for progressive judicial activism certainly concerned the Scouts' lawyers, but many of the court's iconic liberal rulings had been handed down during the 1970s and 1980s, when the court bore the indelible imprint of its two imposing Democratic chief justices: Richard Hughes (1973–1979) and Robert Wilentz (1979–1996). But this was now Chief Justice Poritz's court. And Poritz was a Republican, who had worked as chief counsel to one Republican governor (Kean) and been appointed attorney general and chief justice by another (Whitman). Poritz's elevation to the bench in 1996 meant that the New Jersey high court for the first time in modern memory had more Republicans than Democrats and more justices appointed by Republican than Democratic governors—not surprisingly, since Republicans had won four out of the five gubernatorial contests between 1981 and 1997.

Many observers of the New Jersey court were convinced that Poritz's appointment portended a turn to the right on the once famously progressive court. Her first two opinions as chief justice, both issued in September 1997, did little to dispel that notion. In the first case, Poritz explained why a convicted sex offender did not have a constitutional right to refuse to submit to HIV testing requested by a victim so long as the state had probable cause to believe that the offender had put the victim at risk of contracting HIV (*State of New Jersey in the Interest of J.G., N.S. and J.T.*). In the second, Poritz upheld the government's right to impose random drug and alcohol testing on police officers employed by the state transportation department (*N.J. Transit PBA Local 304 v. N.J. Transit Corp.*). In both cases, Poritz wrote for a unanimous court—a court that in the 1970s and 1980s had pioneered an expansive understanding of the New Jersey constitution's protections against unreasonable searches.

Dale's case, moreover, was markedly different from the school funding and criminal rights cases on which the New Jersey court had erected its progressive reputation for protecting individual rights and promoting equality. None of the justices, each of whom was nearly old enough to be Dale's grandparent, was known as a champion of gay rights. Handler, considered the court's staunchest liberal, had opined in 1976 that he could not "fathom" a reading of state law that would permit two persons of the same sex to marry.

Although the question of discrimination against gays and lesbians—including the NJLAD's 1991 amendment prohibiting discrimination based on "affectional or sexual orientation"—had never come before the state's high court, in 1990 the court did rely upon New Jersey's antidiscrimination law to rule that ostensibly private eating clubs at Princeton University could not exclude women because they were public accommodations under state law (*Frank v. Ivy Club*). Writing for a unanimous court was Marie Garibaldi, the court's first (and at the time only) female justice. Five of the seven justices who took part in that decision, including Garibaldi, were still on the court as it prepared to hear oral arguments in Dale's case on the morning of January 5, 1999.

The court heard oral arguments on the eighth floor of the massive, ultramodern aluminum and glass Richard J. Hughes Justice Complex in downtown Trenton. The courtroom was often half empty for oral arguments, but not on this frigid January morning. Television cameras lined the packed courtroom. Busloads of people made the seventy-mile journey from Lambda's Manhattan offices to witness the historic occasion and lend moral support to Dale and Wolfson.

An emotional day was made even more so because it occurred against the dreadful backdrop of recent events near Laramie, Wyoming, where a twenty-one-year-old gay college student had been tied to a fence and brutally beaten to death by two young men. Upon hearing of Matthew Shepard's horrifying torture and murder, recalls the gay author and blogger Andrew Sullivan, "a lot of gay people felt sort of punched in the stomach" by an attack that "encapsulated all our fears of being victimized." Shepard's murder riveted national attention as never before on the problem of violence against gays, and the slain Shepard became a virtual "poster child" for gay rights. Shepard's funeral on October 17, 1998, also drew the attention of protesters from Fred Phelps's Topeka-based Westboro Baptist Church, whose picket signs included such messages as "No Tears for Queers" and "Fag Matt in Hell" as well as the group's signature "God Hates Fags" slogan. Now, only days before Dale's oral argument, the Shepard case was back in the headlines as prosecutors announced that they would seek the death penalty against the accused, one of whom ironically was an Eagle Scout.

As the oral argument began, neither side knew quite what to expect from the justices. But it quickly became apparent that most if not all the justices were decidedly skeptical of the Scouts' position. The first to interrupt Davidson was Justice O'Hern, who had clerked for US Supreme Court Justice William Brennan back in 1957. O'Hern seemed doubtful that the Scouts actually had "a message on sexual orientation." Predictably, Davidson pointed to the "morally straight" clause, which, he said, "meant living with purity, virtue, and cleanliness" and that had "obvious dimensions of sexual morality." A skeptical Justice Pollock stepped in. He had spent a portion of the weekend browsing the Internet and could find "no references to homosexuality in the Scouts' charter, bylaws or handbook." The gentlemanly Pollock, whose consensus building and quiet diplomacy on the court were legendary, queried Davidson why a homosexual Scout could not be both "morally straight" and "clean." Davidson's answer was terse: because homosexual conduct was immoral. Then the justices started tossing out hypothetical examples. Justice Stein wanted to know whether the Scouts would remove a gay person who did not publicly reveal or discuss his sexual orientation. Davidson evaded at first ("that's never really been tested"), but after being pressed for an answer he suggested that a Scout would only be kicked out if they made their sexual orientation public. The Scouts' concern, he explained, was with "open homosexuals who might extol their life style to younger, impressionable Scouts." Justice Handler wanted to know if the Scouts would "tolerate" a homosexual who was abstinent. An "interesting" question, Davidson conceded.

The tone and tenor of the two-hour argument augured well for Dale. The justices seemed sympathetic toward his plight and skeptical of the Scouts' claim that opposition to homosexuality was an important part of Scouting's message. There was no trace of the antigay animus that Wolfson felt in Judge McGann's courtroom several years earlier. On the busses back to Manhattan, the atmosphere was celebratory. Dale and Lambda appeared to be on the verge of a historic victory that had seemed unimaginable eight years earlier.

Eight months after hearing oral arguments, the court announced its verdict. It should not have surprised anybody that the ruling was unanimous. The court's big decisions often were. Nor could the result have shocked anybody who had been present at the oral argument. The justices agreed with the appellate court that the Boy Scouts were a place of public accommodation and that the law prohibited the Scouts' discriminatory policy. More of a surprise was the author of the opinion: Chief Justice Deborah Poritz.

Under the state's 1947 constitution, the chief justice is charged with overseeing the management of the entire state judiciary, which includes roughly four hundred trial and appellate judges. As a dying Wilentz explained to Poritz, she was taking on "two full-time jobs in one: justice and administrator." The onerous administrative duties mean that the chief justice typically writes substantially fewer opinions than the other justices. So long as she votes with the majority, the chief justice decides who writes for the majority. In 1997 Poritz assigned herself only three court opinions, a tiny fraction of the court's roughly one hundred signed majority opinions. In 1998 she wrote only twice, and neither time in a case that attracted public interest; one involved the disbarment of a lawyer who had stolen from his law firm and the other involved the propriety of litigation tactics that had been used in a foreclosure case. In her first two terms, Poritz consistently gave the biggest cases to her more experienced senior colleagues. But now in the most high-profile case of the term, Poritz assigned herself the task of writing for the court.

Poritz's carefully reasoned ninety-page opinion covered the same terrain as the appellate court and reached the same conclusion: the Boy Scouts qualified as a place of public accommodation under New Jersey law and therefore the Scouts' policy of discriminating on the basis of sexual orientation violated the NJLAD. Like the appellate court, Poritz followed the reasoning of the US Supreme Court in *Roberts v. United States Jaycees* (1984) in dismissing the Scouts' argument that enforcing the law violated the organization's First Amendment rights of expressive association. On the basis of the record before it, Poritz explained, the court was "not persuaded . . . that a 'shared goal' of Boy Scout members is to associate in order to preserve the view that homosexuality is immoral." Although the Scouts continued to insist that the words "morally straight" and "clean" "stand for the proposition that homosexuality is immoral," Poritz declared this interpretation to be implausible on its face. The words, she wrote, did not "express anything about sexuality, much less that homosexuality, in particular, is immoral." Indeed, she doubted that "young boys would ascribe any meaning to these terms other than a commitment to be good." Poritz concluded that New Jersey had not violated the Boy Scouts' freedom of expressive association because "the organization's ability to disseminate its message is not significantly affected by Dale's inclusion" since "Boy Scout members do not associate for the purpose of disseminating the belief that homosexuality is immoral; Boy Scouts discourages its leaders from disseminating *any* views on sexual issues; and Boy Scouts includes sponsors and members who subscribe to different views in respect of homosexuality."

Poritz's decision to write the court's opinion herself must have disappointed the court's longest-serving and best-known justice. During his more than two decades on the court, Justice Handler was often described as its "conscience." Many of the court's most influential and well regarded opinions dating back to the late 1970s were Handler's handiwork. Justice O'Hern, who acknowledged Handler to be the court's "deepest mind," likened his colleague to the court's "cleanup hitter," the one his colleagues wanted at the plate at its "crucial moments." Having determined to retire at the end of the 1999 term, Handler would have liked nothing better than to cap his distinguished career by speaking for the court in a case that underscored the law's capacity to affirm the dignity and worth of every human being.

Although denied the opportunity to speak for the court, Handler opted to pen a concurring opinion. A concurring opinion is normally used when a justice agrees with the result but differs about the reasoning the court used to reach that result. But Handler conceded at the outset that he "fully endorse[d] the Court's reasoning." Ostensibly he wrote to "further emphasize" the role of "genuine membership selectivity" in determining whether an organization was a place of public accommodation, but one would be hard pressed to distinguish the two opinions in their interpretation of the NJLAD. Both Handler and Poritz agreed that the Scout Oath and Scout Law were not "genuine selectivity criteria" and that the Scouts' policy in practice was to accept "all boys who meet entrance age requirements." As a result, both justices noted, the Scouts were a huge organization, with over one hundred thousand youth and adult members in New Jersey and five million in the United States.

The real point of Handler's forty-four-page concurring opinion was not to articulate a different or broader interpretation of the NJLAD. Instead, it was to disavow the antigay prejudice that animated the Scouts' discriminatory policy and the trial judge's opinion. Handler upbraided Judge Patrick McGann for having "impermissibly invoked stereotypical assumptions about homosexuals," the same stereotypes that the Scouts invoked to justify their discriminatory policy. Stereotypes about gays and lesbians were as unacceptable under New Jersey law as "stereotypes about an individual based on sex or race." The stereotype that Handler was most eager to "renounce" was the "archaic" notion that "homosexuals are inherently immoral." That "myth," Handler wrote, had been "repudiated by decades of social science data that convincingly establish that being homosexual does not, in itself, derogate from one's ability to participate in and contribute responsibly and positively to society." That an individual was homosexual, Handler insisted, revealed "nothing about that individual's moral character, or any other aspect of his or her personality." A lesbian or gay person, he underscored, was "no more or less likely to be moral than a person who is a heterosexual."

Without explicitly saying so, Handler's opinion suggested that even if opposition to homosexuality had been found to be an important part of the Scouts' expressive message, the Scouts' discrimination against gays should still be illegal.

For Wolfson, the New Jersey Supreme Court's decision was "a giant moment." For a decade, Wolfson had listened to well-meaning people tell him that this was an unwinnable battle, that it was the wrong battle, that it would not help improve the lives of ordinary gay men and lesbians, that it would set back the cause of gay rights. But now Wolfson basked in the knowledge that "one of the nation's most respected state supreme courts" had unanimously and emphatically sided with Dale. The ruling seemed to vindicate his determination to take on the big cases and the most iconic institutions, whether it was the Boy Scouts, marriage, or the military. This was the only way, he believed, to "get non-gay people talking" about discrimination against gays, and the only way to ensure that "gay and lesbian people have the ability and the right to participate equally in every part of society."

For Dale, too, the victory was immense. Flanked by Wolfson, a beaming Dale appeared at a news conference at Lambda's Manhattan office and told a gaggle of reporters that the court's ruling demonstrated the truth of what Scouting had always taught him: "believe in the system and goodness will prevail." The triumph of goodness and love over intolerance and hate was a theme echoed that Sunday at James's parents' church by its longtime pastor, William A. Hanson—known affectionately by the congregants as "the Rev"—who singled out James's mother and father for the love and support they had offered their son throughout his brave battle against discrimination. That love and support, preached the seventy-six-year-old Hanson, was "what being Lutheran is all about." After the sermon, Dale recalled, "some old timers" at the church who had been giving his father "the cold shoulder" came over to warmly congratulate his parents.

Among those quickest to praise the court's decision was New Jersey's Republican governor Christine Todd Whitman. Discrimination "in any form" was wrong, she intoned. Sexual orientation was a purely private matter and had no more bearing on whether one could be a good Scout leader than did one's race or ethnicity. So long as "a troop leader is a good leader, there's no reason to worry," she insisted.

So intense was the media interest in the New Jersey court's decision that President Bill Clinton's press secretary, Joe Lockhart, was asked about the president's reaction at the White House daily press briefing just hours after the ruling was announced. Clearly unaware of the ruling, a surprised Lockhart told reporters that he was unfamiliar with the case, and that he thought the president was too. However, he reiterated the president's general position "that he opposes discrimination, whether it's based on race, gender, or sexual orientation." "Unless it's in the Armed Service," shot back the reporter acidly—a reference to the military's Don't Ask, Don't Tell policy that Clinton had signed into law in 1993 (and which remained in place until its repeal in 2011). The briefing then reverted to the expected fare of budget negotiations, tax cuts, and farm bills, but as it was winding down the insistent reporter tried again: would the president contemplate using "his authority as Commander in Chief of the Boy Scouts" to help end the BSA's discrimination against gays? Having already twice tried to deflect the question by pleading ignorance, Lockhart now tried humor: "Can I refer that to the Pentagon?"

At the next day's briefing, the dogged reporter returned to the question: now that the president had had twenty-four hours to review the ruling, did he have a reaction? This time Lockhart was prepared and terse: no, next question. The White House clearly had no intention of being drawn into the middle of the contentious battle over gay rights that had bloodied the administration in 1993 and 1994. Clinton's team remembered not only the president's ignominious, forced retreat on his campaign promise to end the ban on gays in the military but also the controversy stirred by Surgeon General Jocelyn Elders's comments in the summer of 1994, when she told reporters that she thought that the Boy Scouts and Girl Scouts should admits gays and lesbians, and that Scouting officials shouldn't worry "about anyone's bedroom but their own." The outspoken Elders lasted less than a year and a half in her post before being fired (the proverbial last straw was her remark that masturbation was "a part of human sexuality, and it's a part of something that perhaps should be taught" in schools).

Reporters weren't the only ones trying to cajole the White House into joining the fight against the Scouts' policy. One week after the New Jersey court handed down its ruling, the fourteen-year-old Eagle Scout Steve Cozza sent a letter to Clinton asking him to resign his post as honorary president of the Boy Scouts in protest of the Scouts' discrimination. Eighteen months earlier, Cozza, who was straight, had launched a drive to gather a million signatures for a petition protesting the Scouts' discriminatory policy, and now he asked the president to affix his name to the petition and thereby "take a stand with me for gay kids and adults."

Although Cozza did not know it, this was not the first time the issue had been raised in the Clinton White House. Two years earlier, in 1997, President Clinton had been invited to address the quadrennial Boy Scouts jamboree. Not everybody was happy when the appearance was approved at the weekly White House scheduling meeting. Among those offended by the decision was Richard Socarides, one of the most senior openly gay officials in the Clinton White House. (Socarides was also, in a bitter irony, the eldest son of the notorious psychiatrist and psychoanalyst Charles Socarides, who taught that homosexuality was an illness that could be cured, pioneered "conversion therapy," and published, in 1995, *Homosexuality: A Freedom Too Far*, which blamed the AIDS epidemic on the American Psychiatric Association's decision to remove homosexuality from its list of mental disorders.) As a special assistant to the president, Socarides was tasked with being the administration's liaison to the gay and lesbian community as well as the principal advisor to the president on gay and lesbian issues. Socarides lobbied other staffers and Clinton directly, maintaining that it was inappropriate for the president to attend the jamboree since the Scouts' discriminatory policy was inconsistent with the president's public positions on nondiscrimination. Even to remain as honorary chair was problematic. The president and others in the White House readily acknowledged the inconsistency, but nobody wanted to take the political heat that would result from Clinton refusing the Scouts' invitation, let alone resigning the honorary post as president of the Scouts.

Pressure on the Scouts, however, now appeared to be mounting. Two days after Cozza fired off his letter to President Clinton, a circuit court judge in Cook County, Illinois, ruled that the Boy Scouts'

Chicago Area Council could not consider sexual orientation in employment decisions. The judge granted that the Scouts could refuse to employ a person who they had reason to believe was using the Scouts to "discuss issues regarding sex," but the judge found that in the case of Keith Richardson the Scouts had refused to hire him merely because he disclosed he was gay. That the law did not allow.

The Scouts, though, remained as defiant as ever. Although expressing disappointment at the New Jersey court's ruling, spokesman Paul Stevenson vowed that it would be "business as usual" for the Scouts. The Scouts' attorney George Davidson informed reporters that it was "a sad day when the state dictates to parents what role models they must provide for their children," but he stressed that there was a "silver lining" in the state court's misguided ruling. For now the Scouts had their "first opportunity to go to the US Supreme Court and get a definitive ruling to put an end to these lawsuits." Davidson was confident that they would prevail and that the Court would affirm the Scouts' right to select their leaders without interference from "an all-powerful state."

But in order to prevail in the US Supreme Court, the Court first had to accept the Scouts' appeal. And notwithstanding the swagger of Stevenson and Davidson, the odds of the Court accepting the appeal appeared long. The Supreme Court only agrees to hear a small fraction (roughly 1 percent) of the seven or eight thousand petitions for writ of certiorari it typically receives each year. Many close observers of the Court thought it unlikely that the Court would take the case. *Time* magazine claimed that "experts doubt the Supreme Court will take up the case." Among the doubters was Georgetown University law professor David Cole, who told *Time* that although "on a symbolic level this is an extremely important decision" for gay and lesbian rights, "on a technical level, this applies only to the Boy Scouts in New Jersey."

Bolstering the experts' confidence was the knowledge that the previous November the Supreme Court had declined to hear the appeal of the California police officer Chuck Merino, who after prevailing in superior court had subsequently lost on appeal because the BSA was determined not to be a business establishment under the meaning of the state's antidiscrimination statute. And five years before that the Court had refused to hear the appeal of the atheist

Mark Welsh, who had lost his case in federal appeals court. One thing was different this time, however. Whereas in the previous cases, either a gay man or an atheist was asking the Supreme Court for help, now the loser asking the Court to step in was the iconic Boy Scouts of America.

PART THREE

In the US Supreme Court

CHAPTER 10

Preparing for the Supreme Court

Evan Wolfson was at his Lambda office on Friday, January 14, 2000, when the call came: the US Supreme Court had acceded to the Scouts' request to hear the *Dale* case. The decision to grant cert was cause for celebration in the Scouts' national headquarters. For more than a decade the BSA had tried to get the Supreme Court to take a case like this in hopes that it would bring down the curtain on the endless lawsuits. The mood at Lambda, in contrast, was somber.

Lambda had argued strenuously that the Court should deny the Scouts' petition because the Court "traditionally does not disturb the decision of a state's highest court when that court has properly and meticulously followed" the Court's precedents and when there is "no confusion or conflict" in the manner that lower courts have applied those precedents. The Court's decision to grant cert suggested that at least four justices (granting a writ of certiorari requires four affirmative votes) believed that either the New Jersey court had failed to follow the US Supreme Court's precedents or that the precedents themselves needed to be modified. Either way, it seemed highly probable that the Scouts started with at least four votes for reversing the judgment of the New Jersey Supreme Court. The Scouts could count on the votes of William Rehnquist, Antonin Scalia, and Clarence Thomas—each of whom certainly voted to hear the case—and probably the vote of either Anthony Kennedy or Sandra Day O'Connor, at least one of whom must have voted to grant cert. Lambda's victory was clearly in grave jeopardy.

Wolfson called to tell Dale the bad news. But whereas Wolfson and his Lambda colleagues were disappointed, Dale was delighted. He had been hoping all along that the Supreme Court would take his case. Having won handily at the state appellate and supreme court level, with the support of both Republican and Democratic judges, Dale was convinced that he would prevail once more. He could not believe that the highest court in the land would countenance discrimination grounded in irrational prejudice. For Dale, it was a matter of right versus wrong, and he seemed to have no doubt that justice would win out.

Wolfson characterizes himself as an "innate optimist," but he found it impossible to share Dale's enthusiasm. This was not only because Wolfson was keenly aware of the very real prospect that Dale could lose but also because his mind raced to the daunting workload and awesome responsibility that lay ahead. Wolfson felt "a giant, immense weight settling on [his] shoulders," a weight that remained with him for the next three-and-a-half pressure-packed months in which he worked feverishly to prepare for the oral argument scheduled for the end of April. He went to bed with the pressure and woke up to the pressure. On the advice of an experienced litigator who knew what it was like to be awake most of the night rehearsing arguments in one's head, Wolfson began taking sleeping pills for the first and only time in his life. Every waking moment—of which there were far too many—seemed to be consumed with thinking, talking, and brainstorming about Dale's case.

Wolfson had never argued a case before the US Supreme Court; indeed no Lambda attorney had ever argued before the Supreme Court. Discussion ensued about whether to bring in an experienced Washington litigator who would be known to the justices, somebody like Paul Smith, who had argued a half dozen cases before the Court dating back to the 1980s. (In 2003, Lambda would turn to Smith to argue *Lawrence v. Texas*, the landmark case that decriminalized sodomy.) Lambda also got "lots of offers" from legal luminaries from top law schools, but the decision was made to stick with Wolfson. It had been his case from the beginning and he knew the facts and arguments better than anyone, having been involved in drafting and editing every brief. He was also a skilled and confident orator who had argued the case successfully at both the appellate and the state supreme court levels. There was little reason to think that a hired gun, no matter how experienced or distinguished, would improve Dale's chance of success.

Although Wolfson was confident in his ability to handle the rigors of oral argument, he was keenly aware of his limitations as a brief writer. For help with the brief, he turned to the obvious candidate: Lambda's deputy legal director (and soon to be legal director) Ruth Harlow. After graduating from Yale Law School in 1986, the year that the Supreme Court decided *Bowers v. Hardwick*, Harlow quickly emerged as the gay and lesbian movement's most formidable constitutional advocate and legal strategist. She worked for the American Civil Liberties Union's Lesbian and Gay Rights Project for a number of years before joining Lambda in 1996. Harlow had drafted many influential briefs, including the American Bar Association's important amicus brief in *Romer v. Evans*, the landmark 1996 case in which the US Supreme Court struck down a voter-approved constitutional amendment that would have prevented any government entity in Colorado from protecting gays and lesbians against discrimination. Harlow's reputation for sagacity would be fully vindicated by the legal strategy she masterminded as Lambda's lead attorney in *Lawrence v. Texas*. Ironically, a decade earlier Harlow had turned down the opportunity to represent Dale, shunting him off to Wolfson and Lambda. Now, however, Wolfson and Harlow worked side by side, honing the legal arguments on Dale's behalf.

The Boy Scouts' legal team faced the same dilemma as Lambda: should they go for a hired gun with experience arguing before the Supreme Court or should they stick with the attorney who had represented them throughout the lower court proceedings? Like Wolfson, George Davidson had never argued a case before the US Supreme Court, and plenty of distinguished law professors and lawyers would have jumped at the opportunity to argue the Scouts' case before the nation's highest court. The Boy Scouts made the same decision that Lambda did: stick with the litigator who knew the case best. Davidson was a safe choice not only because he was familiar with Dale's case but because he had spent the past decade ably—and largely successfully—defending the Scouts against charges of discrimination in courts all across the country.

Although the Scouts were content to have the experienced Davidson argue the case before the Supreme Court, the decision was made to get outside assistance in preparing the all-important Supreme Court brief. For this task, they recruited Michael W. McConnell, a distinguished law professor as well as an assistant Scoutmaster of the Presbyterian-sponsored Scout Troop 38 of the Great

Salt Lake Council. McConnell brought a towering intellect and star power that the Scouts' legal team had hitherto lacked. After a decade at the University of Chicago Law School in which he established himself as one of the nation's preeminent legal scholars of religious liberty, the forty-year-old McConnell had moved to the University of Utah in 1996 to become a presidential professor, a rank reserved for the school's most elite scholars. A father of three young children, McConnell preferred Salt Lake City for its "more family-friendly environment." He found its "Mormon culture" to be "welcoming and attractive." A devout Presbyterian, he felt more comfortable in the company of Mormons, "who are involved in their religion and are interested in it," than he did around people of little or no faith. In McConnell's view, "the greatest divide in American culture" was not between religious faiths but between religious believers and those who were "either indifferent or hostile" to religion.

Unlike many lawyers, McConnell was as skilled at writing for a public audience as a legal one; indeed before deciding on a career in the law, he had contemplated a career in journalism. He could be ideologically combative, as in a 1998 *Wall Street Journal* op-ed, written on the twenty-fifth anniversary of *Roe v. Wade*, in which he excoriated the Supreme Court's historic abortion rights opinion as an "embarrassment to those who take constitutional law seriously." And the year he moved to Utah, he signed a statement that called for a constitutional amendment not only to overturn *Roe* but to secure the right to life of the unborn child. Yet McConnell also counted many liberals as friends, and he knew how to craft legal arguments that reached across ideological lines. At the same time that he railed against abortion rights, he co-chaired the Emergency Committee to Defend the First Amendment, an ideologically diverse coalition that was set up to combat the Republican-led effort in Congress to pass a constitutional amendment to outlaw flag burning. And despite his social conservatism, he had clerked for two iconic liberal jurists: appellate judge J. Skelly Wright, a John F. Kennedy appointee who had spearheaded the struggle against segregation in New Orleans, and the legendary Supreme Court Justice William Brennan. Both clerkships were secured on the recommendation of a liberal University of Chicago law professor, Geoffrey Stone, who had himself clerked for both Wright and Brennan.

McConnell, who served as assistant to the solicitor general during the Reagan administration before joining the University of Chicago faculty, also brought invaluable US Supreme Court experience to the Scouts' legal team. Among the Supreme Court cases that McConnell had argued was *Rosenberger v. University of Virginia*, a landmark case from 1995 that involved a challenge to the University of Virginia's decision to prohibit mandatory student activity fees from being used to fund a Christian magazine called *Wide Awake*. A 5–4 majority of the Court agreed with McConnell that the First Amendment principle of "viewpoint neutrality" required a state university like the University of Virginia to make funding available to all students groups, including religious groups. The justices who decided *Rosenberger* were the same nine justices who would hear *Dale*, and the Scouts hoped that McConnell could help them win over the five conservative justices (Kennedy, O'Connor, Rehnquist, Scalia, and Thomas) who had sided with the First Amendment rights of *Wide Awake*.

In short, McConnell was an ideal advocate for the Scouts. He was an intellectual but not one who sneered at the values of the Boy Scouts. He was a widely respected, nationally known First Amendment scholar. He wrote with clarity and grace. He possessed a brilliant legal mind and a mastery of constitutional law. And he knew what it took to win in a Supreme Court in which the outcome so often depended on the votes of Kennedy and O'Connor.

The brief that the Scouts had submitted to the New Jersey Supreme Court had arguably done their cause more harm than good. The appellate court ruling had clearly annoyed the Scouts' legal team, and those feelings showed in the sometimes snarky tone of their New Jersey Supreme Court brief—for instance, when the brief declared that the "First Amendment protects the right of freely associated Americans to promote views with which judges disagree as well as those with which judges agree." One two-and-a-half-page footnote chided the appellate court for "tak[ing] up arms in the cultural debate" about the morality of homosexual conduct, and quoted a host of conservative Republican politicians who had voiced their disapproval of "the homosexual lifestyle," including Mississippi senator Trent Lott and House Majority Leader Dick Armey (who the brief misidentified as a Texas senator). The brief noted, too, that when President Clinton nominated an openly gay businessman as ambassador to Luxembourg, the senators Donald Nickles (R-OK)—misspelled "Nichols" in the brief—and Tim Hutchinson (R-AK) opposed his confirmation, arguing that gays and lesbians could not serve as ambassadors since their promotion of "immoral behavior" meant they could not represent the nation's "values, views, and policies." The footnote stressed, too, that public opinion polls showed that a large majority of the American people shared the Scouts' view that homosexuality was immoral and sinful. It even cited a Princeton study that showed that only 6 percent of Americans believed that homosexuals raising children was a "good thing." The footnote closed by observing that "this cultural war is not confined to the United States," and that "in Great Britain, the House of Lords last month rejected the House of Commons' legislation which sought to lower the age of consent for homosexual sex from 18 to that for heterosexual sex, which is 16 years of age."

Riled by the appellate court's judgment that its policy against homosexuals was only "of recent vintage," the Scouts spent many pages of their brief attempting to demonstrate to the New Jersey Supreme Court that it was "absurd" to suggest that the Boy Scouts of America could *ever* have believed that homosexual conduct was "clean" or "morally straight." Following down the furrow plowed by Judge McGann, the Scouts detailed the abhorrence that Americans had long felt toward homosexuality and homosexual conduct. Like McGann, the Scouts noted that up until 1979, consensual sodomy was a criminal offense in New Jersey. The brief then dug up an array of mid-century state and federal appellate court rulings that harshly condemned the immorality of homosexuality. Among them was a New Jersey appellate court ruling from 1959 that granted a man a divorce after he had discovered his wife was an "active homosexual." Adding "to the insult of sexual disloyalty *per se*," the court said, "is the natural revulsion arising from the knowledge . . . that the spouse's betrayal takes the form of a perversion, [for] few behavioral deviations are more offensive to American mores than is homosexuality." The brief also recounted a federal court case from

1970 in which a judge upheld the discharge of an army civilian employee for homosexual conduct on the grounds that "any schoolboy knows that a homosexual act is immoral, indecent, lewd, and obscene," and a federal court case from 1967 that upheld the deportation of a homosexual on the grounds that the law prohibiting immigration by persons "afflicted with psychopathic personality" was clearly intended by Congress to bar "homosexuals and other sexual perverts" from coming to the United States.

The Scouts' aim was to demonstrate that the absence of a policy statement prior to 1978 could not be construed as evidence that the organization did not have a long-standing opposition to allowing gays in the Boy Scouts. After all, the Scouts were suggesting, everybody hated homosexuals in those days. But what the Scouts adduced as evidence for their side served as a painful reminder to the New Jersey justices of the widespread bigotry and invidious discrimination that gays and lesbians had historically faced. The history of legalized bigotry recited by the Scouts only underscored why the state of New Jersey had felt it was so important that the protections of the NJLAD be extended to gays and lesbians. Framing the issue in this way all but invited the New Jersey high court's cosmopolitan justices to distance themselves from the judicial bigotry of the past, a past to which the Scouts seemed only too eager to return.

McConnell helped to give the Scouts' brief a makeover. The new brief dispensed with the string of antigay quotations from politicians and judges. Gone, too, was the effort to demonstrate the prevalence of antigay beliefs among the American public. Instead, the brief focused squarely on the Boy Scouts' First Amendment rights of freedom of speech and association.

"Long ago," the Scouts' brief instructed the justices, Alexis de Tocqueville observed that voluntary associations lay "at the heart of American civic life." He marveled that "Americans of all ages, all stations in life, and all types of disposition are forever forming associations," and that "this powerful instrument of action has been applied to more varied aims in America than anywhere else in the world." He recognized that free associations were crucial to the preservation of freedom in a democratic society. And he insisted that "the right of association" was "by nature almost as inalienable as individual liberty" because "the most natural right of man, after that of acting on his own, is that of combining his efforts with those of his fellows and acting together." The case, in other words, was about more than this or that legal precedent. It was about the preservation of an essential principle of liberal democracy.

The brief's final summation was calculated to appeal not only to the conservatives on the court but to the liberals as well. "American pluralism thrives on difference," the brief affirmed in a passage that bears McConnell's mark. The examples trotted out included an African American big sisters organization, a Jewish dating service, and an Asian American theater company that accepted only second-generation Asian Americans. The autonomy of groups such as these was "vital" to sustaining "a diverse and free civil society." In support of this proposition, the brief quoted a recent article by the liberal political theorist and former Clinton advisor William Galston: "If we insist that each civil association mirror the principles of the overarching political community, meaningful differences among associations all but disappear; constitutional uniformity crushes social pluralism." The brief also referred the justices to the political theorist Nancy Rosenblum's recently published book *Membership and Morals: The Personal Uses of Pluralism in America*, which made a powerful liberal case for the importance of group autonomy in promoting individual development.

The brief closed by stressing that the justices could find in favor of the Scouts without endorsing the Scouts' views on homosexuality. "We recognize," the brief's final paragraph began, "that many people of good will believe that Scouting's position [on the morality of homosexual conduct] is misguided. That is not the issue in this case." Instead, the issue was about toleration even for those views that government officials deemed to be repellant. "We can respect the plea of many gay and lesbian Americans not to have the majority's morality imposed upon them," the brief concluded, but "by the same token, we ask that a contrary morality not be forced upon private associations like the Boy Scouts of America." Ultimately, the brief concluded, "controversial questions of personal morality, often involving religious conviction, are best tested and resolved within the private marketplace of ideas, and not as the subject of government-imposed orthodoxy." At stake was a philosophical issue of freedom, not the morality of homosexuality.

This final paragraph appears to have been aimed especially at Justice Kennedy, whom both sides suspected could be the pivotal fifth vote. The brief's philosophical flourish about "the private marketplace of ideas" was calculated to appeal to Kennedy's libertarian instincts as well as his philosophical pretensions; Kennedy, as the Yale law professor William Eskridge notes, "regards himself as the Court's political philosopher." But most of all, the explicit recognition that "people of good will" could regard the Scouts' position as "misguided" was designed to reassure Kennedy (and O'Connor too) that this case need not be a litmus test of their views about the morality of homosexuality or even about the civil rights of gays and lesbians.

Looming over the brief's last paragraph was the specter of Kennedy's historic opinion in *Romer v. Evans*, the most recent case in which the Court had wrestled with gay and lesbian rights. Writing for a 6–3 majority (that included a conflicted O'Connor), Kennedy had rebuked Colorado's Amendment 2 in the strongest possible terms. According to Kennedy, the amendment's effort to nullify all statutes, ordinances, and regulations that prohibited discrimination based on sexual orientation flunked even the Court's lowest standard of judicial review: that a policy bear a rational relationship to a legitimate government purpose. In Kennedy's view, the amendment reflected nothing more than a "hostile animus" toward gays and lesbians. The "desire to harm a politically unpopular group," Kennedy wrote, "cannot constitute a legitimate government interest." Colorado's law, in short, violated the Constitution's equal protection guarantee by removing protections against the exclusion of gays and lesbians "from an almost limitless number of transactions and endeavors that constitute ordinary civic life in a free society."

Kennedy's opinion brought a biting dissent from an almost apoplectic Scalia (signed also by Rehnquist and Thomas), who accused his colleague of having "mistaken a *Kulturkampf* [German for 'culture war'] for a fit of spite." What Kennedy saw as irrational animus toward gays was in fact "an entirely reasonable" effort by Coloradans to express their disapproval of homosexual conduct and "to preserve traditional sexual mores against the efforts of a politically powerful minority to revise those mores through the use of the laws." Scalia could see nothing wrong with society expressing "animus" toward "reprehensible" behavior, whether it was murder, polygamy, cruelty to animals, or "homosexual conduct." On Scalia's understanding of the Constitution, federal courts had no business intervening to protect homosexuals against discrimination because the Constitution "says nothing" about it. In striking down Amendment 2, Scalia thundered, the Court was arrogantly substituting the politically correct values and morality of "the lawyer class" for the moral and political judgments of ordinary Colorado voters.

Kennedy's opinion emphasized the unprecedented nature of Amendment 2; in oral argument he declared that he had "never seen a case like this." But Scalia was not buying the idea that *Romer* was a one-off. In Scalia's view, Kennedy's rejection of antigay animus as a legitimate government purpose threw into question the constitutional validity of a whole host of government policies, including the military's ban on openly gay service members, state restrictions on gay adoption, and, most importantly, statutes criminalizing sodomy, which ten years earlier, in *Bowers v. Hardwick*, a five-justice majority of the Court (including Rehnquist and O'Connor) had upheld as constitutional. To Scalia, it was plain that "in holding [that] homosexuality cannot be singled out for disfavorable treatment," Kennedy's *Romer* opinion contradicted the Court's verdict in *Bowers*. Scalia charged Kennedy with not only getting it wrong but being dishonest about the reach of the decision.

Scalia had a point. Kennedy's opinion nowhere mentioned, let alone repudiated, *Bowers*, despite the antigay animus behind the criminalization of sodomy. The omission of *Bowers* was influenced by the majority's fear of losing O'Connor's vote. Scalia was right, too, that it was difficult to imagine the author of *Romer* voting to uphold the criminalization of sodomy. (Indeed in 2003, in *Lawrence v. Texas*, Kennedy would write the opinion—with the identical 6–3 majority as in *Romer*—that explicitly overturned *Bowers*.) But was Scalia also right that Kennedy had placed "the prestige of [the Supreme Court] behind the proposition that opposition to homosexuality is as reprehensible as racial or religious bias"? If Scalia was right about that, then it was not difficult to imagine that Kennedy would cast a skeptical eye on the Scouts' antigay policy, particularly since the New Jersey Supreme Court had ruled the Scouts counted as a public accommodation.

Kennedy's *Romer* opinion certainly did link civil rights for gays and lesbians with the long struggle for racial equality for African Americans. His opening sentence invited the comparison by quoting Justice John Marshall Harlan's famous admonishment that the Constitution "neither knows nor tolerates classes among citizens." Harlan had penned those words exactly one hundred years earlier in his dissent in *Plessy v. Ferguson*, the Court's famously wrong-headed decision that "separate but equal" public facilities for whites and blacks did not violate the Constitution. But while Kennedy did seem to equate discrimination on the basis of sexual orientation with discrimination on the basis of race, the legal standard he adopted in *Romer* suggested that the two were not constitutionally equivalent. In cases involving race the Court required that a statute withstand "strict scrutiny," that is, there must be a compelling government interest and the policy must be narrowly tailored to achieve its ends. In *Romer*, in contrast, Kennedy had used the lowest "rational basis" standard of review.

But if Scalia exaggerated the constitutional equivalence that Kennedy drew between discrimination based on race and sexual orientation, he was not wrong to highlight Kennedy's sympathy toward gay and lesbian rights. The gulf in attitudes between Kennedy and Scalia—both Catholic and born within a few months of each other—was evident even in the language they used. Whereas Kennedy's majority opinion in *Romer* spoke easily and respectfully of "gays and lesbians," Scalia's dissent clung to the older term "homosexual."

Kennedy's *Romer* opinion surprised many people—thrilling the gay and lesbian community as much as it disappointed Scalia—but a close reading of Kennedy's career suggests that he had long been more accepting of homosexuality than his conservative colleagues, including O'Connor. As an appellate judge on the Ninth Circuit in the 1970s and 1980s, Kennedy hired law clerks he knew to be gay. One of those clerks helped Kennedy craft an opinion in a 1980 case (*Beller v. Middendorf*) that upheld the constitutionality of the military's discharge of gays but also suggested that "some kinds of government regulation of private consensual homosexual behavior may face substantial constitutional challenge." Kennedy wrote those words six years before the *Bowers* Court ruled that there was no constitutional bar against sodomy laws. Kennedy publicly voiced some of his misgivings about *Bowers* only a month after the ruling was announced, in a lecture on "unenumerated rights" at a conference sponsored by the Canadian Institute for Advanced Legal Studies and hosted by his alma mater, Stanford University. (In that lecture, Kennedy also spoke about a decision in 1981 by the European Court of Human Rights [*Dudgeon v. United Kingdom*] that struck down a sodomy law similar to the one the *Bowers* majority had upheld.) Indeed, concerns within the Reagan White House about Kennedy possibly being "prohomosexual" played a part in the president's decision in 1987 to nominate the ultraconservative and unrelentingly antigay Robert Bork instead of Kennedy to replace Lewis Powell, who had provided the crucial fifth vote in *Bowers* (a vote Powell later regretted). Only after Bork was rejected by the Senate (and the second choice Douglas Ginsburg withdrew after allegations that as a young law professor he had smoked pot with his students) did Reagan settle on Kennedy.

Kennedy was no Bork. That much was clear. But the Scouts' lawyers could not be certain that the author of *Romer* would take the Boy Scouts' side, nor could Dale's lawyers count on Kennedy's support. To begin with, *Romer* involved the state nullifying all government provisions that protected gay and lesbian citizens against discrimination. In contrast, the Boy Scouts only asked to be exempted from a state law that prohibited discrimination. Moreover, whereas *Romer* pitted state power against individual rights, the Scouts' case set the BSA's First Amendment rights against Dale's right not to be discriminated against. As much as *Romer* incensed Scalia and thrilled gay and lesbians, it was far from clear what the case signified for Dale's prospects.

A clerk involved in *Romer* cautioned against reading too much into how Kennedy, let alone O'Connor, would rule in other gay rights cases. Although *Romer* offered a valuable "counterbalance" to *Bowers*, he thought that *Romer* didn't necessarily reveal "that much about what [the Court would] do in the next case." Nonetheless, the clerk was hopeful that *Romer* had created a "level . . . playing field" so that "you'd have to make normal constitutional arguments now.

There's no huge thumb on the scale against gay people." At a minimum, *Romer* showed that six of the justices were "pledging not to let prejudice rule them."

The prominent gay legal scholar Arthur Leonard, whose *Lesbian/Gay Law Notes* had been a must read in the gay and lesbian legal community since 1980, sized up *Romer*'s significance for future cases in similar terms. The case suggested that for the first time in the nation's history a majority on the Court might be "comfortable with the idea of gay people as citizens, as people who exist beyond sex acts." If true, that was a "real breakthrough." But the gay community, he cautioned, "shouldn't build castles in the sky on the basis of suddenly proclaiming Anthony Kennedy as the great hero of civil rights."

In truth, Kennedy was not the Court's most reliable vote for any cause. His changes of heart were legendary among Court insiders. His penchant for taking "one position with his clerks, then . . . another after a day or two of thinking it through," according to one account, "drove his law clerks crazy, especially if they'd already started writing the draft opinion." Admirers saw this as a sign of Kennedy's thoughtfulness, moderation, and flexibility. Critics saw it as unprincipled or, even less flatteringly, as owing to a grandiose sense of his own importance and a deep-seated desire to be the center of attention.

But Kennedy's reputation for indecisiveness or inconsistency is easily exaggerated. Worryingly for Dale's team, Kennedy was consistently the justice most likely to strike down a government regulation for violating freedom of speech and association, and the justice most likely to strike down state and federal laws for violating the Constitution. Moreover, despite Kennedy's reputation as a swing justice, he much more frequently swung with the conservatives than the liberals. In the preceding five Court terms (1994–1995 through 1998–1999), the Court had split 5–4 on seventy-six occasions. In only ten of those seventy-six cases (13 percent) did Kennedy side with the four liberal justices; in contrast, he took the same side as the other four conservative justices in thirty-two (42 percent) of the 5–4 cases.

Wolfson's team did have one advantage over the Scouts. Assuming the four liberal justices sided with Dale, the Scouts needed the votes of both O'Connor and Kennedy in order to prevail, whereas Dale needed only one of the two to take his side. The lawyers on both sides, however, surmised that O'Connor was more likely to side with the Scouts than Dale.

True, Dale's team could take heart from the knowledge that O'Connor and her husband were known to have a number of openly gay friends in Washington. And O'Connor's vote in *Romer* showed that she'd come a long way in her attitudes in the decade since she cast her lot with the *Bowers* majority. Moreover, O'Connor had played a pivotal part in articulating "the *Roberts* trilogy" (*Roberts v. United States Jaycees*, *Board of Directors of Rotary International v. Rotary Club*, and *New York State Club Ass'n v. City of New York*) upon which Dale's case rested. Moreover, O'Connor was the only justice who had served as a state legislator and state judge, which made her inclined to find ways to defer to state legislatures and state courts—certainly she was much more inclined to defer to legislatures than Kennedy.

There were several reasons, though, for thinking that O'Connor's vote would be more difficult to get than Kennedy's. First, in *Romer*, as Joyce Murdoch and Deb Price's *Courting Justice* makes clear, "Kennedy led and O'Connor followed." Those privy to the Court's internal deliberations suspected that while O'Connor was willing to provide the sixth vote in *Romer* she would have been unlikely to cast the decisive fifth vote against Amendment 2. Even had she been willing to be the fifth vote, she would never have authored the forceful opinion in favor of gay rights that Kennedy did.

The second reason to suspect that O'Connor's vote was more likely to go to the Scouts was perhaps more consequential, and it had less to do with what O'Connor thought about gay rights and more to do with what she had written nearly sixteen years ago in her concurrence in *Roberts*. That concurrence rested on a distinction between commercial and expressive associations (the Jaycees, O'Connor maintained, were "predominantly commercial"), but it also recognized that determining when an association was "predominantly expressive" would "often be difficult, if only because a broad range of activities can be expressive." It was "easy enough," O'Conner explained, "to identify expressive words or conduct that are strident, contentious, or divisive, but protected expression may also take the form of quiet persuasion, inculcation of traditional values, instruction of the young, and community service. . . . Even the training of outdoor survival skills or participation in community service might become expressive when the activity is intended to develop good morals, reverence, patriotism, and a desire for self-improvement." In a footnote to this passage, O'Connor cited the 1979 *Boy Scout Handbook*, and quoted the historian Paul Fussell's observation that "for all its focus on Axmanship, Backpacking, Cooking, First Aid, Flowers, Hiking, Map and Compass, Semaphore, Trees, and Weather, [the *Handbook*] is another book about goodness." O'Connor's explicit acknowledgment that the Scouts, unlike the Jaycees, could qualify as an expressive association meant that securing O'Connor's vote was likely to be difficult for Wolfson.

The Wolfson-Harlow brief did its best to confront this passage from O'Connor's opinion by stressing that the *Roberts* Court "of course . . . did not have before it any of the evidence regarding either BSA's unique government entwinement or its commercial enterprises." Now, though, the Court did have the advantage of a detailed record of the Scouts' activities, which showed that "while its members undoubtedly engage in valuable recreational and expressive activities, BSA is in many respects also a commercial entity." The brief noted that in 1992 the Boy Scouts "operated more than 700 residential camps around the country" and that the Scouts conducted "aggressive recruitment through national television, radio, and, magazine campaigns." The brief drove home the commercial aspect of the Scouts by quoting, as the New Jersey appellate court had done, the BSA spokesman's affirmation that Scouting is "a product and we've got to get the product into the hands of as many consumers as we can." It seemed unlikely, though, that this record would be sufficient to persuade O'Connor to change her mind about the expressive nature of the Scouts.

Wolfson and Harlow understood that the success of Dale's case rested instead on the Court—and particularly Kennedy—accepting that the Scouts' freedom of expressive association did not trump the state's compelling interest in sustaining its antidiscrimination law. "This Court," Harlow and Wolfson wrote, "has time and again rejected efforts by would-be discriminators to claim a First Amendment freedom to disassociate as a defense against civil rights laws targeting discriminatory conduct." Invoking the *Roberts* trilogy, Harlow and Wolfson maintained that "where the law at issue regulates a large membership organization's ability to exclude human beings based on their personal characteristics or identity, rather than its ability to express its ideas, the Court has upheld the state's power to act." And the record before the Court, they maintained, plainly showed that Dale's case involved "identity-based discrimination, not any policy about or examination of views."

Dale's team hoped that the Court might also be influenced by the impressive array of amicus briefs filed on Dale's behalf, especially the extraordinary brief filed by the American Bar Association (ABA). Friend of the court briefs allow those who are not parties to the litigation to weigh in on a case. At one time a rarity, these days there is nothing at all unusual about amicus briefs, although the nearly forty amicus briefs filed in Dale's case was an extraordinarily high number at that time. Only a handful of cases prior to Dale's case had attracted more amicus filings. Among the hundreds of organizations listed as amicus curiae in support of Dale were the American Civil Liberties Union, the American Federation of Teachers, the Anti-Defamation League, the Mexican American Legal Defense and Education Fund, the NAACP Legal Defense and Educational Fund, the NOW Legal Defense and Education Fund, the American Psychological Association, the American Public Health Association, the National Association of Social Workers, the Society of American Law Teachers, and the American Association of School Administrators. In addition, Dale was supported by the New York City Board of Education, Los Angeles Unified School District, and San Francisco Unified School District; the cities of Atlanta, Chicago, Los Angeles, New York, San Francisco, Portland, and Tucson; and the states of California, Hawaii, Maryland, Massachusetts, New Hampshire, New Jersey, New York, Oklahoma, Oregon, Vermont, and Washington.

From the Court's point of view, however, none of the amicus briefs was as eye-catching or important as the one from the ABA. Every member of the Court understood that an ABA brief (unlike, for instance, an ACLU brief) was a relatively uncommon occurrence; indeed, Dale's case was one of only two cases argued before the Court in the 1999–2000 term that featured a brief from the ABA. The ABA's standing committee on amicus briefs is a daunting gatekeeper, entrusted with ensuring that only briefs of the highest professional quality bear the stamp of the ABA. That rigorous approval process and a reputation for top-quality briefs mean that when the ABA speaks the Court is inclined to listen.

The idea to have the ABA file an amicus brief on behalf of Dale came from Mark Agrast, a savvy congressional staffer who had been instrumental over the previous decade in helping to transform ABA policy toward gays and lesbians. As an aide to the first openly gay member of Congress (Gerry Studds), Agrast had watched a "hidebound" ABA sit on the sidelines during *Bowers v. Hardwick*, a case in which the ABA's involvement could have been decisive. The disappointment of *Bowers* spurred Agrast and other gay and lesbian lawyers to push the ABA to develop a body of policies that would enable the association to file amicus briefs in future cases affecting gay and lesbian rights. In February 1989, the ABA's policy-making body (called the House of Delegates) adopted a resolution urging the federal government and state and local governments to adopt legislation banning discrimination on the basis of sexual orientation in employment, housing, and public accommodations. Three years later, the ABA granted the National Lesbian and Gay Law Association (subsequently renamed the National Lesbian, Gay, Bisexual and Transgender Bar Association) a permanent seat in the ABA House of Delegates (a seat occupied first by Abby Rubenfeld, then by Agrast). In 1995, Agrast orchestrated the filing of the ABA's influential *Romer* brief, the first amicus brief in the association's long history to make the case for gay and lesbian civil rights.

Agrast knew that a brief on behalf of Dale would be a tougher sell than *Romer*. Many ABA leaders had been Scouts, and many more had children in the Scouts. Because the case involved the relationship between gay men and young boys, Agrast also knew that it had the "potential to be radioactive." He also conceded that as a legal matter it was a closer call than *Romer*, which involved discrimination by the state. Dale's case undeniably raised legitimate concerns about freedom of association and expression. Even those who were convinced of the merits of Dale's legal arguments worried about putting the ABA's reputation on the line in a losing cause.

Still, Agrast was determined to try. In the *Hurley* case, Agrast and others had toyed with the idea of proposing an ABA brief on behalf of the Irish American Gay, Lesbian, and Bisexual Group of Boston, but decided against it. It was too easy to imagine "the shoe being on the other foot" in the form of a gay pride parade that wanted to exclude antigay protesters. But Dale's case bore no meaningful resemblance to *Hurley*. Unlike the small, unincorporated clutch of citizens who organized an annual parade in Boston, the Boy Scouts were a ubiquitous, nationwide organization that was inextricably connected to growing up male in the United States. Too much was at stake not to at least attempt to leverage the ABA's considerable reputation and influence to advance equality for gays and lesbians.

Agrast's plan for the ABA brief was straightforward: the argument would be that the New Jersey Supreme Court had successfully applied the *Roberts* framework, and that framework was still the right one for weighing the conflict between antidiscrimination laws and the freedom of association. This was a careful, precedent-based argument that he believed the ABA could approve. Time, however, was short. They had only three weeks to write the brief and submit it in finished form to the ABA amicus committee. Agrast needed someone at a big law firm "with big firm resources" who wrote well and quickly, and who would start work immediately. Agrast's old mentor Abby Rubenfeld suggested Jim Hough, an attorney at Morrison & Foerster (and the father of Rubenfeld's two young children). During the mid-1980s, Hough had worked as a Lambda intern, where he not only met Rubenfeld (who was then Lambda's legal director) but was assigned to help a young pro bono lawyer who was writing Lambda's amicus brief in *Bowers*. That lawyer was Evan Wolfson.

Hough immediately accepted Rubenfeld's request to draft the brief. Working at a rapid pace, with Agrast "heavily involved" in the editing, Hough produced a brief that was a model of clarity and concision. The only question that remained: would the ABA approve the brief? At first it looked as if the answer was "no." The seven-person standing committee on amicus briefs was divided, with the majority voting to reject the brief. The opponents' motives were not all or even mostly bigotry. Opposition, as Agrast anticipated, was rooted in legitimate concerns about the freedom of association as well as the likelihood of success. But there were also some who expressed views that struck Agrast as nothing short of "antediluvian" in their imaginings of the dangers that gay Scout leaders posed to young boys. Agrast asked the ABA's Board of Governors to take the highly unusual—albeit not unprecedented—step of rejecting the amicus committee's recommendation. The thirty-eight-member board was polled on the question, and a majority agreed that the ABA should file the brief.

Even with the support of the ABA, however, most impartial observers believed that Dale faced long odds. The Scouts' attorneys remained confident that they would prevail. Even a unanimous verdict in their favor did not seem beyond the realm of the possible—after all *Hurley* had been decided unanimously. The Scouts weren't the only ones who thought a unanimous ruling in the Scouts' favor was possible. Arthur Leonard, a law professor and former Lambda trustee, was among those in the gay and lesbian legal community who thought that Wolfson could well have difficulty securing the support not only of Kennedy and O'Connor but of the four liberal justices as well. *Romer* may have shown that a majority on the Court could deliberate about gay rights without letting prejudice dictate their decision, but the unanimous *Hurley* case, decided the year before *Romer* by the same nine justices who would hear the Scouts' case, indicated that a unanimous ruling in the Scouts' favor could not be ruled out. To be sure, there were "crucial distinctions between the factual contexts of *Dale* and *Hurley*," but Leonard thought the "core issues" were "similar enough" to make the case "rather daunting" for Dale's side. Leonard predicted that Wolfson would have "his task cut out for him" at oral argument, even apart from the "hostile" questioning he could expect from Scalia and Rehnquist.

CHAPTER 11

On the Supreme Stage

Oral argument in Dale's case was scheduled for ten o'clock Wednesday morning, April 26, 2000, the last case of an eventful term. Already this term the Supreme Court had heard oral arguments on a host of controversial social issues, including "partial-birth" abortion, prayer at public high school football games, nude dancing, sexually explicit programs on cable television, government aid to parochial schools, and the constitutionality of a federal law allowing victims of rape and domestic violence to sue attackers in federal court.

Oral arguments in controversial cases frequently attract colorful protests on the marble plaza in front of the Supreme Court building, and Dale's case was no exception. When James Dale arrived that morning, accompanied by his parents and Evan Wolfson, he was greeted by a gaggle of antigay activists. Among them was Flip Benham, a Dallas-based evangelical minister and president of the antiabortion group Operation Save America, better known as Operation Rescue until a schism split the group. "Save yourself from this awful, horrible lifestyle!" shouted the Reverend Benham. "Mr. Dale, Jesus will set you free!" Benham's antigay message was amplified by Dan Martino, a forty-two-year-old self-described "street preacher" from Chattanooga, who like Benham had spent the previous day on the plaza protesting abortion as the Court listened to oral arguments in *Stenberg v. Carhart*, a case involving a challenge to a Nebraska statute that criminalized all "partial-birth abortions" except those necessary to save the life of the mother. For Dale's case, Martino donned the same giant wooden cross but traded in his antiabortion placards for a large handwritten sign that read: "A Homosexual Boy Scout Leader is Like Asking a Fox to Guard the Chickens! It is Stupid and a Sin!" Martino may have been "slightly deranged-looking," but he certainly knew how to attract media attention. In fact, twelve years earlier, at the Democratic National Convention in Atlanta, Martino landed himself on the front page of a national newspaper by sporting a cardboard sign proclaiming, "God is a Republican."

Martino was an eccentric, but he expressed a view that lurked just beneath the surface of the case. The Scouts never relied on the pedophile argument in court—and explicitly repudiated it whenever it was raised—but the Scouts' backers were not so circumspect. Two days after the oral argument, for instance, the *Washington Times* editorialized that the Scouts' dislike of "the idea of a young, gay man heading off into the woods on camping trips with a troop of young boys" was not "hateful" or "bigoted" but simply "what used to be called common sense." After all, "most people would not be comfortable with the idea of sending their young daughters off into the woods with a single, heterosexual young male, either." And wasn't it just a little bit "well, odd" that "'twenty-something,' single, unattached young males," like Dale, would be "clinging to merit badges and campfires"? The *Times* implied that Dale could only have wanted to remain in Scouting to prey upon young boys.

Most of those who gathered at the Supreme Court on this Wednesday morning, however, were not there to protest against the sin of homosexuality or the bigotry of the Boy Scouts but to get a seat inside the "Marble Palace." In fact many of these eager citizens had spent the night camped on the sidewalk outside so as to have the opportunity to watch the oral argument in person. The seventy-five hundred square foot chamber where the Court hears oral arguments can accommodate about four hundred people, but many of the seats are reserved for the press, the justices' law clerks and special guests, as well as attorneys who have been admitted as members of the Supreme Court bar. In a controversial case, there may be no more than fifty seats available to members of the general public who wish to watch the entire oral argument; a glimpse of the proceedings, however, can be gained by waiting in the "three-minute line," which allows visitors to observe from the rear of the room for a few minutes.

Those privileged to attend an oral argument witness an event that precious few American citizens ever see. Since no cameras are allowed inside, nobody can watch the show on television. The subversive idea that citizens in a democracy should be able to view Supreme Court oral arguments on television has consistently been rejected by both liberal and conservative justices, never more adamantly than when, in 1996, Justice David Souter told the House Appropriations Committee that cameras in the Supreme Court would have to "roll over my dead body." An audio recording is made of every oral argument, but it is not released to the public until months later. Beginning in 2006 a written transcript has been released on the day of the oral arguments, but at the time of Dale's oral argument even a written transcript was unavailable to the public until after the Court's decision was announced.

Among the lawyers, dignitaries, and ordinary citizens who filed into the room that day was, of course, Dale himself. Seated next to him was David Buckel, the Lambda attorney (and former Boy Scout) who had been assigned the task of watching out for Dale and answering any legal questions he might have during the proceedings. A couple rows in front of them were a number of top-ranking Boy Scouts officials. Although all of them recognized Dale, none turned to acknowledge his existence. Buckel was struck not only by their calculated snubbing of Dale but by the ostentatiously boisterous backslapping and pumping of hands with which the Scouts officials greeted one another. To Buckel, their "very loud" behavior seemed to belong in a locker room not a court room. These older men seemed oblivious to the hurt that they were inflicting on the young Eagle Scout sitting behind them.

At precisely ten o'clock, every spectator in the room—among them New Jersey Chief Justice Deborah Poritz—rose from their seat as the Court crier announced, "The Honorable, the Chief Justice and the Associate Justices of the Supreme Court of the United States." At the utterance of those seventeen words, nine black-robed justices emerged from behind an impressive red velvet curtain and filed solemnly into the room. The seven men and two women took their customary positions in their high-backed, black leather chairs, with Chief Justice William Rehnquist in the center, flanked to his right by the next most senior justice, John Paul Stevens. At the far ends of the curved bank of nine chairs were the two most junior justices, Clinton appointees both, Ruth Bader Ginsburg and Stephen Breyer.

The curved nature of the justices' seating arrangement enables the justices to more easily see and hear one another, a not unimportant consideration for an institution generously stocked with geriatrics (in 2000 the Court's oldest member, John Paul Stevens, was eighty years old, and the average age of the justices was nearing seventy). In front of—and beneath—the justices' perch are two tables. Seated at one table were the Scouts' attorneys, George Davidson, Michael McConnell, and Carla Kerr; at the other were Dale's attorneys, Evan Wolfson and Ruth Harlow. The elevated bench ensures that attorneys "have to look up to address the judges," while the justices' curved seating means that they seem "almost to encircle the attorney." Both architectural features help to make an appearance before the US Supreme Court that much more intimidating, especially for litigators like Davidson and Wolfson who were making their first appearance before the Supreme Court.

As the attorney for the petitioner, Davidson would be up first. "We'll hear argument now," Rehnquist announced, "in Number 99-699, Boy Scouts of America and Monmouth Council v. James Dale." The chief justice then invited Davidson to commence. Davidson rose, stepped toward the justices, and began. This was a case, he told the justices, about "the freedom of a voluntary association to choose its own leaders." He got through another two sentences before the justices began to interrupt.

First to cut in was Justice Kennedy, a Boy Scout in his youth, who asked Davidson whether Dale was kicked out of the Scouts because of "the reasonable likelihood that he would use his position to advocate for his cause." Davidson answered that by appearing in the New Jersey newspaper article, Dale had "created a reputation for himself [that] would have carried into the troop meeting and affected his ability to be a role model to the youths in his troop." Kennedy wanted to know whether the Scouts could have terminated Dale if he had only revealed his homosexuality to his family. Davidson tried to dodge the question. The Scouts had only terminated individuals who were "open about their sexual orientation," so the Scouts had never faced the hypothetical situation posed by Kennedy.

This was untrue, as Davidson should have known. In the late 1970s, in the first documented case of a Boy Scout being expelled for being homosexual, two Scouts from Mankato, Minnesota, were kicked out after the mother of one of the boys revealed her concerns regarding the boys' homosexuality to their Scout leader. And in 1993, in a case in Connecticut that made national headlines, the Scouts ousted David Knapp, a sixty-seven-year-old volunteer Scout leader and Eagle Scout, after his ex-wife's disgruntled daughter notified the Scouts that he was gay, a fact known at the time only to "close family members." Kennedy refused to be put off by Davidson's evasion: "Well, what is the position of the Scouts in the case that I have posited?" Davidson relented: he was willing "to defend any decision" the Scouts made if they found out that someone was a homosexual because that was "their right under the Constitution."

Kennedy seemed troubled by the sweep of this contention and sought to steer Davidson onto narrower ground. Did the Scouts take their position, Kennedy asked, "on the grounds that from his [homosexual] status a certain amount of advocacy is likely"? Recognizing Kennedy's concern, Davidson assured him that the Boy Scouts were "not concerned about status." All the Scouts cared about were "expression and conduct inconsistent with the [Scout] oath and law."

Now it was Justice Souter's turn to pose a hypothetical. If a troop leader came to BSA officials and privately and discreetly disclosed his homosexuality, could the Scouts exclude him for that honest admission alone? Davidson again tried to avoid the hypothetical question, but Souter was unrelenting. On the third attempt, Davidson at last answered the question. "I believe," he said, "that there would be the right to do that." And in fact—though Davidson did not reveal this—the BSA had done precisely that on a number of occasions over the past decade when leaders had written to the Scouts to inform them that they were gay.

Justice Ginsburg now took up the baton. She expressed confusion about the Boy Scouts' policy. Was is it "don't ask, don't tell" or was it that "if you are gay you are not welcome in the Boy Scouts"? The policy, Davidson explained, "is not to inquire" about a person's homosexuality but to "exclude those who are open" about their homosexuality.

Sandra Day O'Connor now joined the cue of justices expressing confusion about the Scouts' policy. "Where do we look," O'Connor asked, "to determine what the policy is?" O'Connor also tossed in another hypothetical for Davidson to address: "What about the heterosexual Scout leader who openly espouses the view that homosexuality is consistent with the Scout law and oath, and that it's not immoral?" Is the Scouts' policy to exclude that person too? And where could the justices find the Scouts' policy on this? Davidson could point to no written policy, but he explained that it was permissible for a heterosexual to advocate the position that homosexuality was consistent with the Scout Law and Scout Oath, so long as the advocacy was done "through Scouting channels in an effort to change policy." What was not allowed was for a person "to advocate the morality of homosexual conduct to youth in the program." That person, Davidson assured the Court, "would be excluded."

The more conservative justices now came to Davidson's aid. Chief Justice Rehnquist was the first to throw the struggling counsel a lifeline. "I take it from what you're saying, Mr. Davidson," Rehnquist suggested, "that perhaps the Scouts have not adopted a comprehensive policy covering every single conceivable situation that might come up." Davidson grabbed hold. "Mr. Chief Justice," the grateful counsel began. "The Scouts have general moral principles in the morally straight and clean requirements of the oath and law, and they have to be interpreted by Scout leaders in situations as they have come up." But while the general principles left room for interpretation in some cases, in the case before the Court the policy was crystal clear: those like Dale who were "openly homosexual" could not be Scout leaders.

Justice Scalia, like Kennedy a former Boy Scout, was up next with another sympathetic intervention. He wanted Davidson to clarify what he meant by the "exclusion of people who are openly homosexual." What if a person was "homosexual in the sense of having a sexual orientation in that direction but does not engage in any homosexual conduct"? Again Davidson gratefully accepted the help. If the person admitted to a "homosexual orientation" but declared that they didn't engage in homosexual conduct because they believed—and communicated this view to young Scouts—that such conduct was "morally wrong," then Davidson thought "that person would not be excluded."

None of the hypothetical cases offered by Kennedy (the gay person who does not reveal his sexual orientation in public), Souter (the gay person who discloses his orientation only to the BSA), and O'Connor (the heterosexual who publicly states that homosexuality is moral) was in fact hypothetical. The Scouts had dealt with each of these cases. Scalia's hypothetical, however, was fanciful, and Davidson's answer even more so. In none of the cases in which the BSA excluded gay leaders did the Scouts make any effort to discover whether the person actually engaged in homosexual "conduct." Nor had the BSA ever tried to define what counted as homosexual conduct. Moreover, the policy did not call for the BSA to investigate a person's views on the morality of homosexuality. The BSA policy stated only that known or avowed homosexuals could not be Scouts.

Davidson's reply brought Justice Ginsburg back into the fray. How about "somebody who was homosexual and celibate" but who also avowed that homosexual conduct was not morally wrong? Would the Scouts' policy allow that person to hold a leadership position? Davidson replied that as he understood the policy, such a person "would be eligible for leadership." It is unclear, however, how Davidson came to this conclusion. The Scouts had never articulated such a policy, nor had they (unlike the LDS Church) ever shown any interest in discovering whether a gay person was celibate or sexually active. Neither Dale nor any other gay Scout leader had ever been asked by the BSA about their sexual conduct. If a Scout admitted to being a homosexual that was sufficient for the BSA to expel him.

Still struggling to understand the Scouts' policy, Ginsburg offered another hypothetical case. How about "cohabiters," that is, "people who live together [in] heterosexual unions but [are] not blessed by marriage." Davidson assured the justice that there had been "adulterers" who the Boy Scouts had excluded on the grounds that they were not "morally straight." A surprised Ginsburg reminded Davidson that she wasn't asking about adultery, just "living together before marriage," which was "not so uncommon these days." Davidson admitted that he knew of "no particular instances of application of the policy in that connection." Indeed, the Scouts had never excluded any leader for heterosexual cohabitation outside of marriage, even though the Scouts and many of the churches that sponsored Scouting units pronounced such conduct to be immoral.

Souter steered the conversation back to the BSA's policy regarding homosexuality. It seemed to Souter that the policy that Davidson had been explaining to the Court did not appear to be stated "anywhere in a Boy Scouts manual, or even a troop leader manual." It seemed instead to be "in effect sort of Boy Scout common law" that was then interpreted by the regional councils or national office in particular cases. Davidson took umbrage at any suggestion that this was a "stealth policy." He pointed out that in 1992, *Scouting* magazine, which is sent to all Scouters (that is, registered adult members of the BSA), included an article that clearly communicated the Scouts' policy that avowed homosexuals could not be members of the Boy Scouts. And Davidson assured the justices that "the general principle of morally straight is really very, very widely known in the Scouting movement." Souter still wanted an answer to his question about the policy in the BSA's official handbooks. Here Davidson fell back on the 1972 edition of the *Scoutmaster's Handbook*, which included "a reference in dealing with incidents of sexual activity that might occur in a troop that speaks disapprovingly of homosexual conduct." But that was hardly a policy statement, Souter pointed out. Davidson conceded that point, but noted that the handbooks also didn't contain any policy statements about adultery or any number of other related moral transgressions that could get one kicked out of Scouting.

Worried that Davidson had conceded too much, Justice Kennedy drew Davidson and the Court's attention to the BSA's memorandum from 1978 that declared, in Kennedy's words, that "homosexuality in its troop leaders is incompatible with Scouting." Kennedy thought that was "a rather strong statement" of the Scouts' policy. Davidson welcomed the assistance, and added that the 1978 statement was only the first of "several position statements" that the Scouts had issued in the succeeding years declaring that they did not allow avowed homosexuals to serve as leaders. (The policy actually applied not just to Scout leaders but to all Scouts, though that was something Davidson did not mention.)

Souter pressed for clarification on one further point. Was it true that "the Scouts' position [did] not in any way depend on a judgment that Mr. Dale . . . presents or would present an undue risk of homosexual conduct with the Scouts in his troop"? There was no evasion or hesitation in Davidson's response this time. The Scouts took sexual abuse very seriously, he assured the justices, but that concern was totally unrelated to the policy excluding homosexuals. It was "not the basis of [the] policy in any way," he repeated for emphasis.

The Court's only Eagle Scout, Justice Steven Breyer, now entered the argument for the first time. Noting that Dale was terminated after the Scouts became aware of the *Newark Star-Ledger* article, Breyer wanted to know whether a heterosexual who "said every word exactly the same" as Dale did in the article would also have been terminated. This was an awkward hypothetical since Dale's comments in the article recounted how he had gradually gathered the strength to come out as a gay man. It made no sense to ask Davidson to imagine a hypothetical in which a heterosexual was relating his coming out story. But putting aside the particulars of what Dale had told the reporter back in the summer of 1990, Breyer's hypothetical was essentially the same as the one O'Connor had posed. Davidson's answer, however, was different this time. He had told O'Connor that a heterosexual advocating the morality of homosexuality would be eligible for a leadership position, so long as the person was not advocating homosexuality to Scouting youth. But he now told Breyer that he had "no information as to how that situation would be resolved," though he noted that Scouting officials could reasonably conclude that someone "who is himself presenting a personal example, as well as advocating, might be more unacceptable than somebody who was merely advocating."

Justice John Paul Stevens wanted to know why the policy was applied only to open homosexuals. If the Boy Scouts sincerely believed that homosexual conduct was not morally straight, why did it matter whether the person was open about their sexual orientation? Either way, their conduct violated the Scout Oath. If nobody knew, Davidson responded, then "it doesn't become an issue"—though that still didn't address the question of why the Scouts didn't take steps to find out, for instance, by asking prospective leaders if they were gay. Stevens's follow-up inquiry took a different path, one that returned the Court to the issue raised at the outset by Kennedy: what if the Scouts inadvertently discovered a person's sexual orientation but the person had not wanted the Scouts or anybody else to know about it? When Kennedy had posed essentially this same question, Davidson had tried to evade it on the grounds that it had never come up. But this time Davidson forthrightly described the Scouts' de facto policy: if the Scouts found out a person was homosexual, that was sufficient for the Scouts to terminate the person. Stevens pounced on the admission: in that case "the policy is not limited to open gays." Davidson agreed. The policy was "known or avowed" homosexuals. That is, the Scouts' policy was to exclude all homosexuals even if nobody in the person's troop or community knew they were gay. The word "avowed" was in fact entirely superfluous to the BSA policy, since every "avowed" homosexual was, by definition, "known." The policy, Davidson asserted unapologetically, was that the Scouts had a fundamental right "to choose the moral leaders it wants for the children in the program."

Justice Breyer picked up on the thread that Stevens had left hanging. If homosexual conduct is so immoral, why don't the Scouts make any effort to find out whether prospective leaders engage in conduct that violates the Scout Oath? That the Scouts did not ask this question left Breyer wondering whether the Scouts genuinely believed that "this is very, very bad conduct" or whether they were simply "concerned about public reaction." Thinking Davidson needed help, Scalia jumped in:

> Justice Scalia: Do you ask, Mr. Davidson, if Scouts or proposed Scout leaders are adulterers? Is that one of the questions?
>
> Mr. Davidson: No, Justice Scalia.
>
> Justice Scalia: Do you ask if they're ax murderers?
>
> Mr. Davidson: No, Justice Scalia.

A reasonable person might think that the Scouts *should* make an effort to screen out ax murderers—or pedophiles—from their leadership ranks. A reasonable person might also conclude that comparing homosexuals with ax murderers was offensive. Sensing that Scalia's analogy wasn't helping his cause, Davidson steered his answer in a different direction. He respectfully suggested to Breyer that "as a matter of First Amendment law" he was "not sure" that it mattered whether the policy was grounded in concerns about how the public might react to homosexual leaders or in the organization's belief that homosexual conduct was not morally straight. "That [the legal relevance of this distinction] was something I was going to figure out later," the good-humored Breyer admitted, bringing laughter from the audience for the first time.

O'Connor had a different question. Should it matter "in the balance that the Court strikes," she wanted to know, "that the Scouts are a federally chartered institution and that government entities such as schools and fire departments and police departments and so on sponsor troop units"? Davidson dismissed the significance of the federal charter: "virtually everything conducted in the corporate forum," he said, "is necessarily chartered by a government entity." As for the sponsorship question, every sponsor of a Scout troop, whether governmental or not, "signs on to follow Scouting's values and procedures." If a governmental entity decided that they could not, "for political or legal reasons," sponsor a Scout unit, then "their remedy is to not continue to support Scouting." Kennedy followed up with the obvious next question: wouldn't New Jersey's public schools and fire and police departments be *required*, in order to comply with New Jersey law as interpreted by the state supreme court, "to sever their relations with the Scouts"? Davidson admitted, "that may well be." Scalia jumped in: so the Scouts' position was that if government assistance to the Scouts presented a problem "you'd rather . . . not have the assistance than have to change your policies"? Absolutely, Davidson agreed: "The Scouts have said many times that their policies are not for sale, and if it costs the sponsorship, . . . so be it."

Davidson's time was running out, but Souter wanted a final crack at the Scouts' attorney. Souter was clearly vexed by the Scouts' reliance on the Court's decision in the 1995 case *Hurley v. Irish American Gay, Lesbian, and Bisexual Group of Boston*. Writing for a unanimous Court in *Hurley*, Souter had argued that the parade organizers had a First Amendment right to exclude the Gay, Lesbian and Bisexual Group (GLIB) because the inclusion of GLIB would create a situation in which a person watching the parade could reasonably infer that the parade organizers were sending an expressive message that they endorsed gay and lesbian rights. Davidson maintained that the Scouts' case was in fact "far stronger" than the parade organizers' case in *Hurley* because "there was no readily apparent . . . message in the parade," whereas in the case of the Scouts there was "a moral code, which has been recited in unison at virtually every meeting by all the adults and boys in the program since 1910, in which they promise to be morally straight and clean in thought, word, and deed." Souter objected to the parallel. In *Hurley*, GLIB was trying to use the parade to express a message, whereas in giving an interview in the New Jersey newspaper Dale was not "using the Boy Scouts, or proposing to use the Boy Scouts for expression." Indeed Dale's association with the Boy Scouts was not even mentioned in the story.

Unlike GLIB, Souter insisted, Dale had "not, in effect, asked to carry a banner." Davidson countered that Dale "put a banner around his neck when he . . . got himself into the newspaper." Having "created a reputation" for himself, Dale necessarily "requires Boy Scouting to identify with that message that [he] has created," namely, that it is OK to be homosexual. With that, Davidson was done. Now it was Evan Wolfson's turn to spar with the justices.

Although this was the first time Wolfson had argued a case before the US Supreme Court, it was not the first time he had had a good seat at the Court. Fourteen years earlier, in the spring of 1986, he sat next to the plaintiff Michael Hardwick as the Supreme Court heard oral arguments in *Bowers v. Hardwick*. Listening to the questions that the justices posed that day left Wolfson with the lasting impression that the Court was "a very hostile place" for gays. Not to mention ignorant: Justice Lewis Powell, the decisive fifth vote in *Bowers*, told his law clerk at the time that he had never met a homosexual. (Unbeknown to Powell, the clerk was gay.) The defeat in *Bowers* had plunged Wolfson into an uncharacteristic funk, and he spent the next few days "wondering how I could be a lawyer, how I could be part of [a] system" that seemed so patently unjust. But Wolfson never really seriously contemplated leaving the law. Instead, *Bowers* only fueled his determination to use the law to change public attitudes and public policies toward gays and lesbians.

Bowers had been a searing personal experience for Wolfson, one that he literally carried with him every day in the form of a pink triangle-shaped pin that he wore to protest the Court's judgment.

Court etiquette frowned upon counsel wearing protest pins, particularly when the protest was aimed at them (two of the justices, Rehnquist and O'Connor, sided with the *Bowers* majority), so Wolfson defended Dale sans pin. But the depth of Wolfson's feelings was evident in his choice of tie, which "subtly incorporated the image" of the pink triangle pin.

Wolfson began by addressing the Court in the same words used by every lawyer appearing before the Court: "Mr. Chief Justice, and may it please the Court." Davidson had managed another two sentences before being interrupted; Wolfson managed to squeeze in three:

> The State of New Jersey has a neutral civil rights law of general applicability that is aimed at discriminatory practices, not expression. The law protects gay and nongay people within New Jersey against discrimination based on their sexual orientation. Although it is one of the least private public accommodations in the country, BSA is here today asking this Court to specially excuse it from compliance with that content-neutral. . . .

That was as far as Wolfson got before Justice O'Connor cut him off: "Mr. Wolfson," O'Connor started, "I suppose literally the policy of New Jersey would require the Boy Scouts to admit girls as well." Did he take the position, then, that New Jersey law required the BSA to admit girls?

Wolfson responded that there were "several reasons" that the exclusion of girls did not follow from New Jersey's policy. The first of these was that the New Jersey statute specifically exempted public accommodations that were "reasonably restricted exclusively to individuals of one sex." Before Wolfson could identify reason number two, Justice Souter jumped in with a hypothetical. What if New Jersey eliminated its exemption? Would the BSA then have to accept girls? Wolfson thought that an "unlikely event," but even if the state dropped its exemption, the Scouts would be able to prevail on the First Amendment grounds that admitting girls impermissibly burdened the organization's expressive message. Souter seemed skeptical. Did the Scouts have "an antigirl message"? Wolfson agreed that the Scouts did not have such a message. In that case, Souter noted, wasn't the constitutional case for excluding girls weaker than the constitutional case for excluding gays since the Scouts claimed to have an "antihomosexual . . . message" but did not claim to have an antigirl message? Wolfson disagreed. The Scouts' explicit "self-identity and purposes," he countered, were far more closely related to gender, "beginning with the name of the organization," than they were to homosexuality.

Wolfson's suggestion that the Scouts might have a First Amendment right to exclude girls brought Justice Ginsburg into the argument. Wolfson was, in many ways, a younger version of Ginsburg. Both were Brooklyn-born, liberal Jews. When Ginsburg was Wolfson's age, she was head of the pioneering Women's Rights Project at the American Civil Liberties Union, a project that she cofounded in 1971 and which provided the model for the ACLU's Sexual Privacy Project (later renamed the Gay and Lesbian Rights Project). As the chief litigator for the Women's Rights Project, Ginsburg argued several landmark cases in the 1970s that made the Equal Protection Clause applicable to women. As the head of Lambda's Marriage Project, Wolfson aspired to do for gay and lesbian rights what Ginsburg had done for women's rights.

The parallels were not lost on Ginsburg. But she was nonplussed that Wolfson defended gay rights by seeming to diminish the importance of gender equity in the Scouts. Ginsburg noted "a certain irony" that Wolfson was relying on *Jaycees* and *Rotary*, both cases involving sex discrimination, and yet suggesting that New Jersey's antidiscrimination laws were more permissive toward sex discrimination than discrimination based on sexual orientation. Ginsburg took issue with Wolfson's speculation that the Boy Scouts' exclusion of girls would be protected by New Jersey's "single sex" exception. The "reasonable" exceptions envisioned by the law, after all, were aimed at public accommodations such as restrooms and changing rooms, not an organization like the Boy Scouts.

Wolfson was caught between a rock (O'Connor) and a hard place (Ginsburg). Realizing that there was no way out from the trap O'Connor had laid for him, he confessed to Ginsburg that "the best I can come up with in regard to the admission of girls is that obviously that question is not presented before this Court" and that therefore there was no reason for the Court to reach that question.

After assuring Ginsburg that he was "certainly not here to defend [the] exclusion of girls" from the Scouts, Wolfson tried to guide the conversation back to the question before the Court, namely, whether admitting Dale would unconstitutionally burden the "Boy Scouts' ability to convey or express any message with regard to sexual orientation or homosexuality." Wolfson maintained that admitting Dale would not burden the Scouts because the record before the Court showed that an antigay message, "in fact, is not conveyed to youth members and is not conveyed to any adult member or sponsoring organization or Scoutmaster."

O'Connor accepted Wolfson's plea to return to the question of exclusion based on sexual orientation. "What about," she now asked, "a gay or lesbian group that takes the position that it does not want heterosexual members to participate, or be admitted?" Would the New Jersey law prevent such a group from discriminating against heterosexuals? Wolfson was quick with an answer. Assuming the organization was deemed a public accommodation, then, the answer was clearly yes: the gay and lesbian group could not exclude on the basis of a person's sexual orientation.

Next O'Connor pushed Wolfson on the distinction between commercial and expressive associations that she had made the crux of her concurring opinion in *Roberts*. O'Connor said that she understood that "a public accommodation law should apply to commercial groups, or even to groups such as Jaycees, which essentially depend on a commercial nexus for its membership." But should the Court apply the same scrutiny to the membership policies of "private membership groups" that did not have a commercial purpose or provide economic advantages in the workplace?

Wolfson was prepared for this question and pushed back forcefully. He reminded O'Connor that the Court had "never held that the State's important interest in eliminating discrimination . . . is limited to the commercial sphere." In *Roberts* the Court held instead that the state had an interest in ending discrimination in public accommodations that limited not only economic but also political and cultural opportunities. To restrict the application of public accommodations laws to commercial associations would radically restrict the state's ability to eradicate discrimination. Little League, for instance, would still be free to exclude girls if antidiscrimination statutes applied only to commercial associations and economic opportunities.

Rehnquist, who had been uncharacteristically quiet, now stepped in to move the conversation in a different direction. Rather than focus on what type of organization the Scouts were, Rehnquist wanted to discuss whether sexual orientation was a category that deserved constitutional protection. The Fourteenth Amendment's equal protection principles focused on "immutable characteristics" such as race and national origins. Homosexuality seemed to be "not quite the same." Rehnquist then posed a hypothetical: What if New Jersey amended its antidiscrimination law to include "ex-convicts"? In such cases did the state really have a compelling interest in ending discrimination?

It was not the first time a judge in Dale's case had likened being homosexual to being a criminal; Judge McGann had done the same thing in his opinion. Still, Rehnquist's bizarre hypothetical must have taken Wolfson by surprise. He stumbled initially: "Well, first of all, we do not honor, Mr. Chief Justice . . . sorry." Then he found his feet. It was not necessary, he told Rehnquist, for the Court to find that the state had a compelling interest in banning discrimination against gays and lesbians. Rather the appropriate analysis was to ascertain the burden that the application of the law placed on the "expressive purposes" of the Scouts, and then to "weigh" that burden against the state's interest in ending discrimination against gays and lesbians. That interest need not be compelling for Dale to prevail, especially if the burden on the Scouts' expressive purposes was minimal.

Rehnquist wasn't satisfied with the answer. Nor did he want to give up on his offensive analogy between homosexuals and ex-cons. "Wouldn't the State's interest be weaker," he asked, "if we're talking about, say, ex-convicts being discriminated against than it would [if we were talking] about blacks being discriminated against?" Rather than assent to the obvious, Wolfson reminded Rehnquist that just four years ago, in *Romer v. Evans* (1996), the Court noted "the legitimacy and appropriateness of State civil rights laws that include sexual orientation discrimination within the cluster of prohibited classifications." Gays and lesbians, in other words, weren't the same as ex-cons in the law's eyes; states could and did deprive ex-cons of voting rights; they could not deprive homosexuals of that right. Rehnquist, of course, had been one of the three *Romer* dissenters who would have allowed Colorado to make gays and lesbians second-class citizens. Wolfson's invocation of *Romer* clearly annoyed the chief justice, who huffed: "Well, that doesn't really answer my question at all." Still Rehnquist persisted in getting Wolfson to answer a question to which both men already knew the answer. "I asked you," the chief justice repeated, "if the State interest would be weaker if we were talking about ex-convicts." If Rehnquist expected an answer on the third asking, he was to be disappointed. "I think on this record it's difficult to answer that question," Wolfson told the chief justice.

With Wolfson and Rehnquist at loggerheads, Justice Breyer directed the conversation back to the question of the Scouts' expressive rights. Breyer noted that the Court was bound by the state court's interpretation of its public accommodation laws. So what if New Jersey decided that its public accommodation law applied to the Knights of Columbus or B'nai B'rith, for instance? Would the Knights of Columbus then have to accept Jews and B'nai B'rith have to accept Catholics? Could the Court do anything about that?

Wolfson thought it highly improbable that a state court would ever find that explicitly religious organizations such as the Knights of Columbus qualified as public accommodations. The New Jersey law, after all, explicitly exempted religious organizations, as did most all public accommodation statutes. But in that unlikely event, Wolfson said, "the constitutional question [was] whether the organization has born its heavy burden of winning an excuse from compliance with the law based on its ability to show . . . a specific expressive purpose that brings its members together that is being significantly burdened" by being forced to admit non-Catholics or non-Jews or, in the case of the Scouts, homosexuals. For an explicitly Jewish organization to be forced to admit non-Jews might be just such an exemption. Wolfson's answer here seemed in tension with the answer he had given earlier to Justice O'Connor when he assured her that a gay or lesbian group deemed a public accommodation could not exclude heterosexual members. Under the methodology Wolfson now offered to Breyer, it appeared possible that a gay and lesbian group, even if it was deemed a public accommodation, could demonstrate that it should not be forced by the state to include heterosexuals.

Breyer did not pursue that tension, but he did want to know how Wolfson thought the Court should go about determining whether heterosexuality was fundamental to the Boy Scouts' identity and expressive purpose. Breyer's question brought Scalia into the conversation. Scalia thought that there could be no doubt "that one of the purposes of the Boy Scouts, if not its primary purpose, [was] moral formation, the Scout's oath, and all that good stuff." And if the leaders of the Boy Scouts asserted that one important element of that moral formation project was teaching that homosexuality is immoral, Scalia could not see "why we have any power to question" the organization's claim.

Wolfson countered that New Jersey's law did not restrict what the BSA could say or what messages it wished to express. It did not even stop the Scouts from restricting what individual Scouts could express. What the law did prohibit, Wolfson insisted, was "identity-based discrimination in its membership practices." Scalia's next question probed to the heart of the Boy Scouts' case: "You think it does not limit the ability of the Boy Scouts to convey its message to require the Boy Scouts to have as a Scoutmaster someone who embodies a contradiction of its message, whether the person wears a sign or not? . . . If the person is publicly known to be an embodiment of . . . a contradiction of its moral message, how can that not dilute the message?"

Dale's case rested upon the argument that opposition to homosexuality was not in fact integral to the moral message taught by Scouting. But for the sake of argument, Wolfson granted Scalia's premise that opposition to homosexuality was an important part of Scouting's expressive purpose. Even if opposition to homosexuality was part of Scouting's purpose, Wolfson contended, "a human being such as Mr. Dale is not speech." Scalia batted away that answer by noting that the Court had long accepted that expression need not be limited to speech. Flag burning and wearing armbands were protected under the First Amendment, even though neither is literally speech. Under the Court's First Amendment jurisprudence, Scalia noted, government was prevented "from diluting or imperiling the message that an organization wants to convey." Whether the message was conveyed by speech was not essential.

By conceding Scalia's premise, even if only for the sake of argument, Wolfson had invited trouble. Kennedy immediately seized on the admission, noting that Wolfson's answer "seemed to assume . . . that the Boy Scouts do have a moral message." Wolfson reminded Kennedy that it was Scalia who posited that the Boy Scouts had a moral message against homosexuality, and he had explicitly stated that he granted that premise purely "arguendo" (for the sake of argument). Kennedy backed off on that point, but returned to a question similar to the one Scalia had posed earlier: "who is better qualified to determine the expressive purpose and expressive content of the Boy Scouts' message, the Boy Scouts or the New Jersey courts?" Wolfson answered that the courts had an obligation to make their own inquiry into whether the law burdened the Boy Scouts' "ability to deliver the specific expressive purpose for which they come together." Judges could not just take the organization's word for it, but must look to the record to evaluate whether the organization had the expressive message that its leaders claimed. If the courts simply deferred to the organization, then the organization would prevail over civil rights law every time.

Rehnquist pushed Wolfson on his insistence that an organization must have a specific expressive purpose to warrant constitutional protection. Couldn't an organization such as the Knights of Columbus exclude non-Catholics even if it didn't have an anti-Protestant or anti-Jewish expressive purpose? Maybe the members "just feel much more comfortable with Catholics" or they "do Catholic work." Rehnquist intended his question to direct Wolfson "away from freedom of speech to freedom of association." Wolfson conceded that freedom of association was protected by the First Amendment but said that it was "an instrumental right in furtherance of the expression of the members." Rehnquist demanded to know on what "authority" Wolfson based this claim. Wolfson replied that his authority was the Court's ruling in *Roberts* as well as subsequent cases in which the Court "declined . . . to recognize some kind of free-floating . . . freedom [of] disassociation that can be exercised in the absence of some kind of expressive purpose as a defense against civil rights laws." The Court had rightly rejected a broad conception of freedom of association that was divorced from expressive—or intimate—association because otherwise the right to disassociate "would swallow civil rights laws." Indeed it was this broader, "free-floating" right of disassociation that the Boy Scouts had proposed in their amicus brief in *Roberts* and that the Court had rejected.

Souter wanted to know what would happen if tomorrow the Boy Scouts took steps to amend all their official statements and their handbooks to make it clear to members and the general public that opposition to homosexuality was central to the Scouts' understanding of morality? What if the Scouts, for instance, changed the handbook's explication of morally straight so that it included a denunciation of homosexual conduct? Wolfson conceded that this would indeed make it a very different case since the Scouts would then have a far stronger case that they had an expressive message regarding homosexuality that was systematically communicated to members.

Scalia pounced on this admission to point out the paradox of the Court finding against the Scouts. If Wolfson's position prevailed, Scalia noted, then he "will have succeeded in . . . inducing the Boy Scouts of America to be more openly and avowedly opposed to homosexual conduct in all of its publications." Instead of opening the Scouts to gays, the Court would only turn the BSA into an avowedly antigay institution. Wolfson said he thought that was highly unlikely. The Boy Scouts had been in litigation on this issue for nineteen years and yet in all that time they had never modified the *Boy Scout Handbook* or the *Scoutmaster's Handbook* to make opposition to homosexuality an explicit part of their expressive message. They had not done so, Wolfson speculated, not because they feared losing gay people but because they were "afraid of losing the nongay people who . . . do not agree with this policy" and who thought sexual orientation was irrelevant to the purposes of Scouting.

Scalia proposed "a distinction between being an antigay organization and having a policy of disapproving of homosexual conduct." The Boy Scouts' position was not that opposition to homosexuality was its "raison d'etre" but rather that its "moral code" included a disapproval of homosexual conduct. The BSA, Scalia reiterated, should not have to turn itself into an antigay organization to assert a constitutional right to exclude gays.

Wolfson clearly hadn't persuaded Scalia or Rehnquist, but then he had never expected to. Clarence Thomas had remained characteristically mute throughout the oral argument, but nobody doubted where the Court's most rigidly conservative justice would come down. The Court's four liberal justices, especially Breyer, Souter, and Ginsburg, were more difficult to read. All had asked Wolfson skeptical questions, but they had asked even tougher ones of Davidson, leaving Wolfson hopeful that he had secured their votes. That would leave the case in the hands of the two swing justices, as both sides had assumed all along. Kennedy's questions, though, strongly suggested he was looking for a way to side with the Boy Scouts. O'Connor's intentions were more difficult to divine from the grilling she meted out to both counsels. Wolfson had gone into the oral argument believing that Kennedy was the most likely candidate for a fifth vote in Dale's favor, but he left convinced that if Dale was to prevail it would be O'Connor and not Kennedy who would provide the crucial vote.

The Court's questioning left many experienced Court observers feeling genuinely uncertain about the outcome. The *Washington Post*'s Supreme Court correspondent Joan Biskupic reported that having "bombarded both sides with pointed questions," the justices had left "no clear sign" of how they would decide the case. Many observers sympathetic to Dale had gone into the oral argument believing that the Scouts would prevail on First Amendment grounds, but now they were not so sure. After viewing the oral argument, Georgetown law professor Michael Gottesman, who had argued eighteen cases before the US Supreme Court dating back to the 1960s, declared that "the case can go either way." Gottesman was encouraged that the justices' questions, apart from those posed by Rehnquist and Scalia, "suggested that this was really a hard case and there will be a delicate line between what [the Scouts] can do and what they can't."

The litigants would have to wait several months to find out the Court's decision, but on this day at least Wolfson found himself thinking less about what the Court would do than how far the movement for gay civil rights and the Court had progressed since the dark days of *Bowers*. As he emerged that morning onto the sunlit steps of a plaza "swarming with press and demonstrators," Wolfson was "suddenly hit" with what a "genuinely glorious day this was." It was a day of great celebration, almost "like a bar mitzvah," Wolfson recalled. His mood grew more ebullient still when on his return that evening to New York City he learned that Governor Howard Dean had signed a bill making Vermont the first state in the nation to legalize civil unions for same-sex couples—a law that was a direct response to the state supreme court's groundbreaking ruling in *Baker v. Vermont* (1999), a case in which Wolfson had played an important part as the author of an amicus brief filed on behalf of Lambda Legal and the Vermont Coalition for Lesbian and Gay Rights. Win or lose in *Dale*, the future for gay and lesbian civil rights seemed brighter than it ever had before. "However the Court decides," predicted Dale, "we've already won."

CHAPTER 12

A Decision Is Announced

Many of us carry around visions of Supreme Court justices thinking long and hard about which side to take in a case, and arguing vigorously with one another about the proper outcome. The reality, though, is usually different. Typical of the justice's "deliberations" was their morning conference in Dale's case.

On Friday morning, forty-eight hours after hearing oral argument in Dale's case, the justices convened for their twice-a-week conference (they also meet Wednesday afternoons). The conference began the same way it has since the late nineteenth century: with the traditional handshakes between the justices. Chief Justice William Rehnquist took his accustomed place at the head of the large conference table, Justice John Paul Stevens sat at the other end, and the other seven justices took their assigned seats along the table's two long sides: the three next most senior (Sandra Day O'Connor, Antonin Scalia, and Anthony Kennedy) on one side, the four most junior (David Souter, Clarence Thomas, Ruth Bader Ginsburg, and Stephen Breyer) crowded on the other side. Nobody else is allowed in the room, ever. No clerks, no secretaries, no guards, nobody.

Especially under Rehnquist's stewardship, the conference was no place for debate. Instead, each justice briefly outlined their views of the case and stated how they intended to vote. A justice who "went on too long" could be expected to be cut off by an impatient chief. "It will come out in the writing," he would tell them. Votes cast in conference can be changed but they rarely are. One of the most famous postconference switches came in *Planned Parenthood v. Casey* (1992), when Justice Kennedy initially voted at conference to uphold all of Pennsylvania's restrictions on abortions, only to later change his mind and join Justices Souter and O'Connor in a historic plurality opinion that saved the constitutional right to an abortion established in *Roe v. Wade* (1973). But postconference vote switches are the exception, occurring maybe once or twice a term at most. In the overwhelming number of cases, the initial vote is the decision.

As with the seating arrangements, the order in which the justice speaks at conference is dictated by seniority. The chief justice speaks first. To nobody's surprise, Rehnquist declared his support for the Boy Scouts' position. Next up was Justice John Paul Stevens, who explained, for the fortieth time this term, why he disagreed with the chief. O'Connor, the next most senior justice, agreed with Rehnquist. O'Connor's vote would hardly have come as a surprise to her fellow justices. It was the forty-fourth time out of fifty nonunanimous votes this term in which O'Connor took the side of her chief, a dear friend (briefly boyfriend) whom she had known since their days together at Stanford Law School (Rehnquist graduated first, O'Connor third). No other two justices, not even Scalia and Thomas, voted together during the 1999–2000 term as often as Rehnquist and O'Connor. There were only a tiny handful of cases in which O'Connor sided with Stevens over Rehnquist, the most significant of which involved abortion, where the two friends had long since learned to agree to disagree.

Dale's only hope now rested with Justice Kennedy. Although Kennedy could sometimes be the Court's wildcard, there was little in Kennedy's questioning at oral argument that would have given Stevens much hope that his colleague would join him in supporting Dale. And even though Kennedy did not vote with Rehnquist as reliably as O'Connor did, Stevens and the other liberal justices knew that Kennedy voted with the chief far more often than he voted with the liberal Stevens—more than three times as often. In fact there was no justice on the Court that term that Kennedy sided with more often than the chief justice, and no justice on the Court that Kennedy opposed more frequently than Stevens. Dale's chances for victory were vanishingly small.

Before Kennedy could cast his vote, though, it was the turn of Justice Scalia, who made it three-to-one for the Boy Scouts. Kennedy spoke next. He brought the drama to an end by announcing his support for overturning the New Jersey Supreme Court and upholding the Scouts' right to exclude Dale. Rehnquist still needed one more vote, but there was no doubting that Thomas, the Court's only African American, would provide it. The only real question remaining was whether this would be yet another 5–4 decision split along conservative and liberal lines, or whether there would be broad agreement across ideological lines that the Scouts' First Amendment rights should prevail. There was some reason to think the latter outcome was possible. Justices Souter, Ginsburg, and Breyer had each peppered Evan Wolfson with tough questions. Moreover, in the recent past, freedom of association cases had not divided the Court into ideological camps. The Court's rulings in *Roberts*, *Rotary*, and *Hurley* had all been issued without a single dissent. The question now was whether the Court would speak with a relatively united voice or an ideologically fractured one.

The answer to that question began to take shape when Souter, the author of the Court's *Hurley* opinion, told the group that he agreed with Stevens, ensuring that there would be at least two votes for Dale. Thomas was next and, as everybody expected, he gave Rehnquist the fifth vote the chief needed. Last to speak were the Court's two most junior justices and the lone Democrats. Ginsburg followed by Breyer confirmed that they would vote in favor of Dale. For the eighteenth time that term, the Court was divided 5–4. And for the eleventh time, the Court's five conservative justices voted together to defeat the Court's four liberal justices.

Still to be decided was who would write the Court's opinion. The choice of author falls to the chief justice when, as in *Dale*, he is in the majority; if the chief justice is in the minority, then the most senior justice in the majority coalition assigns the opinion. Of the previous ten cases that term in which the five conservatives had prevailed over the four liberals, Rehnquist had assigned himself the task of writing the majority opinion in four of them; no other conservative justice got the nod more than twice. One might have expected Rehnquist to use the case to even up the numbers. But instead, for the fifth time this term, Rehnquist decided that he would author the majority opinion in a 5–4 decision.

Without access to Rehnquist's papers—which will not be opened until after the last of the justices he served with at the time is dead—it is impossible to say for sure why Rehnquist opted to write the opinion. And even then the reasons may not be entirely clear. His decision does suggest that he was not worried about either O'Connor or Kennedy defecting. Had he felt that one of their votes was at risk, he likely would have given them the responsibility of crafting the Court's opinion. But that strategic calculation does not answer the question of why he would want to write the opinion rather than assign it to one of the other conservative justices. In other words, why did Rehnquist want his name attached to the Court's opinion in this case? The answer lies in Rehnquist's past.

Four decades earlier, when he was a prominent conservative lawyer in Phoenix, Rehnquist "aggressively fought local antidiscrimination laws." In 1964 he showed up at a city council meeting in Phoenix to testify against a proposed public accommodations ordinance that would have required restaurants, lunch counters, and shops to serve people regardless of their race. Such a law, Rehnquist insisted, was an unprecedented and unconstitutional assault on property rights, understood not just as "the right to make a buck but the right to manage your own affairs as free as possible from the interference of government." Rehnquist was one of only three people (out of thirty-three who spoke) to testify against the antidiscrimination ordinance.

A decade before that, as a law clerk for Justice Robert Jackson, Rehnquist complained bitterly about the "pathological search for discrimination" in society. The case that prompted that complaint was *Terry v. Adams*, a suit brought by African American voters in Texas who had been excluded from voting in the Jaybird Democratic Association, a private all-white club that functioned as the de facto primary for the selection of Democratic Party candidates for county offices. When Rehnquist learned that a majority on the Court agreed that this arrangement violated the right to vote, he urged Jackson to file a dissent. "It is about time," Rehnquist wrote, that "the Court faced the fact that white people in the South don't like the colored people; the Constitution restrains them from effecting this dislike through state action, but it most assuredly did not appoint the Court as a sociological watchdog to rear up every time private discrimination raises its admittedly ugly head." In finding for the black plaintiffs, Rehnquist maintained, the Court dangerously "pushes back the frontier of freedom of association and majority rule." Justice Jackson paid no heed to his clerk's memo and voted with the Court majority. Jackson also disregarded his clerk's advice to take the "unpopular" position in *Brown v. Board of Education* of affirming *Plessy v. Ferguson*'s holding that racial segregation was constitutional—instead, Jackson agreed with the rest of the Court that separate but equal was inherently unequal.

Rehnquist had no success in persuading Jackson or the Phoenix City Council, but he was spectacularly successful in persuading his friend and erstwhile civil rights proponent Barry Goldwater to oppose the Civil Rights Act of 1964. Senator Goldwater had backed local antidiscrimination laws like the one in Phoenix and had worked to end racial segregation in the private sector and the Arizona National Guard. But in 1964, with Goldwater on the verge of accepting the Republican nomination for president, Rehnquist and a young law professor at Yale named Robert Bork persuaded Goldwater that the Civil Rights Act was unconstitutional. Bork and Rehnquist shared a deep-seated belief that the question was "not whether racial prejudice or preference is a good thing but whether individual men ought to be free to deal and associate with whom they please for whatever reasons appeal to them." Rehnquist even drafted Goldwater's televised speech on "Civil Rights and the Common Good," delivered several weeks before the November 1964 election, in which Goldwater strongly opposed efforts to use government power to integrate society. The speech included lines that had been part of Rehnquist's mantra for over a decade—as, for instance, when Goldwater declared that "our aim . . . is neither to establish a segregated society nor to establish an integrated society. It is to preserve a *free* society." Reading from Rehnquist's script, Goldwater went on:

> It is often said that only the freedom of a member of a minority is violated when some barrier keeps him from associating with others in his society. But this is wrong! Freedom of association is a double freedom or it is nothing at all. It applies to both parties who want to associate with each other. . . . We must never forget that freedom to associate means the same thing as the freedom not to associate.

A government that stopped individuals, businesses, or organizations from discriminating, Rehnquist earnestly believed, would no longer be a free society.

In later years, Rehnquist would disavow his earlier segregationist views. Indeed when his 1952 memo endorsing *Plessy v. Ferguson* was revealed immediately prior to the Senate's vote on his Supreme Court nomination in 1971, Rehnquist insisted that the views expressed in the memo were not his, but were instead a summary of Justice Jackson's views that he had been asked to prepare. That was untrue. The memo clearly reflected Rehnquist's own views; indeed, nowhere in the many boxes of Jackson's papers is there an instance of Jackson asking a clerk to write a memo summarizing the justice's own views. But while Rehnquist's views of segregation and race changed with the times (he learned, for instance, not to call African Americans "jungle bunnies," as he had in the early 1960s), his philosophical skepticism about antidiscrimination laws remained undimmed. Although he chose not to write a dissent in *Roberts v. Jaycees*, he conspicuously refused to sign either Brennan's majority opinion or O'Connor's concurrence. He jumped at the chance to write the opinion in *Dale* because the case was an ideal vehicle for him to affirm what he had believed all his life: namely, that applying antidiscrimination laws to private associations posed a profound threat to freedom and violated the Constitution.

Although Rehnquist knew the opinion he wanted to write, that did not mean that he would draft the opinion. Instead, that task was delegated, as always, to one of his three law clerks. That was not a peculiarity of the chief justice, but instead was common practice with all but one of the Court's justices. The only justice who still insisted on writing the first draft of every opinion was Stevens, who believed "that without forcing himself through the exercise—most importantly, reading large parts of the record and summarizing the facts of the case—it would be too easy to avoid engaging fully." Because the relevant portions of Rehnquist's papers have not been opened—and clerks are sworn to secrecy—we can't know the directions Rehnquist gave to the clerk who prepared the opinion, but the chief justice was likely quite precise about how the opinion should be framed. Certainly the clerk was "not off on a frolic of his own" but engaged in what Rehnquist described as a "highly structured task." Kevin Boyle, one of Rehnquist's clerks during that term, confirms that he invariably "received detailed instructions as to how the case was to be decided and the rationale for the decision," as well as clear "instructions as to what the key facts and arguments should be." The one invariant rule under the punctilious Rehnquist was that clerks had to show the chief a draft within ten days. Once Rehnquist had a draft in hand, his role in the opinion-writing process was typically as an editor, and often his edits were minor, particularly later in the term when his clerks had adjusted to Rehnquist's preference for spare language and succinct opinions. Although we don't know how much editing or rewriting Rehnquist did in the *Dale* opinion specifically, we do know that the opinion was characteristically terse, checking in at fewer than twenty pages and with only four footnotes.

Inside the Court there was no suspense about the outcome of the case. But outside the Court, the interested parties waited on tenterhooks for the result to be revealed. The Court sets aside certain days for opinions to be announced, but it does not disclose ahead of time what opinions will be announced on which days, let alone what the verdict will be. Advance texts, media alerts, and strategic leaks are standard operating procedure when the executive branch announces a decision, but the Court cloaks its decisions in the utmost secrecy until they are revealed to the public.

However, the audience in the courtroom on Wednesday, June 28, 2000, did know for certain that the Supreme Court would issue its ruling in *Dale* that morning. That was because it was the final day of the Court's term and Dale's case was one of only four cases that had not yet been announced: the others involved Nebraska's ban on late-term abortions (*Stenberg v. Carhart*), federal support of parochial schools (*Mitchell v. Helms*), and a Colorado law that required protesters to stay at least eight feet away from a person entering an abortion clinic (*Hill v. Colorado*).

At ten o'clock, the expectant audience rose to their feet as the poker-faced justices solemnly filed in and assumed their customary seats. This carefully choreographed legal spectacle is structured to maximize drama and suspense. The morning's events begin with the chief justice announcing that a case has been decided, but he never reveals the outcome, only the name of the justice tasked with writing the Court's opinion. It then falls to the opinion-writing justice to announce the Court's decision. But the justice begins not with the outcome, let alone the vote, but with a summary of the principal facts of the case. Only as the justice elaborates upon the legal analysis—which is condensed or excerpted from the written opinion—does the audience discover what the Court has decided and why. And only at the very close of his statement does the justice reveal how the other justices voted and who dissented.

Chief Justice Rehnquist opened the tense drama on the last day of the 1999–2000 term with the announcement that "the opinion of the Court in No. 99-830, Stenberg against Carhart, will be announced by Justice Breyer." For experienced Court watchers that one sentence was sufficient to signal that the Court's prochoice liberal wing had prevailed and that the restrictive Nebraska state law had been invalidated. When Breyer was finished reading his prepared statement (and after Justice Thomas read a portion of his dissent from the bench), Rehnquist next announced that the Court's opinion in *Mitchell v. Helms* would be announced by Thomas. Because Court opinions are typically announced in reverse order of seniority, a seasoned Court observer could deduce that the opinion in *Dale* would not be authored by Breyer, Ginsburg, or Thomas. But beyond that inference there was nothing yet to indicate the outcome in Dale's case. That was about to change. When Thomas finished reading from his opinion in *Mitchell v. Helms*, Rehnquist announced that "the opinion of the Court in No. 98-1856, Hill against Colorado will be announced by Justice Stevens." To the uninitiated this said nothing about Dale's case. But to those in the know, it said everything. For it meant that Rehnquist, the only justice more senior than Stevens, was almost certainly the author of the Court's opinion in *Boy Scouts of America v. Dale*. And a Rehnquist opinion, both sides were certain, could only have one result: a victory for the Scouts.

After Stevens finished reading from his opinion in *Hill v. Colorado* (and Scalia and Kennedy finished reading from their dissents), Rehnquist for the final time in the 1999–2000 term announced a case: "I have the opinion of the Court to announce in No. 99-699, the Boy Scouts of America versus Dale." It took Rehnquist 350 more words to summarize the facts of the case before he announced the Court's decision to reverse the unanimous decision of the New Jersey Supreme Court and find in favor of the Boy Scouts of America.

Rehnquist explained that the Court reached its judgment after having made four inquiries. First, the Court had to determine "whether the Boy Scouts engage in expressive association sufficient to give them First Amendment protection." The answer to this question was indisputably yes, Rehnquist said, because it was "clear from the record that the mission of the Boy Scouts is to instill a system of values in young boys."

Second, the Court had to determine "whether the Boy Scouts express a view about homosexuality" specifically. And here, too, the answer was easy, according to Rehnquist. The BSA, he noted, "asserts that homosexual conduct is inconsistent with the values it seeks to instill" and that it "teaches that homosexual conduct is not morally straight." The Court, Rehnquist said, was required to "accept the Boy Scouts' assertions" because their views on homosexual conduct were "undoubtedly sincerely held." As evidence of the sincerity of these beliefs Rehnquist pointed to the Scouts' position statement from 1978, signed by the president of the Boy Scouts and the Chief Scout Executive, as well as to the position statements from 1991 and 1993 that the Scouts formulated in the wake of the Curran trial. Although the position statements had been "revised many times" over the years, the "core message [about homosexuality] remained consistent." Even more telling of the Scouts' sincerity, in Rehnquist's eyes, was that the Scouts had "been litigating this position for almost 20 years."

Third, the Court had to determine "whether Dale's presence in the Boy Scouts would significantly burden the organization's message." Rehnquist pointed out that Dale "by his own admission" was "one of a group of gay Scouts who have become leaders in their community and are open and honest about their sexual orientation." Dale was, moreover, co-president of a gay and lesbian organization in college and remains to this day "a gay rights activist." Consequently, Rehnquist concluded, Dale's "presence would force the Boy Scouts to send a message it does not desire to send that the Boy Scouts accepts homosexual conduct as a legitimate form of behavior." A person observing that an organization allowed openly gay leaders would reasonably conclude that the organization approved of or at least condoned homosexuality.

Finally, the Court needed to determine whether burdening the Scouts' expressive message violated the First Amendment. In this analysis, the Court placed "the associational interest in the freedom of expressive association on this one side of the scale, and the State's interest [in nondiscrimination] on the other." And in this case, Rehnquist continued, the state's interests could not "outweigh" the "severe intrusion" on the Scouts' First Amendment rights.

The metaphor of scales and weights is commonplace in court rulings. It makes the judgment sound precise and even mechanical, a matter of objective measurements rather than a reflection of the judge's own values and biases. The metaphor also can be way of avoiding having to explain or argue why, for instance, the "severe intrusion" on the Scouts' right of expressive association was more important than the severe intrusion on Dale's right not to be discriminated against. And indeed Rehnquist offered no explanation as to why one right should "outweigh" the other; instead, it was announced as if it were a measurable fact, as if any impartial observer looking at the scale could see that one right outweighed the other.

Rehnquist went out of his way to take issue with Justice Stevens's dissent, which noted that homosexuality was "gaining greater social acceptance." Rehnquist said that social acceptance of homosexuality was "scarcely an argument for denying First Amendment protection to those who do not accept these views." The First Amendment, Rehnquist intoned, "protects expression, be it of the popular variety or not. The fact that an idea may be embraced and advocated by increasing numbers of people is all the more reason to protect the First Amendment rights of those who wish to voice a different view." Rehnquist turned the Boy Scouts of America into the unpopular minority that needed judicial protection from the gay-loving majority.

In closing, Rehnquist insisted that the Court's decision was "not guided by our views of whether the Boy Scouts' teachings with respect to homosexual conduct are right or wrong." Instead, it was guided by a principled commitment to the First Amendment and free speech. The claim echoed directly the position that he had articulated forty years ago in his attacks on laws aimed at eradicating discrimination of blacks.

Rehnquist's pose as a principled champion of the First Amendment rings hollow. The University of Chicago law professor Geoffrey Stone has shown that in Rehnquist's thirty-three years on the Supreme Court, no justice was more consistently hostile to First Amendment arguments. Of the roughly 150 nonunanimous cases involving freedom of speech, Rehnquist voted to uphold the First Amendment claim on only eighteen occasions. In contrast, his colleagues sided with the First Amendment well over half the time. Even the Court's most conservative justices, Scalia and Thomas, voted to sustain First Amendment challenges more frequently than Rehnquist. Stone further finds that thirteen of the eighteen occasions in which Rehnquist upheld a First Amendment claim came in cases involving commercial speech, campaign finance, or religious expression (with the majority coming in campaign finance cases). A cynic, Stone notes, "might say that Rehnquist's First Amendment reads, 'Congress shall make no law abridging the freedom of speech of corporations, the wealthy, or the church.'"

What about the other five instances of nonunanimous decisions in which Rehnquist lined up behind the First Amendment? Four of these, Stone tells us, were "relatively minor decisions." Only one of the five could be counted an important case, and that one was *Boy Scouts of America v. Dale*. In other words, the only time in an important nonunanimous case not involving commercial speech, campaign finance, or religion that Rehnquist voted to uphold the First Amendment was to uphold the Scouts' right to discriminate against homosexuals.

Stone also counted twenty-seven occasions in which Rehnquist wrote the majority opinion in a First Amendment case involving freedom of speech. In twenty-one of those opinions, Rehnquist rejected the First Amendment claim. Of the six Court opinions he wrote that upheld the First Amendment claim, all but one were unanimous decisions. In thirty-three years on the US Supreme Court, the lone time that Rehnquist wrote for the Court in upholding a First Amendment claim in a nonunanimous decision was in *Dale*.

In short, Rehnquist's position in *Dale* cannot be explained by a principled commitment or instinctive bias toward the First Amendment and freedom of expression. Nor can it be attributed to Rehnquist's well-known jurisprudential philosophy that courts should defer to state legislatures, since Rehnquist was overriding the judgment of the New Jersey state legislature. Instead, his judgment in *Dale* seems to have been driven more by his long-standing distrust of antidiscrimination statutes, his unfavorable view of homosexuality, and his favorable attitude toward the Boy Scouts.

Having announced and explained the Court's judgment, Rehnquist's final, customary task was to reveal which justices had dissented. The audience by this time knew there was a dissent by Justice Stevens because Rehnquist had mentioned it, but nobody knew whether the decision was by an 8–1 or 5–4 margin. With his final words of the term, Rehnquist revealed that four justices disagreed with the Court, and that each of the other dissenters signed Stevens's dissent.

Justices who feel particularly aggrieved by the Court's judgment will often read portions of their dissent from the bench, as Thomas, Scalia, and Kennedy had already done that morning. Stevens, however, chose not to read from his opinion. Yet Stevens's dissent, which was twice as long as the chief justice's opinion and with eight times the number of footnotes, made clear the depth of the liberal dissenters' disagreement with the conservative majority.

Stevens traversed the same terrain as the appellate court and New Jersey Supreme Court. Whereas Rehnquist perceived a serious intrusion on the Scouts' expressive message, Stevens accented the "serious and tangible harm" caused by antigay prejudice. And like the lower courts, Stevens found no evidence that the expressive message communicated to Scouting youth had anything to do with homosexuality. On his reading of the record, there was no evidence of a "shared goal or collective effort to foster a belief about homosexuality." The Boy Scouts were "simply silent on homosexuality." Instead, the record demonstrated that the Scouts, beginning in 1978, adopted "an exclusionary membership policy," but the Court, Stevens insisted, had never before allowed "a claimed right to associate in the selection of members to prevail in the face of a State's antidiscrimination law. To the contrary, we have squarely held that a State's antidiscrimination law does not violate a group's right to associate simply because the law conflicts with that group's exclusionary membership policy." Stevens was particularly concerned that the Court majority was willing to defer to the Scouts' claims about their organization's views on homosexuality. "Unless one is prepared to turn the right to associate into a free pass out of discrimination laws," Stevens wrote, "an independent inquiry is a necessity."

In the name of the First Amendment, according to Stevens, the majority had created a constitutional shield for antigay prejudice, a shield that it would not have allowed had Dale been excluded because of his race. "The only apparent explanation for the majority's holding," Stevens wrote,

> is that homosexuals are simply so different from the rest of society that their presence alone—unlike any other individual's—should be singled out for special First Amendment treatment. Under the majority's reasoning, an openly gay male is irreversibly affixed with the label 'homosexual.' That label, even though unseen, communicates a message that permits his exclusion wherever he goes. His openness is the sole and sufficient justification for his ostracism. Though unintended, reliance on such a justification is tantamount to a constitutionally prescribed symbol of inferiority.

Stevens worried that the Court was helping to make gays second-class citizens.

As soon as the Court's decision was announced, reporters rushed to get Dale's reaction. Working in New York City as an advertising director for *POZ*, a magazine dedicated to serving people living with HIV/AIDS, Dale patiently explained that of course he was disappointed by the ruling, just as he was saddened that "small-minded people at the top" had hijacked an organization that had meant so much to him and to so many other gay youth seeking acceptance and community. He worried that by perpetuating the Scouts' policy the Court's decision would "teach gay kids to hate themselves," yet he remained "very, very hopeful" about the future of gay rights. He pointed, for instance, to the "more than 700 gay-straight alliances that have sprung up in high schools across the nation." The Scouts, he told reporters, were increasingly out-of-step with American society, and just as "dinosaurs became extinct because they didn't evolve," so the Scouts were "making themselves extinct" by holding on to antiquated prejudices. The Court's decision was only "a minor setback . . . in the big picture," and Dale was confident that in the near future "people are going to look back on this in shame."

Dale was not alone in feeling that history would not judge the Court or the Scouts kindly, though his reaction was measured compared to the harsh response of many liberals. Roger Wilkins, an African American lawyer and journalist who had been assistant attorney general during Lyndon Johnson's administration, likened Rehnquist's arguments to the "disgraced reasoning" of *Plessy v. Ferguson* and declared *Dale* to be "a constitutional monument to the enduring power of bigotry in our culture." Writing in the *Atlanta Journal Constitution*, the African American columnist Cynthia Tucker reached even further back in history for a still more damning analogy: *Dred Scott v. Sanford*, in which a Supreme Court dominated by Southerners infamously held that African Americans were not citizens under the Constitution. "It may not be quite as bad as the *Dred Scott* decision," Tucker acknowledged, "but it is close." Although Rehnquist had eschewed the blatant homophobia of Judge Patrick McGann, Tucker insisted that the chief justice's opinion "lent legitimacy to the bigotry of not just the Boy Scouts but also that of institutions all over America that still treat gay men and women as if they are dangerous and immoral." Tucker predicted that "one hundred years from now, historians will look back on the US Supreme Court's ruling against a gay Boy Scout troop leader as an unfortunate act of cowardice." As for the Scouts: "later generations will wonder how an otherwise good organization could have been so blinded by bigotry."

Most liberals were disturbed less by the Court's opinion—many allowed that it was a tough call that involved competing values—than the Boy Scouts' bigotry. And here especially there was an unshakable conviction that history was on their side. Typical was the opinion of Jim Fisher, an opinion writer for the *Lewiston Tribune* in Idaho. "In the end," Fisher wrote,

> it probably won't make much difference that the Boy Scouts has chosen to play the role of the Klan in the drive to full equality for gays. . . . To tell the truth, I have little doubt how it will turn out. Society's attitudes toward gay men and lesbians are changing with amazing speed. One of the reasons for that is young people are rejecting the fears and prejudices of their parents. Even the most conservative young people I meet are more tolerant toward homosexuals than the generation before theirs.

Like the bigotry of the Ku Klux Klan, that of the Scouts' leadership would be consigned before long to its rightful place in the reactionary dustbin of history.

Whereas those on the left viewed *Dale* through the prism of the righteous struggle of the civil rights movement and the nation's disgraceful history of racial discrimination, conservatives viewed the case through the lens of the culture wars, especially what they believed to be a war on religion. Liberals' responses were leavened by the smug conviction that history would bear them out, that tolerance would triumph over bigotry, and that the Court's "tragic decision" (in the words of the Feminist Majority Foundation president Eleanor Smeal) would "not stand the test of time." In contrast, conservatives harbored a darker, at times almost apocalyptic vision of the nation's future, a future from which the nation had fortunately been saved—at least for now—by the Supreme Court.

After the oral argument back in April, a small cadre of conservative attorneys who had filed amicus briefs in the case had rushed to the microphones outside the Court building to warn of the calamitous effects of the Court deciding in favor of Dale. The executive director for the Christian Legal Society predicted that public universities would "kick off campus groups that have a message with which they disagree." The general secretary to the National Clergy Council warned that "the government will have the right to tell private organizations, including religious organizations, . . . to dictate . . . what they may practice and what they may believe." Herb Titus, who ran as the vice presidential candidate on the Constitution Party ticket in the 1996 presidential election, put it most simply: if Dale prevailed "we will no longer be a free people." The *Washington*

Times agreed: a victory for Dale would mean that there would be "no privacy, no freedom of association left in this country."

Conservatives who believed that the future of freedom was at stake greeted the Court's ruling with tremendous relief. A lawyer for the Family Research Council explained that "every private association in the country [had been] in danger: student religious groups, churches, and their schools." In confirming that the Scouts were "not an appendage of the state," the Court had struck an important blow for the freedom of all groups.

For the Boys Scouts, however, the decision's significance was more prosaic. It was important not because it furthered a broader ideological crusade for freedom, but because it held out the prospect of a return to normalcy and an end to the countless lawsuits. The BSA spokesperson (and Edelman vice president) Gregg Shields told reporters that the Scouts were "very pleased" with the ruling because it would "allow us to continue in our mission of providing character building experiences for young people." James Kay, the New Jersey Scout executive who sent the initial expulsion letter to Dale, described the organization as "delighted" with the ruling. "Hopefully," he added, "this now gets put behind us."

The losing side was determined, though, not to let the Scouts put this behind them. Instead, they lobbied to brand the Scouts as a bigoted organization and vowed that the Scouts would suffer for their bigotry. They predicted that the Court's ruling would lead public agencies, schools, corporations, and even religious groups all across the country to reconsider their support for an organization that embraces an avowedly "antigay message." Wolfson predicted that the reconsideration would extend beyond sponsors and patrons to the parents and boys who participated in Scouting. "Most fair-minded members and parents," he told reporters, "are going to question whether this is the youth program they want to expose their kids to when there are other organizations out there." Ruth Harlow characterized the case as a "hollow, Pyrrhic victory," because in order to prevail the Scouts "had to demonstrate to the court's satisfaction the centrality of its opposition to homosexuality." The Scouts had "fought long and hard," she said, "for something that has marginalized and diminished them." Lambda's legal director Beatrice Dohrn agreed that this "was a lose-lose decision for everybody." Dale had lost the opportunity to be a Scout and the Scouts had "won the right to be labeled a discriminatory organization." Wolfson and the rest of Lambda's legal team were convinced that "in this day and age" that was "not a label that the Scouts could live with in the long term."

The Scouts insisted that they were unconcerned about a backlash. They believed that their values were the same as those shared by the vast majority of "American families." Shields maintained that "a lot of people like the fact we've stood up for our beliefs [and] it's made them want to get involved and get their sons involved." As evidence, he pointed to a 7 percent increase in the Scouts' membership since Dale's case "became a cause célèbre." If some donors or sponsors withdrew their support, the Scouts would have no trouble finding alternative sponsors and sources of financial support. "We'll be just fine," Shields assured reporters.

PART FOUR

In *Dale*'s Wake

CHAPTER 13

Backlash

The US Supreme Court's ruling ended Dale's decade-long legal odyssey, but victory brought the Boy Scouts no respite from court or controversy. Certainly it did not bring the return to normalcy hoped for by James Kay and other Scouting officials. Over the subsequent decade, the Scouts became ever more entangled in legal and political wrangling over its exclusion of gays. After *Dale*, the non-profits and granting agencies on which the Scouts depended for support came under mounting pressure to reconsider whether they should fund an organization that unapologetically discriminated on the basis of sexual orientation. And while the Court settled the issue of whether the Boy Scouts had a constitutional right to discriminate against gays, it raised new legal issues as public entities across the country, including schools, cities, and the military, considered cutting their ties to Scouting.

Many on the left insisted that local governments were ethically and legally obligated to end their association with Scouting. By allowing the Scouts to use public property, explained the liberal political theorist Amy Gutmann, the "state becomes a complicit (and powerful) agent in imposing symbols of inferiority on individuals because of their sexual orientation." In Gutmann's view, the Court's decision granting the Scouts the right to discriminate could only be justified if "public officials and institutions clearly dissociate themselves from [the Scouts'] discriminatory exclusion." What Gutmann called dissociation the libertarian legal scholar Richard Epstein painted as unconstitutional "state retaliation" for the group's unpopular views. Writing in the *National Review*, Epstein warned that "all forms of state retaliation are out of line." But even Epstein conceded that while the Scouts "must be sheltered from government counterattacks," they could not be protected from "the criticisms of outsiders, the loss of private contributions, and discontent among their members. To those risks, everyone is—and should be—vulnerable in a free society."

In the wake of the *Dale* decision, there was certainly plenty of discontent and dissent among Scouting's members, particularly in California and the Northeast. Eagle Scouts returned their badges, parents pulled their sons from troops, and longtime Scoutmasters resigned. A Republican state appellate court judge in California, who had participated in Scouting for more than three decades, not only resigned his post as assistant Scoutmaster but declared that remaining in the Scouts was "ethically questionable" for any judge. By far the most dramatic departure was that of the Hollywood director and Eagle Scout Steven Spielberg, a long-standing member of the Scouts' advisory board and one of the Scouts' most generous donors—he had, for instance, endowed a Scouting award for aspiring filmmakers.

Spielberg's high-profile exit was embarrassing, but the Scouts' greatest concern was the possible erosion of private contributions, especially from United Way. Of course, this was not a new concern. Local United Way chapters had been under pressure to withdraw funding for much of the previous decade. As we saw in chapter 4, Tim Curran's case prompted the Bay Area United Way to pull funding from the Scouts in 1991. Similarly, outrage at the ouster of David Knapp in 1993 by Connecticut's Quinnipiac Council prompted the United Way of Greater New Haven to withdraw funding from 250 Scouting units. But prior to the Supreme Court's ruling in *Dale*, controversy over United Way funding was generally limited to the particular locale in which a Scout had been expelled. Now the controversy became national in scope, as gay and lesbian individuals and groups—including Lambda—intensified their efforts to induce United Way chapters and other benefactors to end their support for the Scouts.

United Way's national office refused to be drawn into the controversy, but there was no easy escape for the more than thirteen hundred local chapters responsible for allocating monies. Local United Way board members found themselves in a "lose-lose situation." Whether they stopped or continued funding the Scouts, they risked angering many longtime United Way contributors and thus having less money to distribute to the other services that depended on United Way support, such as the Boys and Girls Club, day care centers, and hospice care. The dilemma was particularly painful because funding for the Scouts often represented only a tiny sliver of a United Way chapter's giving; the Merrimack County United Way in New Hampshire, for instance, gave less than one-tenth of 1 percent of its money to the Scouts, yet both sides threatened to make the chapter's support for the Scouts a litmus test.

Only about a dozen United Way chapters cut off funding to the Scouts in the months immediately following the Supreme Court's decision in *Dale*. Most instead tried to work out a compromise, believing that it made little sense to punish local Scouting councils for a national policy that the councils neither created nor supported. This was especially true for councils that served urban areas, where United Way funding was often crucial to sustaining Scouting programs. At the BSA national meeting in February 2001, nine of the nation's largest urban councils pleaded with the national office that they be permitted to set their own membership policies. Few councils were as outspoken as the Greater New York Councils, which derided the national policy as "repugnant" and "stupid," but many councils made little effort to conceal their disapproval of the Scouts' policy and pledged, to United Way officials and others, that they would not discriminate against gays.

United Way chapters often negotiated not only with the local Scouting council but with local gay rights groups as well. The Miami-area United Way, for instance, tried to broker a compromise that would satisfy both the Scouts' South Florida Council—which received nearly a half million dollars annually from United Way—and SAVE Dade, a gay rights advocacy organization that was fresh off a successful campaign to get the Miami-Dade County Commission to enact an ordinance banning discrimination based on sexual orientation. In July 2001, after months of negotiation, the Miami-Dade United Way announced a bargain by which United Way funding for the Scouts would continue and in exchange the council would set up a training program that would help Scout leaders "deal more sensitively with gay youth." That deal did not go down well with what the local Scout executive called "the Christian community," nor did it meet with the approval of the Scouts' national office. In a pattern that was repeated time and time again after *Dale*, the local Scouting council found itself blocked by the national office from delivering on the deal it had negotiated. After waiting almost two years for the promised sensitivity training program to materialize, the Miami-Dade United Way announced that it would no longer fund the Boy Scouts.

Many Scouting councils tried to stave off the threat of a loss of funding by adopting nondiscrimination policies. For instance, in May 2003, immediately following Miami-Dade United Way's announcement that it would no longer fund the Scouts, the BSA Cradle of Liberty Council submitted a signed statement to the Philadelphia chapter of the United Way pledging that it did not discriminate on the basis of sexual orientation. News of the statement prompted the eighteen-year-old Scout Greg Lattera to test the council's resolve by publicly disclosing his sexual orientation at a news conference in Philadelphia. Lattera was immediately expelled from the Scouts, and the council was compelled by the national office—which threatened to revoke the council's charter—to rescind its pledge not to discriminate on the basis of sexual orientation. After the *Dale* decision, the Philadelphia-area United Way had decided to continue funding the Scouts, but on the condition that the money ($400,000 annually) go only to Learning for Life, a school-based program that the Scouts established in the 1990s that eschewed the Scout Oath and Scout Law and was open to all youth and adults regardless of gender, religion, or sexual orientation. However, the Lattera controversy prompted United Way's board of directors to cut funding even for Learning for Life, which they now concluded was not really separable from the Boy Scouts.

The backlash, however, should not be exaggerated. Four years after *Dale*, the overwhelming majority of United Way's thirteen hundred chapters continued to fund the Scouts. Only fifty-six chapters scattered across twenty-one states had elected to withdraw funding, and these were concentrated overwhelmingly in urban areas, university towns, and the Northeast and West Coast. Twenty-five hailed from just three states: California, Connecticut, and Washington. The only chapters in southern states to withdraw funding were in Florida (Fort Lauderdale, Gainesville, Orlando, Miami-Dade, and Broward County) and Texas (Austin and, ironically, Dallas, home to the Scouts' national office). The antigay discrimination that outraged those who lived in blue states or blue enclaves seemed of little concern to those who lived in red states. To many people, the real outrage was the effort by the "homosexual lobby" to pressure the Scouts into changing their policy.

In the wake of *Dale*, for-profit corporations that funded the Scouts were subject to many of the same cross-pressures as the nonprofits, but few companies cut off funding to the Scouts. Some initially indicated they would. Chase Manhattan Bank, for instance, made headlines right after the *Dale* decision by announcing that it would no longer support the Scouts. "Diversity," a company spokesperson explained, "is an important issue for our company and our employees, and the ruling doesn't square with our own feeling about fairness." But in an exact replay of what happened in the early 1990s when Wells Fargo and Bank of America responded to the *Curran* case by vowing to halt funding for the Scouts, Chase Manhattan quickly reversed course under pressure from conservative religious organizations that threatened to boycott the bank. The bottom line trumped feelings about fairness. A decade after *Dale*, almost half of the top fifty corporate foundations—almost all of which had policies prohibiting gifts to groups that discriminated on the basis of sexual orientation—still gave to the Boy Scouts; the total dollar amount was around $3.6 million.

The backlash from the *Dale* decision also engulfed government, at both the federal and the local levels. A fortnight after the ruling, eleven Democratic House members, including Nancy Pelosi and Barney Frank, wrote to President Bill Clinton urging him to resign as honorary head of the Boy Scouts of America. The California representative Lynn Woolsey introduced a bill to revoke the BSA's eighty-five-year-old federal charter. The White House even ordered an investigation into whether a federal agency that aided the Scouts—for instance, by allowing the Boy Scouts to hold their jamborees on federal land—would be in violation of Clinton's new executive order banning discrimination against gays in federally conducted education and training programs, an order promulgated less than a week before the Supreme Court's ruling in *Dale* was announced.

But while these actions attracted media attention, the political currents at the federal level still ran strongly in the Boy Scouts' favor. At the Republican National Convention in July 2000, the party pledged, in words that echoed the 1992 platform, to "stand united" with the Boy Scouts of America. Judging by these platforms, the national politics of gays in the Scouts seemed barely to have budged in eight years. Republicans, including presidential nominee George W. Bush, hammered the Clinton administration for plotting to boot the Scouts off of federal lands. The charge was dropped only after the Justice Department announced, on September 1, 2000, that federal agencies could continue to support the Scouts without running afoul of Clinton's executive order. Two weeks later, by a vote of 362–12, Congress rejected Woolsey's proposal to strip the Boy Scouts of their federal charter. It was Republicans, the majority party in the House, who insisted on bringing the bill to a vote, as a way both to underscore how little support there was for the plan and to embarrass the Democrats in an election year. Only Woolsey spoke in favor of the bill, while a "long line" of Republicans denounced the bill, none more vehemently than Utah's Chris Cannon, who assailed it as an "attack on the fundamental values of America" by "a small group of extremists."

The congressional vote on Woolsey's bill was political theater, but at the local level of school boards and municipalities the combat was entered into in earnest. School districts across the country—including a number of those that had signed an amicus brief on behalf of Dale—responded to the Court's decision by announcing that they were reconsidering whether to allow public schools to sponsor Boy Scout troops, about one in ten of which was sponsored by a public school. Many also considered banning Scout troops from using school facilities for recruitment or meetings.

The Scouts could do little to prevent public schools from withdrawing their sponsorship of Scout troops, but they pushed back aggressively against the effort to bar them from using school facilities. The Scouts' national office fired off letters warning school districts that if the Boy Scouts were barred from school grounds the BSA would take them to court. No district was too small to escape the Scouts' attention. Bethel School District, home to only a few thousand Oregon students, was among those that began the new school year by barring the Scouts from recruiting on school property only to reverse course a few weeks later because of fear of legal action.

Legal threats deterred most school districts, but not the school board in Florida's Broward County, the nation's fifth largest school system. In November 2000, the Broward County School Board decided that the Scouts could no longer meet in school-owned buildings since their discriminatory policy violated the district's requirement that organizations using district buildings could not discriminate "on the basis of age, race, color, disability, gender, marital status, national origin, religion or sexual orientation." The Boy Scouts sued, arguing that Broward County was illegally singling out the Scouts on the basis of its viewpoint, noting that the district allowed school buildings to be used by other organizations that discriminated on the basis of religion and age.

The Scouts' social conservative allies jumped to the Scouts' defense. Robert Knight of the Family Research Council—the self-proclaimed "draftsman" of the federal Defense of Marriage Act of 1996—accused the Broward County School Board of "dragging [the Scouts] through the mud of 'gay' political activism." Antigay activists in Broward County responded to the school board's action by forming the "Equal Rights Not Special Rights" campaign, with the aim of qualifying a ballot measure to repeal the county's five-year-old ban on discrimination against gays and lesbians. For antigay crusaders in Broward County, the showdown with the Scouts over access to the schools was an opportunity to renew the culture wars over gay rights, a battle that had raged on and off in South Florida since 1977 when Anita Bryant launched a referendum that overturned Dade County's pioneering antigay discrimination ordinance, an ordinance that had only been reinstated in 1998.

The Scouts were careful to distance themselves from the stridently homophobic rhetoric of supporters like Knight—who warned that approval of homosexuality was "mainstreaming dysfunction"—and the "Equal Rights Not Special Rights" campaign, whose leader, the *Miami Herald* revealed, had recently been charged with sexually abusing a fifteen-year-old girl. The Scouts instead focused on the legal question of the Scouts' First Amendment rights. The BSA's spokesperson Gregg Shields insisted that the Scouts only wanted to be treated the same as every other organization. If a school district did not want to sponsor troops that was fine. "Nobody is forced to be a Boy Scout," Shields said, "and nobody is forced to be a chartering organization." But while schools were free to choose not to charter troops, they could not bar the Scouts from using public spaces if those spaces were made available to other groups in the community.

The federal judge who heard the case (*Boy Scouts of America v. Till*) acknowledged that the case was a "difficult" one, pitting as it did the school district's desire to ensure nondiscrimination based on sexual orientation and the Boy Scouts' First Amendment right to express its view that homosexuality is immoral conduct. The judge noted, however, that the school allowed many community groups to use the school grounds that limited membership based on sex (for example, pom pom and cheerleading teams), age (the Biddy Basketball League and Florida Youth Orchestra), race (an African American sorority), and religion (Baptist, Seventh Day Adventist, Catholic, and Jewish groups). Presumably, too, the school board would not have excluded a group that limited its membership to gay youth. The school board insisted that it had a compelling interest in combating discrimination based on sexual orientation and in protecting vulnerable gay students from the emotional harm that could result from being excluded from Scout activities held on school property; there was no comparable interest in allowing white women to join an African American sorority or seventeen year olds to join Biddy Basketball. The judge granted that the school board was free "to fashion its own contrary message" about homosexuality as well as to end any special relationship that schools had with Scouting, such as the district's School Night for Scouting, which was promoted by school administrators and teachers through announcements and the distribution of flyers during school hours. But in opening school facilities to a wide range of private groups during after-school hours, the judge ruled, the school board had created "a limited public forum" and therefore could not exclude the Scouts based on the content of their message about the immorality of homosexual conduct.

The Boy Scouts and their allies turned for relief not only to the courts but to federal lawmakers. Slipped into the No Child Left Behind Act of 2001—signed into law by George W. Bush in January

2002—was the Boy Scouts of America Equal Access Act, which required school districts to permit Boy Scout troops (and other "patriotic" youth groups listed in Title 36 of the United States Code) to use school property so long as other outside groups were also permitted to use those facilities. Originally the act passed by both the Senate and House included language (courtesy of amendments sponsored by two southern legislators, Senator Jesse Helms [R-NC] and Representative Van Hilleary [R-TN]) that would have prevented districts from discriminating against the Boy Scouts or any other youth group "that prohibits the acceptance of homosexuals," but the language about homosexuals was scrubbed from the final version signed by President Bush. The intent remained the same, however: to protect the Scouts from the consequences of their discrimination against gays.

In truth, the impact of the Boy Scouts Equal Access Act was more symbolic than real since it essentially codified the reigning judicial interpretation of what the Constitution required of schools that opened their doors to community groups. At the time that Congress was voting on the Equal Access Act in the late spring of 2001, the Congressional Research Service prepared a report that found few if any school districts had followed Broward County's lead in barring the Scouts from school property, in large part because the Scouts' threat of lawsuits had been effective in deterring districts. What many school districts, including in New York City and Minneapolis, were doing instead was terminating their special relationship with Scouting, sometimes under the threat of lawsuits from Lambda Legal and the American Civil Liberties Union. The Equal Access Act did nothing to prevent school districts from refusing to sponsor Scout troops and then charging Scout troops the same fee that other groups not affiliated with the school were charged for the privilege of using school premises. After losing in federal court in March 2001, that is exactly what the Broward County School Board did: it rewrote its meeting policy to require that all groups not affiliated with the school or government pay a fee to use school facilities. Unable to pay the fee, Scout troops had to find a new sponsor and meeting place or fold.

After *Dale*, the percentage of schools sponsoring Scouting units plummeted. Some of this decline in school-sponsored troops predated the Supreme Court's ruling in *Dale*. Chicago's public schools, for instance, stopped sponsoring Scout troops in 1998 as a result of a settlement reached after the ACLU of Illinois sued the Chicago School Board on the grounds that the special relationship between Scouting and the city's public schools violated both the separation of church and state and nondiscrimination laws. In 2005, in the face of persistent legal challenges and the declining number of public school–sponsored troops, the Scouts announced that all BSA units chartered by public schools would instead be sponsored by private organizations.

School districts were not the only public entities to loosen their ties to Scouting in the wake of *Dale*. Some cities took steps to terminate special arrangements that had long benefited Scouting, such as the free use of public lands and buildings. Here, too, the move to end Scouting's privileged position did not begin with the Supreme Court's ruling in *Dale*. Since at least the mid-1990s, the Scouts had been on the defensive against critics who called for an end to "sweetheart deals" for the Scouts.

In 1997, for instance, the city of Berkeley enacted an ordinance that provided free berthing at the city's marina for all nonprofits that did not discriminate on the basis of sexual orientation. On the basis of that policy, the city revoked the free berthing privileges that it had extended to the Berkeley Sea Scouts since the 1930s. Forced to pay the regular $500 monthly berthing fee, the Sea Scouts were compelled to reduce the number of boats they berthed at the marina and their membership plummeted. The Scouts sued, arguing that the city violated its First Amendment rights by withholding a privilege it granted to other organizations. In March 2006, a unanimous California Supreme Court sided with the city, ruling that the government could make subsidies to groups conditional on compliance with nondiscrimination laws. The Scouts were free to discriminate, but the government was not required to subsidize that discrimination. In October 2006, the US Supreme Court announced that it would not hear the Scouts' appeal.

In a darkly ironic postscript to the case, the heterosexual Scoutmaster (Eugene Evans) who was the lead plaintiff in the Scouts' suit against the city was arrested in 2007 for having sexually abused boys aboard a Sea Scouts' boat, a boat that for three decades he had used "as a front for his deceitful acts." One of the abused wrote a letter to the court describing his former Scout leader as "the most vile and disturbing human being I have ever known," and the deputy district attorney described him as a man who "spewed racist and homophobic slurs and showed pornographic pictures of women as he abused young boys." Evans confessed and was sentenced to six years in prison for child molestation and was required to register as a sex offender.

After *Dale*, the Scouts were put on the defensive not only in liberal bastions like Berkeley but in municipalities all across the country. No privilege was too small for those who wished to protest the Scouts' policy and the Court's ruling. The Borough Council in Princeton, New Jersey, for instance, voted to deny free parking for the local Boy Scout troop's annual Christmas tree sale unless it took a stance against the national organization's discriminatory policy. More typical was the unanimous vote of the Los Angeles City Council to sever all ties with the Scouts, including ending the city's policy of waiving fees for the Scouts' use of city facilities for camping and others activities. The council also directed the city's police and fire department to end their relationship with Scouting's vocationally oriented Explorer program and devise an alternative youth program that could be administered without the Scouts' involvement. The directive met with fierce resistance among Scouting's supporters within the LAPD and LAFD, and not until 2009, at the insistence of the city's attorney, did the police and fire departments finally cut all ties to the Scouts and set up their own vocational programs for youth interested in careers in law enforcement and firefighting.

Cities that cut their ties with the Boy Scouts often faced ferocious pushback from conservatives, at both the local and the state level. In Tempe, Arizona, for instance, the announcement that the city would no longer permit public funding to go to the Scouts or other nonprofits that supported the Scouts triggered a recall effort of the city's openly gay mayor. The mayor survived the recall vote but only after reversing course on the proposed funding cutoff. When Tucson, Arizona, stuck to its ban on public funding for the Scouts, Republican state legislators pressed for passage of the Scout Protection Act. Introduced by a follower of the Rev. Sun Myung

Moon's Unification Church, the bill forbade local governments from discriminating against or investigating the Boy Scouts, denying Scout troops access to public property, or withholding funding in an attempt to "compel" the Scouts or any other groups to adopt policies they deemed inconsistent with their "policies, programs, morals or mission." Whereas the city of Tucson insisted it was only trying to enforce its twenty-four-year-old nondiscrimination policy, the bill's proponents argued that the Scouts were being unfairly singled out for their beliefs. The bill passed in committee—as did a similar Defense of Scouting Bill in Georgia—but failed on the floor, in part because even many conservatives believed these decisions properly belonged to local governments and in part because of fears that the bill might compel local governments to fund racist organizations such as the Ku Klux Klan.

A few states also took action against the Scouts. Connecticut, for instance, removed the Scouts from the list of nine hundred charities to which state employees could contribute through payroll deductions, a program that provided about $10,000 annually to Connecticut's BSA council. Worried that other states, public universities, and local governments with similar programs might follow Connecticut's lead, the Scouts sued. As in their suit against the Broward County School Board, the Scouts argued they were being singled out for their viewpoint on homosexuality. The Scouts drew attention to the dozens of organizations to which Connecticut state employees were allowed to contribute despite restrictive membership criteria, including "Catholics for a Free Choice ('pro-choice organization of Catholics'), La Casa De Puerto Rico (a group furthering 'social, economic and political well being of the Puerto Rican community'), the Girl Scouts Council of Southwestern Connecticut (a group 'for girls age 5–17'), the Indian Law Resource Center (an 'Indian organization providing free legal help to Native American tribes'), and the Fellowship of Christian Athletes (a group reaching 'students for Jesus Christ')," as well as gay rights groups such as the Stonewall Foundation that did "not allow persons opposed to the gay rights agenda to 'speak' for it or 'represent' it."

The Scouts' arguments were essentially the same as in the Broward County case, but the outcome this time was different. The district court judge Warren Eggington, a Carter appointee, found this case to be distinguishable from *Till* on two grounds. First, unlike Florida, Connecticut had a state law that explicitly forbade the state from "becoming a party to any agreement or plan which has the effect of sanctioning discrimination" on the basis of sexual orientation. Second, Connecticut's workplace-based charitable contribution campaign did not constitute a "limited public forum" and so the required level of judicial scrutiny of the exclusion was lower. Whereas exclusion from a public forum required a compelling state interest, the US Supreme Court (*Cornelius v. NAACP Legal Defense and Education Fund* [1985]) held that exclusion from a nonpublic forum needed only to be reasonable and viewpoint neutral. Judge Eggington rejected the Scouts' contention that they had been singled out because of their viewpoint on homosexuality. Instead, the Scouts were being excluded because they discriminated against gays. As for the list of other allegedly discriminatory groups provided by the Scouts, the judge pointed out that the Scouts had collapsed the crucial distinction between discriminatory membership and employment policies, which the law forbade, and discrimination in the provision of services, which the state allowed. Moreover, those groups on the list that did discriminate in their employment and membership policies, specifically religious groups and the ROTC, had been explicitly exempted by the Connecticut law. The legislature could have exempted the Scouts as well, but it did not. The judge allowed that *Dale* had put the Scouts in a "unique position" of being able to exclude gays and lesbians, but that constitutionally protected right was not "synonymous with compliance with the non-discrimination laws of the state." The state of Connecticut was neither compelling the Scouts to admit homosexuals (which would violate *Dale*), nor was it excluding the Scouts on the basis of their viewpoint (which would violate the Court's holding in *Cornelius*). Instead, the state was making a reasonable, viewpoint neutral judgment that the Boy Scouts were not in compliance with the state's nondiscrimination law, and only groups that were in compliance could be part of the state-approved list. The Scouts appealed, but the appellate court—consisting of three Clinton appointees—unanimously affirmed the district court's judgment. The Scouts lost again when, in March 2004, the US Supreme Court declined to hear the case.

The Scouts also became embroiled in a bitter legal battle with the city of Philadelphia over the Cradle of Liberty Council's rent-free (actually $1 a year) use of prime real estate owned by the city. The arrangement dated to 1928 when the council was granted permission to build its headquarters on a half-acre parcel of city land. In the wake of *Dale*, Bill Dwyer, the chief executive of the Cradle of Liberty Council, strenuously opposed the BSA's national policy, but ultimately the council's public disavowal of discrimination was not enough to stave off attacks on the Scouts' "sweetheart deal" with the city. After the national office compelled the Liberty Council to dismiss Greg Lattera in the summer of 2003, the city, pressured by gay groups and backed by a legal opinion from the city solicitor, decided to end the rent-free arrangement. If the Scouts wanted to remain in the building, they would have to pay fair market value for using the property, which the city estimated to be $200,000. For the next three years, the city and the Cradle of Liberty Council negotiated to find a way out of the impasse, but to no avail. In 2007 the Philadelphia City Council voted 16–1 to give the Scouts until May 2008 to pay the $200,000, vacate the premises, or promise not to exclude gays. The Cradle of Liberty Council sued the city in federal court to block its imminent eviction.

The case went to trial in 2010. The Scouts maintained that the city's action was "motivated solely by its hostility to the viewpoint" expressed by the Scouts about homosexuality. As in the Connecticut and Broward County cases, the Scouts pointed to other groups with "exclusive" membership policies that used city-owned property at no or nominal cost, including the Roman Catholic Church and the Colonial Dames of America. The city countered that the case was not about the Scouts' speech but about their discriminatory conduct. The city insisted that it had no legal obligation to subsidize an organization that failed to comply with a city ordinance prohibiting discrimination on the basis of sexual orientation. Indeed, it had a legal if not moral obligation not to subsidize such an organization with taxpayer monies. Philadelphia's mayor Michael Nutter explained: "If we were talking about an organization that discriminated against African Americans, Italians, the Irish, Catholics, people of the Jewish faith, or any of a number of other categories, there would be such an outrage that you wouldn't be able to contain it."

To Nutter, it was incomprehensible that an organization could "countenance discrimination and then expect to carry out that activity on public property."

At trial, Dwyer, by then retired as the head of the Cradle of Liberty Council, testified that the council would have liked nothing more than to repudiate the national policy, as the city had been pressing them to do since 2003. But, unfortunately, the council "couldn't repudiate totally the national position" because the national office would have pulled the council's charter and "put us out of business."

After deliberating for two days, a unanimous jury sided with the Scouts. Although rejecting the arguments that the city had discriminated against the Scouts based on its viewpoint and that the city subsidized other organizations that violated the city's nondiscrimination policy, the jury was nonetheless persuaded that the city had violated the council's First Amendment rights. The jury found that the city "would have permitted [the Cradle of Liberty Council] to continue to use its headquarters building on a rent-free basis if it repudiated or renounced" the Boy Scouts' antigay policy. The city had therefore violated the Scouts' constitutional rights because it had tried to compel speech by imposing unreasonable conditions on the group's continued use of the building.

The presiding judge urged the two sides to negotiate a settlement. At first it looked as if that might happen. The mayor proposed that the city sell the half-acre parcel to the Scouts for a half million dollars—roughly half of what the Scouts' attorneys were insisting they be paid in legal fees—but the city council refused to back the plan. Instead, the city requested a new trial on the grounds that the jury's verdict was inconsistent and that the federal judge Ronald Buckwalter had failed to adequately instruct the jury. Judge Buckwalter rejected the city's motion and ordered the city to pay the Scouts $877,000 in legal fees. The seventy-five-year-old Buckwalter, who had been appointed to the bench by George Herbert Walker Bush, agreed with the jury that that the city had placed an "overly broad speech restriction" on the Cradle of Liberty Council. He also objected that the decision to evict had been made under "the improper influence" of the lobbying of a gay rights group that gave the group an "unfair advantage in advancing its agenda"—an observation that appeared to refer to the fact that the city solicitor was openly gay. The city appealed the judge's ruling to the third circuit court of appeals, but in May 2013 the parties finally settled. The city agreed to pay the Cradle of Liberty Council $825,000 and, in exchange, the Scouts agreed to vacate the premises.

In the Philadelphia, Broward County, and Connecticut cases, the Scouts brought suit to defend themselves against actions taken by state and local governments. But the Scouts and local governments also found themselves the target of lawsuits from groups such as the ACLU that sued to end what they saw as the Scouts' special privileges. Two months after the Supreme Court's ruling in *Dale*, for instance, the San Diego chapter of the ACLU and San Diego's LGBT Law Association, on behalf of two couples, one lesbian and the other agnostic, sued to stop the city of San Diego from leasing city land to the BSA's Desert Pacific Council at essentially no charge. The Desert Pacific Council paid $1 annually for the use of "Camp Balboa," sixteen acres in Balboa Park that housed the council's headquarters and public camping facilities that were maintained and operated by the Scouts. The city also granted the council free use of a half-acre parcel in Mission Bay Park on which the Scouts had built an aquatic center at a cost of $2.5 million.

The case (*Barnes-Wallace v. City of San Diego*) was heard by the federal judge Napoleon Jones, a Clinton appointee and only the second African American judge to serve on the federal bench in San Diego County. Judge Jones sidestepped the question of discrimination on the basis of sexual orientation and instead based his ruling on the religious character of the Scouts. He ruled that the leases at Balboa Park and Mission Bay Park violated the separation of church and state because a "reasonable observer" would "naturally view" the city's preferential treatment of the Scouts as government endorsement of religion.

Judge Jones's rulings against the Scouts provoked outrage among many conservatives, a number of whom called for the judge's impeachment. Critics of the ruling were angry not only at the judge but at the city of San Diego, which rather than join the Scouts in appealing the ruling opted to settle with the ACLU. The city agreed to pay nearly $1 million to the ACLU in legal fees and court costs and to take no position on the legality of the leases in future litigation. Although the Scouts were upset by Judge Jones's ruling, the principal target of their ire was the ACLU. Appearing in May 2005 at a Federalist Society–sponsored panel in San Diego devoted to discussing *Barnes-Wallace* (the panel was titled "The Constitution and the Boy Scouts: Equal Access to Government Land and the First Amendment"), BSA's attorney George Davidson reserved his sharpest barbs for the ACLU. *Barnes-Wallace* and *Dale*, Davidson explained, were "just the tips of an iceberg in a quarter century assault by the ACLU on the civil liberties of Boy Scouts." Davidson complained that the ACLU's board had become "dominated by a narrow politically correct ideology" and was "happy to defend the insignificant fringe of any political stripe." He warned that any "mainstream organization" that "departs from the ACLU's view of political correctness may expect [to share] the Boy Scouts' fate."

Davidson's frustration with the ACLU was understandable. For twenty-five years, dating all the way back to the *Curran* case, Davidson had been defending the BSA against lawsuits filed by the ACLU. Worse still, over the previous eighteen months the ACLU had scored a string of notable victories, not only in the San Diego case but also in cases challenging the sponsorship of Scout troops by government organizations. In November 2004, for instance, an ACLU lawsuit had prompted the Pentagon to direct military bases not to sponsor Boy Scouts troops. More worrying to the BSA was ACLU litigation (*Winkler v. Rumsfeld*) aimed at ending the Scouts' use of the Virginia military base Fort A. P. Hill for its quadrennial national jamboree. According to the ACLU, the Defense Department spent $2 million annually to ready the military base for the jamboree. And in June 2005, just a month after Davidson appeared in San Diego, the federal judge Blanche Manning, another Clinton-appointed African American judge, sided with the ACLU and ordered the Pentagon to stop using taxpayer funds and military property to support the Scouts.

Davidson was not the only person unhappy with what BSA supporters portrayed as a "war on the Scouts." As they had in 2001, Republicans in Congress responded by pushing federal legislation to support the Boy Scouts. Senate Republicans introduced the Support Our Scouts Act, which stipulated that no federal agency could provide less support for the Scouts—including hosting an official event such as the jamboree—than they had provided over the previous four years. In addition, the act required local governments that received federal funding to give Scouts the same access to government facilities—whether a public forum, limited public forum, or nonpublic forum—that they provided to other organizations. Local governments that did not abide by this rule would lose their federal funding. In December 2005, five months after speaking to thirty thousand Scouts at the national jamboree (where he warned "against people who say that moral truth is relative, or call a religious faith a comforting illusion"), President George W. Bush signed the bill into law.

The Bush administration also backed the Scouts in court. When the Scouts appealed the rulings by Judge Jones and Judge Manning, the Bush Justice Department wrote amicus briefs backing the Scouts' position. From this point on, the Scouts' legal fortunes improved.

In 2006 the Oregon Supreme Court reversed a state appellate court ruling from the previous year that had found Portland's public schools guilty of discriminating against atheist students by allowing the Boy Scouts to recruit during school hours. Like the great majority of other suits targeting the Scouts, this one was brought by the ACLU. Six of the seven justices on the Oregon high court agreed that since religion was referenced neither by the recruiters nor in the literature they distributed, the schools could allow recruitment during the school day. Although the Scouts won the legal battle, it meant little in the context of Portland's school district, which had changed its policy three years before so that neither the Boy Scouts nor any other community groups could recruit during the school day, a change that the district insisted was driven not by the lawsuit but by the desire to "preserve instructional time."

Things got better still for the Scouts in 2007, when an appellate court overturned Judge Manning's verdict. Rather than ruling on the merits of the case, the appeals court dismissed the suit on the grounds that the taxpayers who had brought suit against the military's support of the Scouts lacked the standing to sue. Although the Scouts had prevailed in court, the scrutiny and uncertainty brought by the case led them to look for an alternative site for the jamboree that would be owned and operated by the Scouts. With generous backing from a number of private foundations and wealthy individuals, the BSA purchased ten thousand acres in West Virginia, and in the summer of 2013 the Scouts for the first time in their history held their jamboree on property that they owned.

For a variety of technical reasons, the San Diego case relating to the use of Balboa Park took much longer for the court of appeals to reach a resolution. But finally, in December 2012, a unanimous appellate court ruled in favor of the Scouts. The appellate court rejected Judge Jones's argument that leasing land to the Scouts at a nominal charge ran afoul of the separation of church and state. The court found "no evidence [that] the city's purpose in leasing the subject properties to the Boy Scouts was to advance religion." Instead, there was "abundant evidence that its purpose was to provide facilities and services for youth activities." In addition, the court rejected the equal protection argument that Judge Jones had sidestepped. The court ruled that the lesbian couple that filed suit had failed to show that they had been excluded from using the aquatic center or the campground facilities because of their sexual orientation. Indeed the record made it "abundantly clear" that they had "never attempted to use the facilities."

A decade after *Dale*, the Boy Scouts had battled their critics to at least a stalemate. They had done so not only by vigorously fighting the ACLU and gay rights groups in the courtroom but by contesting policies adopted by school districts and governmental entities across the country. The BSA's unbending posture contrasted sharply with the assurances that Davidson had given the US Supreme Court justices. When Antonin Scalia asked if "the Scouts' position was that if government assistance to the Scouts presented a problem, 'you'd rather . . . not have the assistance than have to change your policies,'" Davidson answered, "absolutely." Outside the courtroom, the BSA spokesman Gregg Shields offered similar reassurances that the Scouts were not "forcing [their] values on anyone," but were simply asking "people to respect [their] values and beliefs." Yet when governmental entities moved to withdraw their assistance, the Scouts swiftly responded by threatening or taking legal action. The Scouts also turned to supporters—typically conservative Republicans—in the legislative and executive branches to compel support for the Scouts. The constitutional fight for freedom of association became a political, usually partisan fight to ensure that local governments, schools, corporations, and foundations continued to support the Boy Scouts of America in the same stalwart style that they had for the past century.

CHAPTER 14

Freedom of Association after *Dale*

The Supreme Court's decision in *Dale* ended the dispute between the two parties but not the larger political struggle between the Boy Scouts of America and their gay rights adversaries. The broad sweep of Rehnquist's opinion had given the BSA an undoubted warrant to exclude those it deemed "avowed homosexuals," but the opinion necessarily left a host of crucial questions unanswered, particularly whether the Scouts could be denied public benefits because of their exclusionary policy. Getting answers to these questions, as we have seen, engulfed the Scouts in more than a decade of post-*Dale* litigation. However, *Dale* left unanswered questions not only for the Scouts but for anybody interested in the scope of the freedom of association, particularly expressive association.

Prior to *Dale*, courts evaluating a claim of freedom of association were guided by three unanimous Supreme Court decisions from the 1980s: *Roberts v. United States Jaycees* (1984), *Rotary International v. Rotary Club of Duarte* (1987), and *N.Y. State Club Association v. New York* (1988). These cases recognized that the right to exclude some members was an essential part of a group's First Amendment right to define its own identity. But these cases also recognized that the state had a compelling interest in eradicating discrimination. Courts therefore had to balance these two competing values on a case-by-case basis. Neither freedom from discrimination nor freedom of expression was to be a trump card that would prevail in every case. In the seminal *Roberts* case, for instance, the Court determined that admitting women would have only a negligible impact on the Jaycees' expressive message whereas the exclusion of women from the Jaycees would have a substantial adverse effect on the advancement and integration of women in the workforce.

Rehnquist's opinion in *Dale* pointed to a very different calculus. The Scouts' freedom of association was a trump card, a virtually absolute right that could not be restricted even by the state's interest in nondiscrimination. And whereas the *Roberts* Court had embarked on its own independent inquiry into whether the Jaycees' expressive message would be compromised by admitting women, Rehnquist said that courts should largely defer to the organization. If the Scouts or any other organization declared that admitting homosexuals would compromise its expressive purpose, then the courts were in no position to second guess that judgment. In a free society, associations must possess the right to define their own message and to decide which individuals or groups subvert or muddy that message.

Rehnquist's deference to the Scouts made for an easy case because there was little need for the Court to ascertain—as the dissenters insisted on doing—whether opposition to homosexuality was central or peripheral to Scouting's message. Less clear was how useful or workable Rehnquist's deferential standard would prove in future freedom of association cases. Would the conservative majority have the courage of its convictions when the roles were reversed, when freedom of association was invoked on behalf of an expressive purpose they disliked and in defiance of a law they supported? The test would come in 2006 in *Rumsfeld v. Forum for Academic and Institutional Rights*.

The case stemmed from the Solomon Amendment, so named after the legislation's sponsor, Congressman Gerald Solomon (R-NY). Passed by Congress in 1994, the amendment denied certain categories of federal funding—specifically grants and contracts through the Department of Defense—to institutions of higher education that did not allow the US military to recruit on campus. The amendment was in direct response to a growing movement among the nation's law schools to bar military recruiters on campus because of the military's ban on gays and lesbians serving in the armed forces. The military's long-standing discrimination on the basis of sexual orientation was in direct conflict with the guidelines adopted by the Association of American Law Schools in 1990 that exhorted the nation's law schools to enact policies barring discriminations on the basis of sexual orientation and requiring all public and private employers recruiting on campus to abide by the nondiscrimination policy.

Since few law schools relied on Department of Defense funding, those that chose to bar military recruiters from campus could initially do so at little cost. Gradually, though, Congress intensified the pressure. Subsequent iterations of the Solomon Amendment expanded the types of federal funding that would be denied to institutions that barred the military from recruiting on campus. Congress turned the screws still further by clarifying that noncompliance on the part of any "subelement" (such as a law school) within a university would lead to a cutoff of federal funds to the entire university. Because no research university could survive without federal grants and support, the law schools' only option was to challenge the Solomon Amendment in court.

To challenge the law, more than thirty law schools and their faculties formed an association called the Forum for Academic and Institutional Rights (FAIR), the mission of which was "to promote academic freedom, support educational institutions in opposing discrimination, and vindicate the rights of institutions of higher education." In the fall of 2003, FAIR filed suit in federal court (*FAIR v. Rumsfeld*), alleging that that the Solomon Amendment trampled upon their First Amendment rights. The principal pillar upon which FAIR's case rested, ironically, was the Supreme Court's opinion in *Dale*.

The district court judge, a Reagan appointee, dismissed FAIR's argument that the Solomon Amendment violated the law schools' rights, but in November 2004 a divided appeals court reversed. Relying heavily on *Dale*, the appellate court agreed with FAIR that if the Boy Scouts—a public accommodation under New Jersey law—had a First Amendment right to exclude gays, then an association of private law schools had the same First Amendment right to exclude discriminatory employers. "Just as the Boy Scouts believed that homosexual conduct is inconsistent with the Scout Oath," wrote Clinton appointee Thomas Ambro, "the law schools believe that employment discrimination is inconsistent with their commitment to fairness and justice." By requiring law schools to allow military recruiters on campus, the law compelled private schools to communicate a message with which they disagreed. And according to Judge Ambro, the Supreme Court's ruling in *Dale* stood for the principle that an organization could not be so compelled.

A federal district court reached the same judgment two months later in a separate case (*Burt v. Rumsfeld*) brought against the Solomon Amendment by faculty at Yale Law School. Judge Janet Hall, another Clinton appointee, also relied on *Dale* in finding that the Solomon Amendment unconstitutionally burdened the law school's freedom of expressive association. In rejecting the Defense Department's contention that *Dale* did not apply in this case because military recruiters did not speak for the law school and were not members of the law school, Judge Hall pointed to the breadth of the *Dale* court's holding. In the Supreme Court's view, James Dale's mere "presence" in the Scouts "would, at the very least, force the organization to send a message . . . that the Boy Scouts accepts homosexual conduct as a legitimate form of behavior." By the same reasoning, the presence of military recruiters on campus would send a message that the law school accepts discriminatory conduct as a legitimate form of behavior. The government's lawyers argued, as they had in the *FAIR* case, that the presence of military recruiters on campus would not be seen as a sign that the law school endorsed discrimination, but Judge Hall, like Judge Ambro, answered this argument by quoting from Rehnquist's expansive language in *Dale*. The "key" to the *Dale* Court's analysis, Judge Hall explained, lay in "the substantial deference given to a private organization's determination of 1) what its message is and 2) what significantly interferes with its ability to advocate its chosen message." Just as Rehnquist said that the Court must defer to the Boy Scouts about the nature of the association's message and what would impair the expression of that message, so the courts must defer to the law school faculty's definition of its message and its judgment about what would impair the expression of that message.

Supporters of gay rights relished watching the military hoisted by the Boy Scouts' petard. FAIR's lawyer crowed that "now every academic institution in the country is free to follow their consciences and their nondiscrimination policies." But not everybody on the left was as pleased. Many worried that the logic of the court opinions in *Fair* and *Burt*, like the *Dale* opinion on which they rested, placed at risk the antidiscrimination regulations that law schools valued. If law schools did not have to abide by the Solomon Amendment, then why couldn't a university that claimed to support traditional gender roles be exempted from adhering to Title IX, which since 1972 has guaranteed educational equal opportunities for women through the threat of withholding federal funding from educational institutions that discriminated on the basis of sex? And why couldn't universities that declared a commitment to traditional morality claim a First Amendment right to exclude gay or lesbian students or fire gay and lesbian teachers, no matter what state law said? Like the Court majority in *Dale*, Ambro and Hall seemed to offer groups a constitutional right to evade almost any laws they thought (or claimed) impeded their expressive purpose.

In May 2005, the same nine Supreme Court justices who had decided *Dale* agreed to hear the government's appeal of the *FAIR* ruling. By the time the Court heard oral arguments in the case in December, however, Chief Justice Rehnquist had died and been replaced by John Roberts. And by the time the Court issued its ruling the following March, Justice Sandra Day O'Connor was gone too, replaced by Samuel Alito. The change in personnel mattered little. In a unanimous 8–0 ruling (Alito did not participate because he joined the Court a month after the Court heard oral arguments), the Court sided with the government and against the law schools. The new chief justice assigned himself the opinion, an opinion that the law professor Andrew Koppelman has described as "an exercise in damage control." The damage that needed to be contained was "the unsustainably broad implications" of Rehnquist's *Dale* opinion, which taken to its logical extreme seemed to suggest that members of an association might be "entitled to disobey laws whenever obedience would be perceived as endorsing some message."

Almost immediately after *Dale* was decided, litigants across the country had seized on Rehnquist's opinion in *Dale* to try to justify noncompliance with one law or another. Among those quick to try to capitalize on *Dale* were the Central Texas Nudists, who had brought suit against a ban on minors at a county park in which clothing was optional. At oral argument in September 2000, the nudist association likened its plight to that of the BSA, which also had been prevented by the government from instilling its values in children. The Texas Court of Appeals labored to sidestep the *Dale* analogy. The cases were different, the court insisted, because even though the nudists and the Boy Scouts "may share a common goal to instill values in children, the manner in which these values are transmitted is distinguishable." That is, the BSA sought to transmit its values by "having its adult leaders spend time with the youth members, instructing and engaging them in activities like camping, archery, and fishing," whereas the nudists "seek to convey their values to their children by engaging in swimming, sunbathing, and other forms of recreation in the nude." This distinction was decisive, in the court's view, because what mattered to the nudists was "not the activity itself [swimming and sunbathing], but rather, the manner in which the activity is conducted—in the nude and in public." But one could have as easily said, as Koppelman points out, "that the BSA was trying to protect the manner in which its activities [camping, archery, and fishing] were conducted," namely "away from gay people."

The manner in which the Texas appeals court handled *Dale* was typical of the way many other lower courts responded. Faced with *Dale*-based claims, lower courts almost always rejected them on the grounds that the facts in *Dale* were distinguishable from the facts before them. A dodge adopted by some courts was to declare that "conduct that obviously had expressive dimensions was nonetheless not expressive." Another was to read *Dale* as being relevant only to cases in which the state compelled an association to admit members against its will. Some courts even distorted *Dale*'s findings in an effort to limit *Dale*'s reach. An appellate court in Oregon, for instance, ruled (*Lahmann v. Grand Aerie of Fraternal Order of Eagles*) that the Fraternal Order of Eagles's exclusion of women from regular membership violated the state's public accommodation law. Following the Supreme Court's reasoning in the allegedly "essentially indistinguishable" cases of *Roberts* and *Rotary*, the appellate court, like the trial court before it, found that "the record does not support the conclusion that requiring the Eagles to evenhandedly consider women for membership will significantly (or even modestly) impair" the Eagles's mission and purpose. The Oregon court dismissed *Dale* as irrelevant because the Supreme Court had found that in the case of the Boy Scouts "the antihomosexual value was central, frequently asserted, and long-standing." In fact, however, the *Dale* Court determined no such thing. Indeed Rehnquist explicitly disavowed the notion that the BSA had to show that opposition to homosexuality was central to its expressive message—that was instead the threshold that Dale's lawyers wanted to set for the Boy Scouts. Rather, the Court's ruling in *Dale* was premised, as the dissenting judge in *Lahmann* pointed out, on the proposition that courts should not substitute their judgment about the importance of a given message for the judgment of the organization's leadership, and that courts should (in Rehnquist's words) "give deference to an association's view of what would impair its expression."

The lower courts' narrow reading (or, on occasion, misreading) of *Dale* helped to limit its reach, but the rulings in the Solomon Amendment litigation threatened to turn *Dale* into a license for lawlessness by expressive associations. In *Rumsfeld v. Forum for Academic and Institutional Rights*, the Supreme Court set about undoing or at least limiting the damage done by Rehnquist's highly deferential standard in *Dale*.

Writing for a unanimous Court, Roberts sharply distinguished between conduct and speech. The Solomon Amendment, Roberts argued, regulated "what law schools must do—afford equal access to military recruiters—not what they may or may not say." The law did not implicate the law schools' First Amendment rights because schools remained absolutely free to condemn or protest the military's policy. Of course, this was precisely the distinction that Lambda, the dissenters in *Dale*, and a unanimous New Jersey Supreme Court had made about the Boy Scouts. New Jersey's nondiscrimination law regulated what a public accommodation such as the Boy Scouts could do—that is, not exclude members based on their sexual orientation—not what the Boy Scouts may say or may not say about the morality of homosexuality. The conservative majority in *Dale* had rejected this straightforward distinction between speech and conduct—a distinction that Scalia, Thomas, and Kennedy now endorsed—because they evidently believed that for gays and lesbians there could be no meaningful distinction between conduct and speech. A person's status as a gay or lesbian—or at least as a known or "avowed" gay or lesbian—was inherently an expressive message. But somehow a person's status as a military recruiter did not carry an expressive message of any sort.

Roberts's opinion in *FAIR* contained no trace of the deference that the Court showed to the Boy Scouts in *Dale*. Whereas Rehnquist had refused to second guess the Boy Scouts' claims about what would distort their message, Roberts freely substituted the Court's judgment about what would or would not interfere with the expressive purposes of the law schools. And in Roberts's view, the law schools' message of opposition to gay discrimination was not compromised by allowing an antigay organization to recruit on campus. The law schools, Roberts concluded, had "plainly overstate[d] the expressive nature of their activity and the impact of the Solomon Amendment on it." Ironically, while treating the law schools' claims with a robust skepticism, Roberts accepted at face value the government's contention that Solomon Amendment was necessary to national security. Little wonder that the law professor Dale Carpenter derided the *FAIR* opinion as "an exercise in single-entry bookkeeping."

A striking feature of Roberts's opinion is that while the law schools—like the lower court judges—pinned their case on *Dale*, Roberts did not even mention *Dale* until the eighteenth page of a twenty-page opinion. When Roberts finally did get to *Dale*, he hemmed it in by positing a "critical" distinction between *Dale* and *FAIR*. Whereas *Dale* involved the state compelling an association "to accept members it does not desire," *FAIR* involved military recruiters who were, "by definition, outsiders who come onto campus for the limited purpose of trying to hire students—not to become members of the school's expressive association." Roberts conceded FAIR's argument that the "the freedom of expressive association protects more than just a group's membership decisions." For instance, in *NAACP v. Alabama* (1958) and *Brown v. Socialist Workers* (1972), the Court found state-mandated disclosure of a group's membership lists to be unconstitutional. But these restrictions also affected "the group's ability to express its message" because they "made group membership less attractive." The Solomon Amendment, in contrast, had no effect on the desirability of being a member of a law school. Or at least the law schools had failed to demonstrate that the law had had this effect, a failure that was perhaps due to the law schools not knowing that this was the standard the Court would adopt.

So where does this leave the freedom of expressive association? Nobody really knows for sure. Koppelman describes the law of expressive association as "in flux." *FAIR* did not repudiate *Dale* or "impose clear and explicit limitations on *Dale*." Yet, as the law professor Jack Balkin points out, *FAIR* did appear to limit *Dale* by reading it narrowly as "a case about membership and about laws that burden the right of an organization to choose their members or make membership in the organization less valuable and desirable to its members." Certainly the Court showed no interest in the law schools' invitation to exploit the "anarchic potential" at the heart of *Dale*'s deferential standard. The Court's liberals—Stevens, Souter, Breyer, and Ginsburg—had never bought into *Dale*'s permissive standard and they were not about to start now, despite their personal sympathy for law schools' attempt to promote gay rights. The change in litigants, however, made all the difference to Scalia and Thomas, the Court's allegedly most principled conservatives. Trusting in the Boy Scouts was one thing; deferring to the gay rights agenda of elite law schools was quite another.

At his confirmation hearings in 2005, John Roberts told the Senate Judiciary Committee that a Supreme Court justice was like an umpire. The job of a justice, like that of an umpire, Roberts said, was "to call balls and strikes and not to pitch or bat." The analogy is appealing, simplistic, and completely wrong as a description of judicial decision-making. The umpire analogy suggests that justices and judges never show favoritism toward one team or another. We can all agree that an umpire whose calls are influenced by which team is at the plate would be a disgrace to his profession and should be fired immediately. Yet the empirical evidence is clear: liberal justices are more likely to strike down conservative laws and conservative justices are more likely to strike down liberal laws. If judges don't exactly pitch or bat in the game of politics, they are clearly not politically neutral umpires, and especially not when the legal calls are close ones, as they often are in contentious cases.

The *Dale* and *FAIR* cases show how profoundly judges can be influenced by the identity of the litigants. Both Scalia and Thomas—like Rehnquist—have invariably sided against claims made on behalf of gay individuals and groups. When the law is perceived as antigay (as with Texas's sodomy statute, Colorado's ban on "preferential treatment" for gays, the federal government's Solomon Amendment, and, most recently, the Defense of Marriage Act), they have found a way to uphold the law. When the law is perceived to be progay (as with New Jersey's nondiscrimination statute) they have found a way to trump or set aside the state law.

Arguably, the liberal Supreme Court justices showed more umpire-like behavior in *Dale* and *FAIR* since in both cases they deferred to the government, even though in one case (*Dale*) it would have meant a victory for the gay rights side and in the other (*FAIR*) it meant a defeat for the gay rights side. However, beneath the Supreme Court level, liberal judges showed a political bias that was at least as prominent as that displayed by conservative judges. Both lower-court opinions that sided with the gay rights stance of the law schools were penned by liberal judges appointed by President Clinton. Moreover, at no point in the *Dale* litigation in New Jersey's courts did a liberal Democratic judge rule against Dale. And in cases involving the Scouts' use of public facilities, Clinton-appointed judges were far more likely to side against the Scouts and in favor of the gay rights position than were Republican-appointed judges. Some Republican judges did side against the Scouts, most notably the four Republicans on the New Jersey Supreme Court, but none of these judges could be considered social conservatives who shared the Boy Scouts' view of the immorality of homosexuality. Judges who sympathized with the Boy Scouts' moral stance—whether a lowly superior court judge such as Patrick McGann or the chief justice of the US Supreme Court—invariably called the Scouts "safe" and the gay litigants "out." The game's outcome usually depended less on the strength of the legal arguments and more on the personal feelings and political biases of the "umpires."

"The Wrong Side of History"

The announcement on July 17, 2012, seemed like business as usual for the Boy Scouts of America. After an allegedly exhaustive and undeniably secret two-year review by an eleven member "special committee" comprised of professional Scout executives and adult volunteers, the BSA emphatically reaffirmed its antigay policy. The policy would continue to be that "while the BSA does not proactively inquire about the sexual orientation of employees, volunteers, or members, we do not grant membership to individuals who are open or avowed homosexuals or who engage in behavior that would become a distraction to the mission of the BSA." The BSA's spokesperson Deron Smith confidently declared it to be "absolutely the best policy" for the Scouts.

The announcement was followed by the usual round of bitter denunciations and resounding cheers. The president of the Human Rights Campaign, the nation's largest gay rights advocacy group, assailed the statement as "a missed opportunity of colossal proportions." Rather than teaching "the value of respect," the BSA leadership had again chosen to "teach division and intolerance." The other side's reaction was equally predictable. Typical was the response of a spokesperson from the Family Research Council, who said that the Scouts deserved "a major pat on the back" for having "defied the winds of political correctness" and for bravely saying "'no' to a culture that wants us to accept as normative a pattern of sexual behavior which clearly violates God's intended design for men and women."

The BSA's forceful reaffirmation of its policy and the polarized responses it engendered made it easy to miss the signs of change. One clue could be found in the BSA executive board's statement, which while affirming the policy also highlighted the divisions that existed not only in the larger Scouting community but on the board itself. The brief statement read: "Scouting believes that good people can personally disagree on this topic and still work together to achieve the life-changing benefits to youth through Scouting. While not all Board members may personally agree with this policy, and may choose a different direction for their own organizations, BSA leadership agrees this is the best policy for the organization and supports it for the BSA."

Signs of change were evident, too, in the language and shifting arguments of Scout executives. In explaining the policy reaffirmation, Chief Scout Executive Bob Mazzuca spoke of "same-sex orientation," not "homosexuals," avowed or otherwise. He explained the policy not by referencing the Scout Oath, the demands of being "morally straight," or even the "traditional values" of the families that Scouting served. Instead, Mazzuca pointed to Scouting parents' preference that "the issues of same-sex orientation" be discussed "within their family, with spiritual advisers, and at the appropriate time and in the right setting." This, of course, had been the argument that James Dale and Lambda Legal had made all along: that the Boy Scouts did not teach anything about sexual orientation but instead taught that questions about sex were best handled within the family. Opposition to homosexuality, Mazzuca was all but conceding, was not actually part of the Scouts' expressive message.

Mazzuca also forthrightly acknowledged the diversity of opinion within the Scouts. "We fully understand," Mazzuca said, "that no single policy will accommodate the many diverse views among our membership." But in accenting the diversity of viewpoints within the Scouts, and the depth of feeling on both sides, the BSA leadership managed only to underscore the powerful case for the "local option" policy that was being pressed by those within the Scouts who were opposed to the current policy. If the Scouts were internally divided on the issue, then why not leave it to local Scouting units to decide whether to admit gays?

The local option idea was not new. For more than two decades, local councils had been lobbying the national office to allow individual units to set their own policies about homosexuality. In April 1992, for instance, the Baden-Powell Council executive board unanimously passed a resolution that called on the national office to "give responsibility for choice of membership" to individual chartering organizations. In communicating the council's position to the BSA national office, the council president Robert Gwinn acknowledged that some of the council's board members were "troubled by the thought of homosexual leaders." Yet Gwinn reported that even board members who were "personally uncomfortable with homosexuals as members" supported the resolution because they were convinced that the antigay position of the national office was damaging "our movement," both in New York and nationwide. The problem, admitted one of those board members who was "uncomfortable with homosexuals," was that "we are just on the wrong side of history on this issue."

In 1992, at the height of the culture war, the staunchly conservative BSA leadership in Irving, Texas, had no interest in compromising their antigay stance. Most of the organization's top leaders could not fathom that opposition to homosexuality would place them on the wrong side of history. Two decades later, however, it had become clear to many in the BSA hierarchy that Gwinn had been prescient. History, it seemed, would judge the BSA leaders not as men of principle or wisdom but as narrow-minded bigots who promoted a policy of invidious discrimination for no good reason other than that they disliked or feared the idea of men having sex with other men.

Those who now wanted to get the Boy Scouts on the right side of history faced a profound dilemma rooted in the organization's increasing reliance on conservative religious institutions, especially the Mormon Church but also the Catholic Church and Southern Baptist Convention. In the two decades since Gwinn's missive, that reliance had grown stronger as the BSA became more closely identified with its antigay position, and as membership and support from public entities and nonprofits declined. When public schools, government agencies, and the military ceased to charter Scout troops, churches often picked up the orphaned troops. At the time that Dale was kicked out in 1990, a little more than half of Scout troops were chartered by religious organizations. By 2012, seven in ten Scout troops were chartered by religious organizations, and the Mormon Church alone sponsored one-third of all Cub Scout packs and Boy Scout troops (the percentage of registered Scouts who are

Mormons is smaller—about 15 percent—but is still higher than any other religious denomination and more than seven times higher than one would expect based on the percentage of the population that is Mormon). The Mormon Church is also by far the Scouts' largest financial contributor. And according to one estimate, roughly one-third of the seventy or so men on the BSA National Executive Board are Mormon, including the current president, Wayne Perry.

Between 2000 and 2012, while the BSA experienced a more than 20 percent drop in membership, membership in Mormon-sponsored packs and troops remained remarkably robust, at well above four hundred thousand boys. The reason for that stability (and even slight growth) is that every Mormon boy, at the age of eight, is enrolled in the Cub Scouts, and every Mormon congregation (or ward) has its own Cub Scout pack and Boy Scout troop. For the Mormon Church, Scouting is an integral part of the boys' spiritual training. Mormon boys become eligible for the Boy Scouts and the Aaronic priesthood at the same age (twelve), and the same person (appointed by the congregation's bishop) is both Scoutmaster (on Wednesday nights) and the boys' guide through the preparatory priesthood (on Sundays). Oversight of all Mormon Scouting units and the spiritual development of all boys are vested in one person: the president of the church's Young Men organization.

The Mormon Church's "all-in support" for Scouting has made the LDS the single most important stakeholder in Scouting, and that stake has only grown in importance as the Scouts' membership has shrunk. As a result, no change to the Scouts' national policy barring "open or avowed homosexuals" is possible without the consent and support of the LDS Church. The BSA's decision to reaffirm the policy in 2012 suggested that the Mormon Church remained unwilling to sanction a shift in policy.

Nothing that happened in the immediate aftermath of the decision to reaffirm the policy indicated that either the Mormon Church or the BSA would have a change of heart. It is true that the BSA announcement prodded the nation's most prominent Mormon, Republican presidential nominee (and father of three Eagle Scouts) Mitt Romney, to issue a statement reaffirming his position that "all people should be able to participate in the Boy Scouts regardless of their sexual orientation." But this was not a new position for Romney. He had adopted the same position nearly two decades before, in 1994, during his unsuccessful run for a Senate seat in liberal Massachusetts. Romney also said then, as he did now, that he supported "the right of the Boy Scouts of America to decide what it wants to do on that issue."

Romney's Democratic opponent, President Barack Obama, was on record as being opposed to the Scouts' policy, but for three weeks the White House refused to comment on the BSA's decision to continue to adhere to its discriminatory policy. Only after a Romney spokesperson issued a statement did the White House finally issue one of its own that reaffirmed the president's opposition to discrimination while also praising the Scouts as "a valuable organization that has helped educate and build character in American boys for more than a century." The White House also indicated that the president had no intention of bowing to calls from the ACLU and others that he reconsider his position as honorary president of the Scouts. Most gay rights groups, however, were not interested in pressing Obama to take a stance against the Boy Scouts. Instead, most seemed to share the view expressed by Congressman Barney Frank (D-MA) that the gay rights community had "bigger fish to fry"—most notably, same-sex marriage, which Obama had already endorsed.

Initially, protests against the Scouts' reaffirmation of its policy seemed, if anything, somewhat more muted than in the past. The Scouts' decision certainly triggered the usual round of adverse publicity, editorial scolding, and returned Eagle Scout badges, but there was little in these all-too-familiar protests to suggest that they would usher in a change in the Scouts' long-standing policy, a policy that was firmly rooted in the Scouts' need to mollify the Mormon Church and its conservative religious allies. The BSA's critics seemed, as ever, to be tilting at windmills.

The protesters, though, had strategic advantages that they had lacked a decade earlier. First, and most important, cultural attitudes toward what Mazzuca called "issues of same-sex orientation" had changed dramatically. In November 2012, for the first time in US history, same-sex marriage was legalized in a state not by courts or legislatures but by a vote of the people (two votes in fact, one in

Maine and the other in Washington). Public opinion polls showed that support for same-sex marriage, which before 2011 had always been a minority position in the country, had now become the majority position. But even while a majority of the public now backed same-sex marriage and nearly two-thirds believed that discrimination against gays and lesbians was a "serious problem," Americans remained uncomfortable with the idea of gay men serving as Scout leaders. A Gallup poll taken in November 2012 found that only 42 percent of the public (26 percent of Republicans and 60 percent of Democrats) agreed that the Boy Scouts should "allow openly gay adults to serve as Boy Scout leaders." Nonetheless, public acceptance of gay and lesbian relationships had grown dramatically in a very short period of time, particularly among younger Americans. As figure 2 shows, around the time that the US Supreme Court heard Dale's case, only four in ten Americans believed gay and lesbian relations were "morally acceptable," but by 2013 six in ten Americans agreed that gay and lesbian relations were morally acceptable.

A second advantage possessed by BSA's opponents stemmed from  technological changes that facilitated grassroots mobilization. No group made more effective use of these new technologies than Scouts for Equality (SFE). Unveiled in June 2012, SFE was backed by GLAAD, which bills itself as "the LGBT movement's communications epicenter." Since its formation in the mid-1980s, GLAAD had been hugely successful in changing the ways in which the media represent gays and lesbians, and now for the first time GLAAD enlisted its public relations professionals in the battle to end the Boy Scouts' policy of excluding gays.

The appealing public face of SFE was its cofounder Zack Wahls, a twenty-year-old, straight Eagle Scout raised by two lesbian parents. On the surface, SFE resembled Scouting for All, the advocacy group launched two decades earlier by Dave Rice. Both organizations had the goal of giving voice to those within the Scouting family—particularly Eagle Scouts—who opposed the BSA's policy of exclusion, and both used petition drives to pressure the Scouts. SFE, however, was able to launch its signature-gathering drive using the hugely successful online petitioning website Change.org. Several years into the petition drive launched by Steve Cozza in 1997,

Figure 2. Percentage of Americans Who Believe Gay and Lesbian Relations Are "Morally Acceptable" or "Morally Wrong"

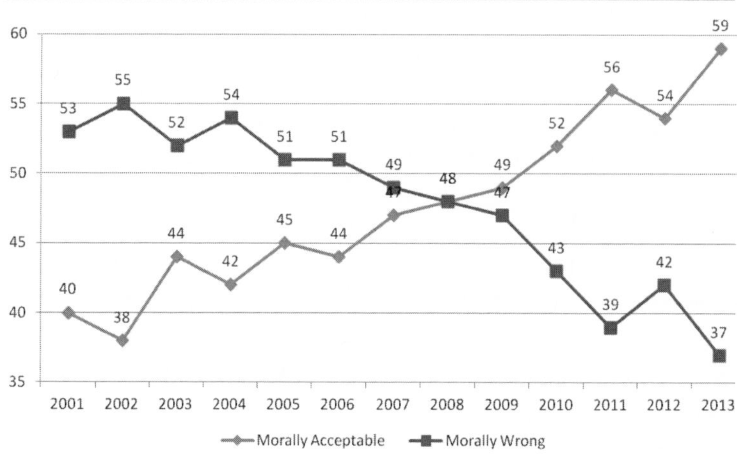

Scouting for All boasted of having gathered fifty thousand signatures in support of ending the Boys Scouts' exclusionary policy. SFE gathered five hundred thousand signatures in less than two months and reached the million mark in six—ten times the number that Scouting for All gathered in ten years, between 1997 and 2006—and delivered 1.4 million signatures to the BSA board of directors at its meeting in the first week of February 2013.

As important as the change in technology was the change in strategy and tactics. Unlike Scouting for All, SFE focused its lobbying campaign not only on the Boy Scouts but on the corporate donors who supported the Boy Scouts. Nearly half of the nation's fifty most generous corporate foundations gave to the BSA in 2010, totaling $3.6 million. Cut off the money, SFE calculated, and the Scouts would have to change.

SFE's first target was the Scouts' largest corporate donor, Intel. The Santa Clara–based company contributed $700,000 to the Scouts in 2010 through a matching program that pegged the corporation's charitable giving to the number of hours volunteered by its employees. Using this formula, nearly half of Intel's annual giving went to Mormon-affiliated BSA troops and councils. SFE's lobbying campaign paid quick dividends. In October 2012, Intel announced that it would no longer fund the BSA, though local Scout troops and councils would still be eligible to receive funds if they refused to adhere to the BSA's national policy of discrimination.

Next, SFE turned up the heat on United Parcel Service (UPS). Although UPS was not even close to the second-largest corporate funder (seven other companies gave more in 2010), three-fifths of its $167,000 contribution in 2010 was earmarked for the BSA national headquarters. SFE also shrewdly calculated that the combination of UPS's visibility and the impending Christmas season would make the package-delivery company particularly sensitive to a campaign of public pressure. They were right: a month later, in the middle of November, UPS announced a new nondiscrimination policy that made the Boy Scouts ineligible for funding. In announcing the change, UPS spokeswoman Kristen Petrella downplayed the effects of SFE's online petitioning, which had garnered more than eighty thousand signatures. UPS, she explained, "is a company that does the right things for the right reasons." The change had been made because UPS believed in "promot[ing] an environment of diversity and inclusion." Yet the fact remains that in September, the month before SFE launched its online petition, Petrella had publicly pledged that the Scouts' reaffirmation of its antigay policy "has not and will not impact the UPS Foundation's decision to provide funding to BSA."

Although Petrella's efforts to downplay the effects of public pressure on company decision-making is unconvincing, it is nonetheless true that SFE and other gay rights groups found a receptive audience in many corporate boardrooms. Business executives had long since become accustomed to company policies that barred discrimination on the basis of sexual orientation. Intel, for instance, prided itself on its inclusive and diverse workforce, and boasted of its 100 percent rating on the Human Rights Campaign's Corporate Equality Index, which measures how accepting corporate policies and practices are toward lesbian, gay, bisexual, and transgender employees. SFE's third target, Verizon, was selected not only because it contributed more than $300,000 to the Scouts in 2010, making it the third-largest corporate donor to the Scouts, but also because, like Intel, it proudly advertised its perfect rating on the Corporate Equality Index.

In fact, the conflict between corporate cultures, in which acceptance of gay, lesbian, bisexual, and transgender employees had become commonplace, and the antigay policies of the Boy Scouts had already begun to generate unprecedented conflict within the BSA's volunteer national board, which traditionally included a substantial number of corporate executives. In June 2012, Jim Turley, CEO of the accounting firm Ernst & Young—a corporation widely recognized for its progressive LGBT policies—became the first BSA board member to publicly voice his support for lifting the national ban on openly gay homosexuals in the Scouts. Shortly thereafter, Randall Stephenson, the CEO of AT&T (a company with close ties to GLAAD), announced that he, too, favored changing the Scouts' policy. Stephenson's position was particularly noteworthy because he was also the BSA president-elect (his term was scheduled to begin in 2014).

Stephenson and Turley had been unable to prevent the BSA from reaffirming its antigay policy in July 2012, but the subsequent loss of financial support from major donors such as Intel and UPS as well as the prospect of other corporations and foundations following suit (the pharmaceutical giant Merck was among those that had since pledged to end funding to the Scouts) spread alarm within the BSA national office. Although the Scouts had faced the threat (and reality) of funding cuts many times before, events this time seemed to be snowballing in a way that shifted the cost-benefit calculus of continuing the policy. The corporate funding decisions strengthened the hand of Turley and Stephenson, who continued to press for a change in policy.

Then on January 28, 2013, only six months after the Scouts had emphatically reaffirmed their long-standing policy of exclusion, word leaked out that the BSA national office "may soon give sponsors of troops the authority to decide whether to accept gays as Scouts and leaders." Under the proposed change, BSA spokesman Deron Smith explained, "the Boy Scouts would not, under any circumstances, dictate a position to units, members, or parents." Smith told reporters that a policy change could be enacted as early as the next week during the upcoming board meeting.

The dramatic announcement was the lead story all across the country. Gay rights groups, of course, hailed the abrupt reversal, while social conservatives deplored it. The president of the Family Research Council warned the BSA board that it would "be making a serious mistake to bow to the strong-arm tactics of LGBT activists and open the organization to homosexuality." Southern Baptist leaders expressed "tremendous dismay" at the decision and warned of a "significant backlash . . . as churches reevaluate whether Scouting comports with their values." One traditional backer of the antigay policy, however, was notably silent. Representatives of the Mormon Church issued no statement and made no comment about the impending policy change. What that silence meant was less obvious. What was clear, though, was that the three key BSA leaders—Wayne Perry, the national president and a billionaire Mormon; Tico Perez, the national commissioner who was also a Catholic Cuban American active in the Republican Party; and Chief Scout Executive Wayne Brock, a Southern Baptist—wanted to nudge the Scouts toward the right side of history.

The BSA leadership knew that Mormon support would be essential to any change in BSA policy. But by the same token, the Boy Scouts of America are also an integral part of Mormon life. And it is not difficult to imagine that many within the Mormon Church, like many of those in the BSA national office, were coming to realize that a local option was in the best long-run interests of the BSA generally and the Mormon Scouting program specifically. However, many evangelical social conservatives, particularly Southern Baptists, were far less vested in the viability of the Boy Scouts than they were in fighting the good fight against the sin of homosexuality.

While the Mormon and Catholic churches avoided wading into the controversy provoked by the leak, the Southern Baptist Convention instructed its congregations "to pray that board members will retain the Scouts' policy." Frank Page, head of the convention's executive committee, warned of an exodus of religious conservatives from the Scouts if the antigay policy was changed. "A lot of parents and students," Page told NBC News, "will make the decision to look for other organizations that are more in line with the principles that they espouse."

The Baptist church leaders' reactions were mild, however, compared to the rhetoric of some social conservative groups, many of whom dusted off the old canard about the dangers of child molestation by gay men, an argument that the Scouts had long ago rejected. The American Family Association (AFA), a Mississippi-based fundamentalist Christian group, sent out an "action alert" on Friday, February 1, 2013, imploring its several million subscribers to "Ask the Boy Scouts Not to Allow Jerry Sandusky to Be a Scout Leader," a reference to the former Penn State football coach, who had sexually abused young boys for decades. The alert acknowledged that Sandusky "isn't actually preparing to be a Scout leader" (there was no acknowledgment that he was a heterosexual father of six who had been married for nearly a half century) but offered it as an entrée to a series of statistics about sexual abuse that allegedly showed "how dangerous it will be for the Boy Scouts to lift the ban on homosexual leaders and members." The alert closed by listing twenty-six BSA board members (and their phone numbers) and urging people to call these board members and "ask them to protect the Boy Scouts and retain the current national policy banning homosexual leaders and members."

The irony of AFA's email alert was that it came on the heels of a string of highly publicized court cases that documented widespread sexual abuse of boys by heterosexual Scout leaders. The Scouts' Ineligible Volunteer Files (aka the "perversion files"), which they had been compelled to turn over in court (and which were subsequently made public), listed several thousand former Scout leaders who were now ineligible to serve because they were believed to be child molesters. These records showed that the national office had often treated those accused of sexual abuse with far greater sympathy and compassion than they treated those who were discovered to be gay. An openly gay individual could count on being immediately placed in the BSA's Ineligible Volunteer Files, often the same day or the day after the national office learned of the person's sexual orientation. In contrast, a person charged with sexual abuse was sometimes allowed to continue as a Scout leader for years, and the Scouts invariably sought to conceal the offender's crime from public scrutiny, just as they strenuously resisted background checks. One Scout leader, for instance, was found to have tied up and fondled three boys, for which he received four years' probation. The Scouts suspended the man for the duration of his probation, but in 1975, at the end of his court-imposed probation, the BSA national office agreed to a local council's request to have him reinstated as a Scout leader. Richard Stenger continued to work as a Scout leader until the spring of 1989 when he was arrested after a Scouting parent reported that he "had padlocked her 11-year-old Scout in a harness and watched him dangle for 15 minutes." A police raid of Stenger's home found "dozens of restraints and hundreds of images of children in bondage, including one of a blindfolded 6-year-old tied to a bed." In December 1989, eight months after Stenger's arrest—and after "two dozen former and current Scouts came forward to say they had been abused by Stenger"—the BSA officially deemed him ineligible to serve as a Scout leader.

Notwithstanding the absence of any evidence linking pedophilia with homosexuality, social conservatives shamelessly exploited the public's fear of sexual abuse to mobilize support against the impending change. On February 4, 2013, the Family Research Council, the American Family Association, and several dozen other social conservative organizations signed a half-page advertisement in *USA Today* that urged the Scouts to "stand firm for timeless values" and to stand up against "political and financial pressure" from activists and corporations. Resorting to a blatant falsehood, the ad declared that the "current policy is part of the BSA's efforts to protect Scouts from sexual abuse." The ad reminded the public that "last year BSA released their so-called 'perversion files,' which contained the names of hundred of sexual predators who had managed to hide their attraction to boys and enter the Boy Scouts." How, the ad asked, "will parents be able to entrust their children to the Boy Scouts if they trade the well-being of the boys for corporate dollars?" Readers were directed to call the BSA national office and demand that the Scouts hold the line on membership standards.

The ferocity of the conservative grassroots campaign seemed to take the Scouts' leadership by surprise. The BSA policy on gays, after all, had no connection to the problem of sexual abuse in the Boy Scouts. Moreover, the local option would have allowed troops to continue to discriminate against openly gay Scouts if they wished to do so. Two days after the publication of the *USA Today* ad, the BSA announced that it would defer a decision until its May meeting when it would put the question to the fourteen hundred voting members of the national council. The BSA spokesperson Deron

Smith explained that the "outpouring of feedback from the American public" showed just "how deeply people care about Scouting and how passionate they are about the organization." A few days later, the Scouts claimed that the announcement of the prospective policy change had not been a trial balloon but a leak from an unknown source, either a person who "didn't like what we were doing, or [who] thought they were going to be helpful to the conversation." Whether trial balloon or leak, the BSA had clearly been preparing the ground for a historic policy shift.

The policy change would be delayed, but the leadership still appeared hopeful of lifting the ban on gays and enacting a local option. The national office commissioned an online membership survey that seemed tailored to soliciting support for a change in the BSA policy. The Voice of the Scout Membership Standards Survey, sent to more than one million adult BSA members (roughly two hundred thousand of whom responded), began by positing six scenarios, four of which asked specifically about the criteria for membership and leadership. (The other two asked about whether an openly gay fifteen-year-old Scout should be allowed to share a tent with a heterosexual boy on an overnight camping trip, and whether a gay male troop leader should be permitted to take adolescent boys on an overnight camping trip.) Three of the scenarios clearly invited respondents to think twice about the fairness of the Scouts' current policy of excluding gays, both as adult leaders and as youth members:

- Tom started in the program as a Tiger Cub, and finished every requirement for the Eagle Scout Award at sixteen years of age. At his board of review Tom reveals that he is gay. Is it acceptable or unacceptable for the review board to deny his Eagle Scout award based on that admission?
- Johnny, a first-grade boy, has joined Tiger Cubs with his friends. Johnny's friends and their parents unanimously nominate Johnny's mom, who is known by them to be lesbian, to be the den leader. Johnny's pack is chartered to a church where the doctrine of that faith does not teach that homosexuality is wrong. Is it acceptable or unacceptable for his mother to serve as a den leader for his Cub Scout den?

- A troop is chartered by an organization that does not believe homosexuality is wrong and allows gays to be ministers. The youth minister traditionally serves as the Scoutmaster for the troop. The congregation hires a youth minister who is gay. Is it acceptable or unacceptable for this youth minister to serve as the Scoutmaster?

Consistent with the local option idea, both the scenario of Johnny's mom and the gay youth minister emphasized that the chartering organization did not believe homosexuality was wrong. The fourth scenario that asked about membership standards probed support for the local option from the other direction.

- David, a Boy Scout, believes that homosexuality is wrong. His troop is chartered to a church where the doctrine of that faith also teaches that homosexuality is wrong. Steve, an openly gay youth, applies to be a member in the troop and is denied membership. Is it acceptable or unacceptable for this troop to deny Steve membership in their troop?

Only after respondents had responded to each of these scenarios were they asked whether they favored the current policy that prohibited "open homosexuals from being Scouts or adult Scout leaders." They were also asked whether they thought this prohibition was "a core value of Scouting found in the Scout Oath and Law," and whether they supported the local option, given that "different organizations that charter Boy Scouts troops have different positions on the morality of homosexuality."

If the BSA leadership hoped that the membership survey would bolster the case for the local option, they were to be disappointed. Nearly six in ten Scouters said the current exclusionary policy was a "core value" of Scouting that reflected the teachings of the Scout Oath and Scout Law. Sixty-one percent favored keeping the current policy and only one-third wanted it repealed. The only age group that opposed the current policy was eighteen- to twenty-four-year-olds; among those over sixty, support for retaining the policy climbed to seventy percent. Even more worrying, 54 percent of the Scouting community "strongly supported" the current policy, more than twice as many as the number who "strongly opposed" it. Asked whether they would "continue to participate if BSA makes a decision that disagrees with your own view," half of those who backed the current policy said "no." Only one in ten of those who wanted to change the policy said the same. Support for the local option was tepid at best, even among those who opposed the current policy. Many Scouters feared that different standards for different troops would sow confusion.

The survey showed that the Scouts' problem was not simply the Family Research Council or a handful of vocal antigay activists but the conservatism of its membership, particularly its older members. Just how out of step the BSA membership was from the rest of American society was evident from two identical surveys the BSA commissioned at the same time: one a nationwide phone survey of eight hundred parents who had boys under the age of eighteen, the other an online survey of one thousand teens between the ages of sixteen and eighteen. Parents were divided, but more (45 percent) opposed the Scouts' policy than supported it (42 percent); the only region of the country in which parents supported the ban on gays was the South. Teens were even more opposed to the Scouts' policy, with less than one-fourth backing it. And as figure 3 shows, parents and teens responded to the Scouting scenarios by coming down strongly on the side of inclusion. In contrast, among Scouters, the only scenario in which a majority supported inclusion was in the case of Tom, the sixteen-year-old gay Eagle Scout candidate.

In carrying out what it billed as the "most comprehensive listening exercise in its history," the BSA also solicited input from each of its 280 local councils. What the Scouts found, unsurprisingly, was a deeply divided organization. Among the councils in the Northeast Region, 92 percent said they preferred a change in the BSA policy, whereas 83 percent of councils in the South Region wanted no change in the policy. The other two regions—the West and Central—were more evenly split in their views, with about half of councils wanting no change, and about a third advocating change.

The Scouts also charged a Finance and Fundraising Study Group with gauging the level of support for change among donors, and found that only about a third of individual donors supported a policy change (half opposed a change), whereas a change in policy was

Figure 3. Percentage of Respondents in BSA Survey Who Believe Discrimination against Gays Is "Acceptable"

Scenario	Scouters	Parents	Teens
Deny Eagle Scout Award to gay 16-year-old	32	18	15
Exclude lesbian as den leader	50	32	22
Exclude gay youth minister as Scoutmaster	55	41	27
Deny membership to 16-year-old gay teen in troop charted to religious organization that opposes homosexuality	61	38	22
Forbid gay Scout leader from taking boys on overnight trip	54	37	32
Forbid 15-year-old openly gay Scout from sharing tent with a heterosexual boy	63	49	26

backed by a majority of corporations that sponsored or had sponsored the Scouts. Change was also backed by a majority of Fortune 500 companies. The study group concluded that the Scouts would see a drop in financial support whether they retained the policy or changed it.

Having collected "a ton of information," the question remained: what was to be done? The local option was clearly dead, even though it had been designed to address precisely the sort of divisions within the BSA that the data so clearly revealed. One reading of the data was that the Scouts should do nothing: after all, a majority of Scouters and Scouting councils supported retaining the current policy. But convinced that the status quo was unsustainable, the BSA leadership was determined to press for some modification in the policy.

Two pieces of data in that "ton of information" were crucial in charting the path forward. First, was the response to the scenario of Tom, the sixteen-year-old Eagle Scout candidate, which showed

that overwhelming majorities, even within Scouting, believed that it was unacceptable to deny a boy his Eagle Scout Award merely because he was gay. Second, and even more important, were the findings of the study group charged with soliciting information from chartered organizations, primarily religious ones. On the basis of their research, the Chartered Organization Study Group estimated that lifting the ban on both gay youth and adults, which the local option would have done, would lead to membership losses of anywhere between 100,000 to 350,000. However, the study group also reported that "many religious chartered organizations stated their concern is with homosexual adult leaders and not with youth."

Armed with these key findings, the BSA leadership set to work on crafting a new compromise that would lift the ban on gay youths but leave in place the ban on gay and lesbian adult leaders. On April 19, 2013, the BSA announced that a proposal to lift the ban on gay youth, and not the local option, would be put to a vote of the fourteen-hundred-member national council at the upcoming annual national meeting in May. Specifically, the resolution to be voted on stated:

> Youth membership in the Boy Scouts of America is open to all youth who meet the specific membership requirements to join the Cub Scout, Boy Scout, Varsity Scout, Sea Scout, and Venturing programs. Membership in any program of the Boy Scouts of America requires the youth member to (a) subscribe to and abide by the values expressed in the Scout Oath and Scout Law, (b) subscribe to and abide by the precepts of the Declaration of Religious Principle (duty to God), and (c) demonstrate behavior that exemplifies the highest level of good conduct and respect for others and is consistent at all times with the values expressed in the Scout Oath and Scout Law. No youth may be denied membership in the Boy Scouts of America on the basis of sexual orientation or preference alone.

The resolution invoked the Scout Oath and Scout Law twice, which only underscored that the BSA no longer made any claim that the commandments of the Scout Law (to be "clean") and Oath (to be "morally straight") were relevant to one's sexual orientation. The effort to divorce the Scout Oath and Scout Law from the debate about homosexuality was also evident in two "whereas" clauses that preceded the resolution. The first of these stated, "Scouting is a youth program, and any sexual conduct, whether homosexual or heterosexual, by youth of Scouting age is contrary to the virtues of Scouting," and the second proclaimed that "the Boy Scouts of America does not have an agenda on the matter of sexual orientation."

If opposition to homosexuality was not grounded in the Scout Oath and Scout Law and was not part of the Scouts' expressive message, on what grounds did the BSA propose to retain its ban on gay Scout leaders? In a memorandum titled "Membership Resolution Points of Clarification," the BSA attempted to address this question. Speaking to those who "have asserted that this proposal didn't go far enough and the Boy Scouts should remove any sexual orientation standard for membership for both youth members and adults leaders," the BSA replied: "The conclusion the executive officers of the Boy Scouts of America reached is that [lifting the ban on gay youth but not gay leaders] is the option that did not, in some way, prevent kids who sincerely want to be a part of Scouting from experiencing this life-changing program. While people have different opinions about this policy, kids are better off when they are in Scouting." Translation: many religious organizations and individuals would have pulled out of Scouting had they lifted the ban on gay leaders, and so the BSA felt compelled to adhere to the existing policy.

Remarkably, the BSA made no attempt to defend its decision by appealing to moral principle. Instead the BSA was perfectly candid in admitting that its decision was based on maximizing the number of kids enrolled in Scouting. As a prudent political calculation, the BSA proposal made sense because (a) lifting the ban on gay leaders would almost certainly have been defeated, and (b) in the unlikely event that it passed it would have led to a hemorrhaging of members and chartering organizations. One wonders how well this argument would work, however, as a legal defense if an openly gay adult were to challenge his exclusion from the Scouts? Can the BSA claim a First Amendment right to exclude gays even if they concede that disapproval of homosexuality is no part of the Scouts' expressive message?

When the Scouts first unveiled the proposal in April, BSA spokesmen pitched it as a sincere effort to reflect the preferences of Scouting families, as revealed in the Voice of the Scout survey. What mattered were not the beliefs of the BSA leadership but the beliefs of the broader Scouting family. If Scouters opposed having gays as adult leaders, for whatever reason, then that was a sufficient reason for the BSA to exclude gay adult leaders. For years, the BSA leadership had insisted in court and in public that their policy was not premised on fears that gay Scouts leaders were particularly prone to prey on young boys. Such fears, BSA spokesmen had repeatedly insisted, were unfounded, a position they strongly affirmed in the "Points of Clarification" memo. Yet the proposed policy implicitly enshrined those unfounded fears in policy, since many Scouters—as the survey results confirmed—opposed gay men serving as Scout leaders because of precisely that fear. Of course, that is not the only reason Scouters might oppose gay men becoming Scout leaders. Some may fear that being around an openly gay Scout leader would make it more likely that Johnny would grow up to be gay. But that fear is equally irrational and unsupported by scientific evidence. Perhaps some Scouting parents merely felt that exposure to positive gay or lesbian role models would make their sons more tolerant toward and accepting of gays and lesbians. It is difficult to comprehend, however, who is harmed by any increased toleration that might result from allowing gays and lesbians to serve as Scout leaders.

From one point of view, then, the proposed policy capitulated to the unfounded fears of religious conservatives. To be sure, it was a step in the right direction, a step that could make a big difference in the lives of the openly gay youth who would otherwise be kicked out of Scouting, like Pascal Tessier, a sixteen-year-old openly gay Boy Scout from Maryland who desperately wanted to stay in Scouting. The proposed policy would also ensure that no boy would be denied an Eagle Scout Award merely because he revealed his sexual orientation, as happened in the fall of 2011 to seventeen-year-old Ryan Andresen, whose plight drew national attention after his mother launched a petition on Change.org that garnered nearly a half million signatures. The Scouts' new policy would allow openly gay boys such as Ryan and Pascal to achieve the rank of Eagle Scout. However, over the past quarter century the legal and political controversy over gays in the Boy Scouts has revolved largely around the question of whether gay *adults* should serve as Scout *leaders*. That was what James Dale's case had been about, as well as the cases of Tim Curran, Keith Richardson, Roland Pool, Michael Geller, and

Chuck Merino. Arguably on the crucial question, then, the Boy Scouts' "compromise" conceded nothing.

That is not the way that many social conservatives saw the proposed new policy, however. Instead, they saw it as the Boy Scouts of America capitulating once again to homosexual activists and corporate pressure. The same social conservatives—particularly leaders of the Southern Baptist Convention and the Family Research Council—who denounced the local option also opposed lifting the ban on gay youth. They complained that both the local option and lifting the ban on gay youth strayed from the moral teachings of the Scout Oath and Scout Law. The local option had suffered from moral relativism, but the Scouts' latest proposal seemed to one FRC spokesman to be simply "incoherent" since it suggested that "homosexuality is morally acceptable until a boy turns 18." These spokesmen promised an exodus of Christian conservatives from the Boy Scouts if the policy was approved in May.

Not all religious conservatives shared this negative assessment, however. Most important for the Scouts, this was not the view of the Mormon Church. When the idea of a local option had been leaked to the press, the Mormon Church had remained conspicuously silent. Now, however, the Mormon hierarchy publicly leapt to the Boy Scouts' defense. In late April, the LDS Church announced that it was "satisfied" with the Scouts' new proposal, which it characterized as "constructively" addressing the issues at stake. The Mormon Church particularly lauded the proposal for "including consistent standards for all BSA partners, recognition that Scouting exists to serve and benefit youth rather than Scout leaders, a single standard of moral purity for youth in the program, and a renewed emphasis for Scouts to honor their duty to God." In fact, duty to God is underscored five separate times in the resolution, including in the second "whereas" clause, which states that "the Scout Oath begins with duty to God and the Scout Law ends with a Scout's obligation to be reverent, and that will always remain a core value of the Boy Scouts of America."

The Mormon leadership could support the BSA proposal because homosexual "conduct," whether among youth or adults, would still be grounds for dismissal from the Scouts. According to the Mormon Church's latest teachings on "same-sex attraction," "the attraction itself is not a sin, but acting on it is." From the church's perspective, then, the proposed policy change did not compromise the values of Scouting so much as align the Scouts' policy more closely with the teachings of the LDS Church. (Unlike the BSA, the Mormon Church allows "chaste" gays and lesbians to remain and hold positions in the Church.)

Having secured the support of the Mormon Church—which the Scouts had presumably lined up privately before publicly unveiling the resolution—the way was cleared for a vote at the May meeting. The BSA leadership lobbied aggressively for a "yes" vote, and ultimately prevailed, with 61 percent of the national council voting for the historic change. Henceforth (beginning on January 1, 2014), openly gay youth would be eligible to be Boy Scouts and Eagle Scouts.

Precisely how enduring this new policy will be is impossible to predict. But it is safe to assume that it will not defuse the cultural struggle over gays in the Boy Scouts. The new policy keeps the BSA on "the wrong side of history," while at the same time tacitly acknowledging that its position is essentially unprincipled (unless one counts maximizing the number of Scouts as a principle). That of course is what so infuriates the Family Research Council and its socially conservative allies. And it is why gay and lesbian advocacy groups will only intensify their efforts to pressure the Scouts to lift the ban on gay adults. If religious conservatives follow through on their threats to leave the organization, it will only speed up the change in policy.

When the day comes that the BSA lifts its ban on openly gay leaders, the Southern Baptist Convention, Family Research Council, and other social conservative who balked at the local option will have only themselves to blame. Whereas lifting the ban on gay youth will likely intensify the struggle over the ban on gay adults, the local option would have enabled the BSA national office to step out of the line of fire in the culture war by decentralizing the decisions to the troop level. The local option, moreover, was a compromise in keeping with the BSA's governing philosophy that Scouting was "locally owned." Scouting's programs, as Chief Scout Executive Jere Ratcliffe explained two decades earlier, were "designed to become a reality in the hands of community groups that hold charters for packs, troops, and posts." The local option both respected the decentralized spirit of Scouting and enabled the national office to avoid taking a position on an issue that sharply divided the Scouts, its financial supporters, and the country. The local option would not have made everybody happy—compromises rarely do. In fact, among the local option's sharpest critics was none other than James Dale, who assailed it for stopping well short of "true equality" since it allowed individual troops to continue to discriminate. Dale was right, of course, that the local option allowed for continued discrimination, but it was also arguably the option best suited to enabling divergent moral visions to coexist within the Boy Scouts. In defeating the local option, religious conservatives may have made their own defeat more likely.

Public opinion about gays and lesbians continues to change with a speed that has taken almost everyone by surprise. A *Washington Post*–ABC News poll conducted in early May 2013 found that 56 percent of Americans supported allowing openly gay adults to serve as Scout leaders, dramatically higher than the 42 percent of Americans who responded that way the year before in a *USA Today*–Gallup poll. The rapid change in attitudes suggests that the BSA's "incoherent" policy of admitting gay youth but not gay adults may not endure long. But however long it takes for the BSA to change its policy, the change in public attitudes inside and outside Scouting vindicates those courageous individuals whose struggles against an unjust policy culminated in the disappointment of the US Supreme Court's ruling in *Boy Scouts of America v. James Dale*. A quarter century ago, Evan Wolfson calculated that whatever the legal outcome in Dale's case, the litigation would bring public scrutiny to a discriminatory policy that could not withstand close examination in a liberal democracy committed to equality. Wolfson wagered that the price the Scouts would pay for winning the legal battle would be to lose the larger culture war over treatment of gays and lesbians. We now know that he was right.

RELEVANT CASES

Barnes-Wallace v. City of San Diego, 530 F.3d 776 (2008)
Board of Directors of Rotary International v. Rotary Club of Duarte, 481 U.S. 537 (1987)
Bob Jones University v. United States, 461 U.S. 574 (1983)
Bowers v. Hardwick, 478 U.S. 186 (1986)
Boy Scouts of America v. Dale, 530 U.S. 640 (2000)
Boy Scouts of America v. D.C. Commission on Human Rights, 809 A. 2d 1192 (2002)
Boy Scouts of America v. Till, 136 F. Supp. 2d 1295 (2001)
Boy Scouts of America v. Wyman, 335 F.3d 80 (2003)
Brown v. Socialist Workers, 458 U.S. 87 (1982)
Chicago Council of Boy Scouts of America v. City of Chicago, 748 N.E.2d 759 (2001)
Christian Legal Society v. Martinez, 130 S.Ct. 2971 (2010)
Cornelius v. NAACP Legal Defense and Education Fund, 73 U.S. 788 (1985)
Cradle of Liberty Council v. City of Philadelphia, No. 08-2429 (2009)
Curran v. Mount Diablo Council of the Boy Scouts of America, 17 Cal. 4th 670 (1998)
Evans v. City of Berkeley, 129 P.3d 394 (Cal. 2006)
Frank v. Ivy Club, 120 N.J. 73 (1991)
Hurley v. Irish-American Gay, Lesbian, and Bisexual Group of Boston, 515 U.S. 557 (1995)
Isbister v. Boys' Club of Santa Cruz, 40 Cal.3d 72 (1985)
Lahmann v. Grand Aerie of Fraternal Order of Eagles, 121 P.3d 671 (2005)
Lawrence v. Texas, 539 U.S. 558 (2003)
Leeds v. Harrison, 9 N.J. 202 (1952)
NAACP v. Alabama, 357 U.S. 449 (1958)
New York State Club Association v. City of New York, 487 U.S. 1 (1988)
Nixon v. Condon, 286 U.S. 73 (1932)
NOW v. Little League Baseball, 67 N.J. 320 (1974)
Powell v. Bunn, 59 P.3d 559 (2006)
Quinnipiac Council, BSA v. Commission on Human Rights, 204 Conn. 287 (1987)
Randall v. Orange County Council, Boy Scouts of America, 17 Cal. 4th 736 (1998)
Roberts v. United States Jaycees, 468 U.S. 609 (1984)
Romer v. Evans, 517 U.S. 620 (1996)
Rosenberger v. University of Virginia, 515 U.S. 819 (1995)
Rumsfeld v. Forum for Academic and Institutional Rights, 547 U.S. 47 (2006)

..unyon v. McCrary, 427 U.S. 160 (1976)
Schwenk v. Boy Scouts of America, 275 Ore. 327 (1976)
Seabourn v. Coronado Area Council, BSA, 257 Kan. 178 (1995)
Terry v. Adams, 345 U.S. 461 (1953)
Welsh v. Boy Scouts of America, 993 F. 2d 1267 (1993)
Winkler v. Chicago School Reform Board of Trustees, 382 F.Supp.2d 1040 (2005)

CHRONOLOGY

1910	The Boy Scouts of America (BSA) is founded.
1911	The president of the United States becomes honorary president of BSA.
1916	A congressional charter for BSA is signed into law by President Woodrow Wilson.
1973	Lambda Legal Defense and Education Fund is incorporated.
1978	First BSA memorandum on "homosexual unit members" is circulated to Scout executives, in response to an incident in Mankato, Minnesota, in which two Scouts, ages sixteen and seventeen, were kicked out because they were gay.
1978	James Dale, age eight, joins Monmouth Council's Cub Scout Pack 242.
1980	Tim Curran's application to become assistant Scoutmaster is rejected because Curran is openly gay.
1982	Wisconsin becomes the first state to outlaw discrimination on the basis of sexual orientation.
1988	Dale becomes an Eagle Scout, and upon turning eighteen is invited to become assistant Scoutmaster of Monmouth Council's Troop 73.
1989	Evan Wolfson joins Lambda Legal.
1989	BSA hires Edelman Public Relations Worldwide to handle its public relations.
July 8, 1990	The *Newark Star-Ledger* publishes a story on a seminar on the "needs of homosexual teens" at which Dale—then co-president of the Rutgers University Lesbian/Gay Alliance—spoke.
July 19, 1990	The Monmouth Council Scout executive James Kay writes to inform Dale that his involvement with the Scouts has been terminated.
August 10, 1990	Kay writes a second letter, informing Dale he has been expelled because the BSA's "standards of leadership . . . specifically forbid membership to homosexuals." Dale then contacts Wolfson at

	Lambda Legal Defense and Education Fund to seek legal assistance.
September 20, 1990	Curran's trial begins in Los Angeles County Superior Court. The Scouts for the first time reveal internal documents designed to show that they have a long-standing policy against admitting gays.
November 27, 1990	Charles Ball writes to inform Dale that the regional review committee affirmed Monmouth Council's decision to terminate Dale's registration with the Scouts.
July 25, 1991	Superior Court judge Sally Disco rules against Curran on the grounds that the Boy Scouts' First Amendment rights trump the state's law against discrimination.
January 19, 1992	New Jersey governor James Florio signs into law an amendment to the New Jersey Law against Discrimination (NJLAD) that makes New Jersey the fifth state in the nation to prohibit discrimination against lesbians and gay men in employment, public accommodations, housing, and credit.
July 29, 1992	Lambda, together with the law firm Cleary Gottleib Steen & Hamilton, files suit against the Boy Scouts of America on behalf of Dale for violating the NJLAD.
November 6, 1992	Dale's case is transferred to the Chancery Division.
February 4, 1994	Superior Court judge Patrick McGann hears the arguments of Donna Costa on behalf of Dale and George A. Davidson on behalf of the Scouts.
November 3, 1995	Judge Patrick J. McGann files his memorandum decision that finds in favor of the BSA.
December 8, 1997	The New Jersey Court of Appeals hears arguments in *Dale v. Boy Scouts of America*.
March 2, 1998	In a 2–1 decision, the appeals court reverses the lower court and finds in favor of Dale. The Boy Scouts, the court concludes, is a "place of public accommodation" under NJLAD.
March 23, 1998	The California Supreme Court rejects Curran's appeal, ruling that the BSA is not a public accommodation.

January 5, 1999	The New Jersey Supreme Court hears oral arguments in *Boy Scouts of America v. Dale*.
August 4, 1999	The New Jersey Supreme Court unanimously sides with Dale and affirms the appellate holding that BSA is a place of public accommodation under New Jersey law.
January 10, 2000	The US Supreme Court grants BSA's petition for certiorari.
February 28, 2000	The BSA submits its brief to the US Supreme Court; twenty-one amicus briefs are also filed in support of the BSA's position.
March 29, 2000	Lambda submits its brief to the US Supreme Court; sixteen amicus briefs are also filed in support of Dale's position.
April 26, 2000	The US Supreme Court hears oral argument in *Boy Scouts of America v. Dale*.
June 28, 2000	The US Supreme Court, in a 5–4 decision, reverses the state supreme court, holding that the BSA has a constitutional right to exclude gays.
November 7, 2002	On the grounds that the US Supreme Court's decision in *Boy Scouts of America v. Dale* is controlling, the DC Circuit Court of Appeals reverses the DC Commission on Human Rights's 2001 ruling in favor of Roland Pool and Michael Geller.
July 17, 2012	The Boy Scouts publicly reaffirm their policy of not granting membership to "individuals who are open or avowed homosexuals."
May 23, 2013	The Boy Scouts vote to end their policy of excluding gay youth. Gay and lesbian adults, however, continue to be excluded from serving as troop leaders.

BIBLIOGRAPHIC ESSAY

Note from the Series Editors: The following bibliographic essay contains the major primary and secondary sources the author consulted for this volume. We have asked all authors in the series to omit formal citations in order to make our volumes more readable, inexpensive, and appealing for students and general readers. In adopting this format, Landmark Law Cases and American Society follows the precedent of a number of highly regarded and widely consulted series.

This book does not attempt to recount the history of the Boy Scouts, but my understanding of the Scouts has nonetheless been informed by that history. Particularly important in making sense of the origins of the Scouting movement generally and the meaning of the Scout Law in particular is Tim Jeal's masterful biography of the founder of the Boy Scouts, Robert S. Baden-Powell. In *Baden-Powell: Founder of the Boy Scouts* (Yale University Press, 2001; originally published 1989), Jeal not only famously suggests that Baden-Powell was a "repressed homosexual" but also shows that Baden-Powell's final and most important commandment that a Scout be "clean in thought and word and deed" was principally a warning against the uncleanliness of women, or at least the wrong kind of women. In Baden-Powell's mind, writes Jeal, "when boys talked 'dirt' they were talking about women." A highly critical but still insightful assessment of Baden-Powell is Michael Rosenthal, *The Character Factory: Baden-Powell's Boy Scouts and the Imperatives of Empire* (Pantheon, 1986). Also relevant to Scouting's relationship to empire is Robert H. MacDonald's *Sons of the Empire: The Frontier and the Boy Scouts Movement, 1890–1918* (University of Toronto Press, 1993).

Useful material related to the early history of the Boy Scouts of America is available in William D. Murray, *The History of the Boy Scouts of America* (Boy Scouts of America, 1937), as well as in biographies of two BSA founders, Edward L. Rowan's *To Do My Best: James E. West and the History of the Boy Scouts of America* (Publishing Works, 2005) and Janice A. Petterchak's *Lone Scout: W. D. Boyce and American Boy Scouting* (Legacy Press, 2003). The best cultural or intellectual history of the Boy Scouts of America's role in early twentieth-century America is David Macleod's *Building Character in the American Boy: The Boy Scouts, YMCA, and Their Forerunners, 1870–1920* (University of Wisconsin Press, 1983). The connection between Scouting and masculinity is explored in Jeffrey P. Hanover, "The Boy Scouts and the Validation of Masculinity," *Journal of Social Issues* (1978), 184–195. A thoughtful introduction to the cultural meaning of the Boy Scouts is Jay Mechling's *On My Honor: Boy Scouts and the Making of American*

Youth (University of Chicago Press, 2001) as well as Paul Fussell's classic short essay on "The Boy Scout Handbook," in *The Boy Scout Handbook and Other Observations* (Oxford University Press, 1982). Less thoughtful but still revealing of the Scouts' centrality to the culture wars in recent decades are Hans Zeiger's *Get Off My Honor: The Assault on the Boy Scouts of America* (Broadman & Holman, 2005), which features a foreword by Oliver North, and Texas governor Rick Perry's *On My Honor: Why the American Values of the Boy Scouts Are Worth Fighting For* (Stroud & Hall, 2008), which boasts a foreword by Ross Perot and gushing endorsements from Newt Gingrich, Sean Hannity, and the presidents of the American Conservative Union and the American Family Association. An earlier warning against the coordinated attack on the Boy Scouts by the "culture warriors of the left" is William A. Donohue's short booklet, "On the Front Line of the Culture War: Recent Attacks on the Boy Scouts of America," published by the Claremont Institute in 1993. The problem of sexual abuse in the Scouts is examined in Patrick Boyle's *Scout's Honor: Sexual Abuse in America's Most Trusted Institution* (Prima Publishing, 1994).

On the "culture wars," see the seminal book by James Davisson Hunter, *Culture Wars: The Struggle to Define America* (Basic Books, 1991). Questions about the utility of the "culture war" concept are raised by E. J. Dionne in "Why the Culture War Is the Wrong War," *Atlantic* (January/February 2006), and by Alan Wolfe in James Davisson Hunter and Alan Wolfe, *Is There a Culture War? A Dialogue on Values and American Public Life* (Brookings, 2006). Two exceptional books that bear on this debate are Bill Bishop, *The Big Sort: Why the Clustering of Like-Minded America Is Tearing Us Apart* (Houghton Mifflin Harcourt, 2008), and Daniel T. Rodgers, *Age of Fracture* (Belknap Press of Harvard University Press, 2012).

The history of gay rights litigation has been told by a number of scholars. Among the works I found particularly helpful were Ellen Ann Anderson's *Out of the Closets & into the Courts: Legal Opportunity Structure and Gay Rights Litigation* (University of Michigan Press, 2005) and Patricia A. Cain's *Rainbow Rights: The Role of Lawyers and the Courts in the Lesbian and Gay Civil Rights Movement* (Westview Press, 2000). Less academic but far more readable and accessible for the general reader is Joyce Murdoch and Deb Price's wonderful *Courting Justice: Gay Men and Lesbians v. the Supreme Court* (Basic Books, 2001). There are also several excellent accounts of landmark gay rights cases. The best of these is Dale Carpenter's masterful *Flagrant Conduct: The Story of* Lawrence v. Texas (Norton, 2012). The litigation that led to the Supreme Court's decision in *Romer v. Evans* is the focus of Lisa Keen and Suzanne B. Goldberg's *Strangers to the Law: Gay People on Trial* (University of Michigan Press, 1998). *Bowers v. Hardwick* is recounted in David A. J. Richards, *The Sodomy Cases:* Bowers v. Hardwick *and* Lawrence v. Texas

(University Press of Kansas, 2009). Also worth reading for charting the long arc of history relating to gay and lesbian civil rights are Linda Hirschman, *The Triumphant Gay Revolution* (Harper, 2012); William N. Eskridge Jr., *Dishonorable Passions: Sodomy Laws in America, 1861–2003* (Viking, 2008); and Eric Marcus, *Making Gay History: The Half Century Fight for Lesbian and Gay Rights* (Harper, 2002). Readers of a more legal or philosophical bent will benefit from Andrew Koppelman, *The Gay Rights Question in Contemporary American Law* (University of Chicago Press, 2002); and David A. J. Richards, *The Case for Gay Rights: From Bowers to Lawrence and Beyond* (University Press of Kansas, 2005). Data on state and local antidiscrimination statutes on which I have relied can be found in William N. Eskridge Jr., *Gaylaw: Challenging the Apartheid of the Closet* (Harvard University Press, 1999).

In thinking about the importance of—and limits on—freedom of association in a liberal democracy, I have benefited enormously from the many excellent essays in Amy Gutmann's edited collection *Freedom of Association* (Princeton University Press, 1998), especially George Kateb's "The Value of Association" and Nancy Rosenblum's "Compelled Association: Public Standing, Self Respect, and the Dynamic of Exclusion." Rosenblum's robust defense of the freedom of association is elaborated at book length in her *Membership and Morals: The Personal Uses of Pluralism in America* (Princeton University Press, 1998), which the Boy Scouts cited in their US Supreme Court brief in *Dale*. Both Kateb and Rosenblum contend that the Court went too far in requiring the Jaycees to admit women on equal terms. For a different balancing of the freedom of association and the freedom from discrimination—one that vindicates Justice William Brennan's opinion in *Roberts v. United States Jaycees*—see Amy Gutmann's *Identity in Democracy* (Princeton University Press, 2003), especially chapter 2 ("The Value of Voluntary Groups") and Stuart White's "Freedom of Association and the Right to Exclude," *Journal of Public Philosophy* (1997), 373–391. Other illuminating perspectives on the relationship between liberal democracy and associations are Paul Hirst, *Associative Democracy: New Forms of Economic and Social Governance* (University of Massachusetts Press, 1994), Robert D. Putnam, *Bowling Alone: The Collapse and Revival of American Community* (Simon and Schuster, 2000), Mark E. Warren, *Democracy and Association* (Princeton University Press, 2001), Jason Kaufman, *For the Common Good? American Civic Life and the Golden Age of Fraternity* (Oxford University Press, 2002), and Theda Skocpol, *Diminished Democracy: From Membership to Management in American Civic Life* (University of Oklahoma Press, 2003).

The best analysis—and critique—of the Supreme Court's ruling in *Dale* is Andrew Koppelman with Tobias Barrington Wolff, *A Right to Discriminate? How the Case of* Boys Scouts of America v. James Dale *Warped the Law of Free Association* (Yale University Press, 2009). In chapter 14, I rely heavily on Koppelman and Wolff's analysis of *Dale*'s impact on the law of free association. I have also benefited from Dale Carpenter's reading in "Unanimously Wrong," *Cato Supreme Court Review* (2005–2006), 217–255, which is sharply critical of the Court's ruling in *Rumsfeld v. Fair*. The impact of the *Dale* decision is also explored in David Bernstein, "Expressive Association after *Dale*," in Ellen Frankel Paul et al., eds., *Freedom of Speech* (Cambridge University Press, 2004), 195–214. In the immediate wake of the *Dale* decision, law reviews were filled with readings of the Court's decision and its significance. A few of the many are Richard A. Epstein, "The Constitutional Perils of Moderation: The Case of the Boy Scouts," *Southern California Law Review* (November 2000), 119–143; Taylor Flynn, "Don't Ask Us to Explain Ourselves, Don't Tell Us What to Do: The Boy Scouts' Exclusion of Gay Members and the Necessity of Independent Judicial Review," *Stanford Law and Policy Review* (Winter 2001); N. Nicole Endejann, "Coming Out Is a Free Pass Out: *Boy Scouts of America v. Dale*," *Akron Law Review* (2001), 893–917; Erwin Chemerinsky and Catherine Fisk, "The Expressive Interest of Associations," *William and Mary Bill of Rights Journal* (April 2001), 595–617; Dale Carpenter, "Expressive Association and Anti-Discrimination Law after *Dale:* A Tripartite Approach," *Minnesota Law Review* (June 2001), 1515–1589; Scott Kelly, "Scouts' (Dis)Honor: The Supreme Court Allows the Boy Scouts of America to Discriminate against Homosexuals," *Houston Law Review* (2002), 243–274; Mark Hager, "Freedom of Solidarity: Why the Boy Scout Case Was Rightly (but Wrongly) Decided," *Connecticut Law Review* (Fall 2002), 129–194; and Stephen Clark, "Judicially Straight? *Boy Scouts v. Dale* and the Missing Scalia Dissent," *Southern California Law Review* (March 2003), 521–598. Among the other law review articles that I found useful in thinking about the freedom of association are Douglas O. Linder, "Freedom of Association after *Roberts v. United States Jaycees*," *Michigan Law Review* (August 1984), 1878–1903; and "Section 1981 and Private Groups: The Right to Discriminate versus Freedom from Discrimination," *Yale Law Journal* (June 1975), 1441–1476.

My view of how Rehnquist's opinion in *Dale* fits into his politics and jurisprudence was shaped by reading Geoffrey R. Stone, "The *Hustler*: Justice Rehnquist and 'The Freedom of Speech, or of the Press,'" in Craig M. Bradley, ed., *The Rehnquist Legacy* (Cambridge University Press, 2006), 11–25; Donald E. Boles, *Mr. Justice Rehnquist, Judicial Activist: The Early Years* (Iowa State University Press, 1987); Sue Davis, *Justice Rehnquist and the Constitution* (Princeton University Press, 1989); David G. Savage, *Turning Right: The Making of the Rehnquist Supreme Court* (John Wiley, 1992); Rick Perlstein, *Before the Storm: Barry Goldwater and the Unmaking of the American Consensus* (Hill and Wang, 2001); and John A. Jenkins, *The Partisan: The Life of William Rehnquist* (Public Affairs, 2012). On the political dynamics of the Rehnquist Court at the time of the *Dale* decision, see the absorbing account in Jeffrey Toobin's *The Nine: Inside the Secret World of the Supreme Court* (Doubleday, 2007). Also see Earl M. Maltz, ed., *Rehnquist Justice: Understanding the Court Dynamic* (University Press of Kansas, 2003); and Mark Tushnet, *A Court Divided: The Rehnquist Court and the Future of Constitutional Law* (Norton, 2005). On Rehnquist's use of law clerks, see Todd C. Peppers, *Courtiers of the Marble Palace: The Rise and Influence of the Supreme Court Law Clerk* (Stanford University Press, 2006), and Artemus Ward, "Making Work for Idle Hands: William H. Rehnquist and His Law Clerks," in Todd C. Peppers and Artemus Ward, eds., *In Chambers: Stories of Supreme Court Law Clerks and Their Justices* (University of Virginia Press, 2012).

My understanding of the New Jersey Supreme Court has been informed by G. Alan Tarr and Mary Cornelia Aldis Porter, *State Supreme Courts in State and Nation* (Yale University Press, 1988); Mary Cornelia Porter and G. Alan Tarr, eds., *State Supreme Courts: Policymakers in the Federal System* (Greenwood Press, 1982); Kevin M. Mulcahy, "Modeling the Garden: How New Jersey Built the Most Progressive State Supreme Court and What California Can Learn," *Santa Clara Law Review* (2000), 863–905; and Gerald Russello, "The New Jersey Supreme Court: New Directions," *Journal of Civil Rights and Economic Development* (Fall 2002), 655–690. For quantitative measures of the influence and stature of state supreme courts, see Jake Dear and Edward W. Jessen, "'Followed Rates' and Leading State Cases, 1940–2005," *UC Davis Law Review* (2007), 683–711; and Gregory A. Caldeira, "On the Reputation of State Supreme Courts," *Political Behavior* (1983), 83–108.

Although the relevant scholarly literature has been invaluable in illuminating my way, the narrative in this book is based overwhelmingly on primary sources, notably court and legal records, BSA publications, contemporary newspaper coverage, and interviews. Legal records have been particularly important in understanding the evolution of the Boy Scouts' policy regarding gays because Scouting officials generally declined to talk with me and because the national office does not open their internal records to scholars.

The *Dale* case was decided by summary judgment and so never went to trial. However, both sides nonetheless deposed numerous witnesses and submitted countless affidavits and certifications in support of their motions for summary judgment. All of the affidavits and certifications, as well as exhibits, motions, and orders, totaling nearly five thousand pages, are available on microfilm at the law library of the New Jersey State Library. All of these documents were transmitted on June 25, 1996, to the appellate court as a Joint Appendix of the Plaintiff-Appellant James Dale and Defendants-

Respondents Boy Scouts of America and Monmouth Council, Boy Scouts of America (Docket No. A-2427–95T3). Judge McGann's opinion, filed November 3, 1995, can also be found in this appendix, as can Dale's complaint, filed July 29, 1992, and the BSA's answer, filed September 25, 1992. Briefs in the case (the sixty-six-page memorandum of law in support of Dale's motion for summary judgment, dated September 10, 1993; the BSA's fifty-eight-page memorandum of law in support of cross-motion for summary judgment, dated November 11, 1993; Dale's eighty-six-page reply memorandum, dated January 7, 1994; and the BSA's twelve-page reply memorandum, dated January 28, 1994) were not available in the appendix, and were instead obtained from the law firm Cleary Gottlieb Steen & Hamilton.

Included among the hundreds of exhibits are excerpts from depositions that were taken by the two sides in the first half of 1993. I was not able to locate all of the original depositions, either because they had not been preserved or were not available, but Jon Davidson, Lambda's legal director, tracked down and sent me the two-hundred-page deposition by Blake Lewis, who at the time of his deposition (May 1993) was vice president at Edelman Public Relations Worldwide and had worked on the BSA account since first joining Edelman in March 1991. Only a tiny fraction of Lewis's deposition was submitted into the court record because, as the visibly frustrated BSA counsel Carla Kerr complained at the time, the questioning of Lewis seemed "gruesomely irrelevant" to the legal case. For the historical researcher, though, a deposition such as Lewis's is a treasure trove of information about the organizational relationships and decision-making that would otherwise be impossible to reconstruct from the public record.

I supplemented my research into the evolution of the Boy Scouts' antigay policy by examining court records in other cases that challenged the Boy Scouts' policy of exclusion. By far the most important of these were the voluminous records in *Boy Scouts of America v. Roland D. Pool and Michael Geller*, which include a transcript of a dozen evenings (between January and March 1998) of evidentiary hearings before the DC Commission on Human Rights; the hearings took place in the evening (roughly 5 to 10 pm) because the commissioners are volunteers. Particularly useful as a guide to the Scouts' evolving policy are the complainants' proposed findings of fact and conclusions of law, totaling two hundred pages, which I read along with the respondents' proposed findings of fact. The findings of fact collected by the legal team for Pool and Geller are also available at www.bsa-discrimination.org/POOL004.htm. Pool and Geller's counsel Merril Hirsh also sent me, among other things, a massive binder of "C" exhibits that included a cornucopia of Boy Scout documents, including publications, position statements, and correspondence.

The opinions of the New Jersey Court of Appeals, New Jersey Supreme Court, and the US Supreme Court are all available online, as are the amicus briefs and oral arguments in the US Supreme Court. The appellate court opinion is available at www.bsa-discrimination.org/Dale_NJ_Appellate_Opinion.pdf, as well as at http://caselaw.findlaw.com/nj-superior-court-appellate-division/1456467.html. The New Jersey Supreme Court opinion (734 A.2d 1196) can be accessed at www.lambdalegal.org/in-court/legal-docs/boy-Scouts-v-dale_nj_19990804_decision-nj-supreme-court. The briefs filed by Lambda and the BSA in the US Supreme Court can be found at www.lambdalegal.org/in-court/cases/boy-Scouts-of-america-v-dale. The US Supreme Court oral argument can be read or listened to at http://www.oyez.org/cases/1990-1999/1999/1999_99_699, and the opinions by Rehnquist, Stevens, and Souter, can be accessed at www.law.cornell.edu/supct/html/99-699.ZO.html. The many amicus briefs filed before the Court can be found at www.bsa-discrimination.org/html/dale-documents.html. Briefs filed at the appellate and state supreme court level, however, are not to my knowledge available online. They are available, however, from the law section of the New Jersey State Library; the filings for the state supreme court are on Reel 1869. Unfortunately, no tape or transcript survives, if any were ever made, of the lower court proceedings in the case. However, the *New York Times* dispatched a reporter to the oral argument before the New Jersey Supreme Court, leaving a record of some of what the justices said. As of this writing, none of the papers of the US Supreme Court justices who participated in the *Dale* decision are open to the public.

An extraordinary resource for anyone interested in the myriad legal cases in which the BSA has been involved is a website maintained by David Peavy: www.bsa-discrimination.org/. The site includes hundreds of legal documents as well as extensive media coverage of cases challenging the Scouts' exclusionary practices and policies, including cases relating not only to gays and lesbians but also to atheists and girls. The industrious Peavy also maintains another incredibly useful website focused on the history of Scouting around the world called Paxtu (http://paxtu.org/index.html). Among the treasures of this site are the dazzling bibliographies (http://paxtu.org/html/bibliographies.html). On the BSA, the reader will find a baker's dozen of bibliographies (http://paxtu.org/html/bsa_bibliography.html), arranged by subject, including a forty-one-page bibliography made up solely of articles on the Scouts published in the *New York Times*. The official website of the BSA is www.scouting.org.

Dale's case as well as the broader controversy about gay Scout leaders has obviously attracted intense media coverage, and that coverage is the source of many of the details and profiles in this book. To list the couple thousand newspaper and magazine articles I read is neither feasible nor useful, but a good starting place for readers wishing to understand the religious and organizational dimensions of the conflict are Chuck Sudetic, "The Struggle for the Soul of the Boy Scouts," *Rolling Stone*, July 6, 2000; Patrick Boyle, "Boy Scouts' Holy War over Homosexuals," *Youth Today*, July 2000; Benjamin Soskis, "Big Tent: Saving the Boy Scouts from Its Supporters," *New Republic*, September 17, 2001; and David France, "Scouts Divided," *Newsweek*, August 6, 2001. A valuable piece on the relationship of the Scouts and the Mormon Church is Erik Eckholm, "As Partners, Mormons and Scouts Turn Boys into Men," *New York Times*, October 17, 2012.

James Dale has been profiled many, many times in the press since first filing his legal complaint in 1992. One of the most useful is the in-depth profile by Paul Keegan, "The Gay Boy Scout," *Philadelphia* (January 1993), 76–88. Also helpful for understanding Dale's perspective is the interview with Dale by Erik Meers, "The Model Boy Scout," *Advocate*, April 4, 1998, 46–51; and Dale's February 8, 2013, op-ed in the *Washington Post*, "Why Did I Challenge the Boy Scouts' Anti-Gay Policy? Because I Am a Loyal Scout." There are also numerous press profiles of Dale's lawyer Evan Wolfson. Among the most revealing are Tony Mauro, "The Wedding Ring Leader," *American Lawyer* (June 2004), 94–97; Robin Finn, "Married to the Cause," *New York Times*, February 16, 2007; and an encyclopedia entry for Wolfson on *GLBTQ*, an online encyclopedia of gay, lesbian, bisexual, transgender, and queer culture (www.glbtq.com/social-sciences/wolfson_evan.html). The profiles of Dale and Wolfson in this book are also based on my own conversations with them. For other interviews I conducted, see the names listed among the acknowledgments.

INDEX